Voices of the Civil War

Voices of the Civil War · Charleston

By the Editors of Time-Life Books, Alexandria, Virginia

Contents

CHARLESTON HARBOR

The artist's view of Charleston Harbor shows the ring of island fortifications that fended off the Union fleet and invading ground forces for two and a half years, almost until the end of the war. Guarding the entrance to the harbor is Fort Sumter, beyond which lies the city itself at the confluence of the Ashley and Cooper Rivers.

Charleston & Savannah Railroad

CHARLESTON

Ashley River

Secessionville

James Island

Fort Johnson

Battery Simkins

Cumming's Poi

Morris Island

Battery Gregg

Battery Wagner

Lighthouse Inlet

Cooper River

Cooper River

Wando River

stle Pinckney

Fort Sumter

Fort Moultrie

Fort Beauregard

Sullivan's Island

Fort Marshall

A City under the Gun

The longest-running single campaign of the Civil War was the Union siege of the Confederate port of Charleston, South Carolina. For three years, from the summer of 1862 when Federal troops launched their first attempt to hack a way through Charleston's formidable ring of forts, to virtually the war's last days in 1865, Union and Confederate forces expended prodigious amounts of energy in the struggle for control of the city with its superb harbor and labyrinthine waterways.

Much of the fighting was naval. Federal ships, including a flotilla of the menacing new monitor-class ironclads, hurled shot and shell at the Rebel shore batteries—and were blasted in return by booming cannonades from huge guns mounted in the Confederate bastions. "The thunder of artillery," said one observer, "was as familiar as the noises of

passing vehicles in more fortunate cities."

In the fighting on land, Union troops were put ashore in large, risky amphibious operations that often brought enemy soldiers face to face in desperate close-quarters combat. The Federal attackers charged head-on at massive earthworks in mostly doomed efforts to wrestle the Rebels from spits of sand that might open accesses to the city and its port. The Confederates fought back not only with big guns but also with every new weapon they could devise, from iron-prowed rams to electrically detonated underwater mines to an experimental submarine.

Despite the destruction and carnage, neither side would back off. Battered by repeated attacks, Charleston's defenders clung with tenacity to their forts and redoubts. Repeatedly mauled, the Federal land and naval forces still hammered away, often at tragic cost, to gain the prize.

Federal determination was fueled in part by the Union's grand strategy, the so-called Anaconda Plan formulated by General Winfield Scott, U.S. Army commander at the beginning of the war. Scott's plan was to squeeze the Confederacy as if it were in the coils of a giant snake by gaining control of the Missis-

In a photograph taken shortly after the fall of Fort Sumter on April 14, 1861, Rebel soldiers pose beside cannons on the parade ground of the fort in Charleston Harbor. The Stars and Bars of the Confederacy snaps in the wind atop a derrick used to hoist guns to the fort's upper tier.

sippi River in the West while blockading or seizing the main Southern ports along the Atlantic Coast and on the Gulf of Mexico.

Closing the Confederate ports was essential to the plan. The South, a largely agricultural society with few heavy industries, desperately needed to export huge amounts of cotton to Britain and France to support its economy, and to buy in return European weapons for its armies. To choke off this trade became the Union navy's overriding mission—and Charleston's busy port inevitably became a prime target.

But Charleston was a target for another reason—vengeance. Here the war had begun, with the inflammatory Confederate bombardment and capture of Fort Sumter. To Northerners, the city was the hated "cradle of Rebellion," and a "hornet's nest of sedition." Charleston had to be taken, and made to suffer in the process. The Northern public wanted to kill secession where it began and cheered every attack that gnawed away at Charleston's defenses. "If there is any city deserving of holocaustic infamy, it is Charleston," howled the New York *Tribune*.

For the Confederacy, holding Charleston was essential to morale. To Southerners the city was holy ground, the soul and spiritual center of the cause of Southern independence, and they were prepared to defend it to the last man. Thus, from the outset, Charleston was destined to become a bloody battlefield, the scene of a prolonged and bitter struggle.

The Federal strategists realized that any quick conquest of the notorious city was out of the question. In the war's first months the Union navy, still the size of a peacetime force with only 42 ships in commission and about 9,000 officers and men, was powerless even to mount a blockade of any consequence. By

the end of 1861 the navy had almost tripled its manpower and grown astonishingly to 264 ships—although many of them were merchant ships, coastal vessels, and even ferries converted into gunboats.

Even this fast-growing force was too small for the overwhelming tasks it faced. There was no Confederate navy to contend with aside from a few gunboats and revenue cutters seized from the Federals when the war began. But the Union ships had to patrol almost 3,500 miles of coastline from Chesapeake Bay to the Rio Grande, coasts indented by an infinity of rivers, lagoons, and hidden channels.

The answer, according to Gideon Welles, President Abraham Lincoln's navy secretary, was to seize the more vulnerable Southern ports and anchorages. This would close them up for good. Almost as important, it would give the Union navy handy bases along the Confederate coast where blockading ships could recoal and resupply instead of beating back to their remote Northern ports whenever fuel, rations, and ammunition got low.

Welles' strategy focused first on the North Carolina coast and specifically on Pamlico and Albemarle Sounds with their half-dozen small but busy ports. Ready to move in late August 1861, a little makeshift flotilla that included five steam-powered warships and two chartered merchantmen loaded with 900 soon-to-be-seasick soldiers rounded down the coast from their base at Hampton Roads, Virginia.

Turning for the attack, the warships pounded the two small forts guarding Hatteras Inlet, the sole gateway through North Carolina's Outer Banks deep enough for oceangoing vessels. A landing party of Federal troops quickly took control of the forts. Then after some delay the navy dispatched a force of shallow-draft vessels for a follow-up

attack on Roanoke Island, key to the control of both the wide, shallow sounds. By early spring of 1862 the Federals had seized or neutralized all the area's ports including the main ones, New Bern and Elizabeth City. "The whole of the eastern part of the State," lamented a local reporter, "is now exposed to the ravages of the merciless vandals."

Meanwhile, farther down the coastline, the U.S. Navy struck a strategic blow in the fall of 1861. The target there was Port Royal Sound, a huge island-strewn anchorage about 60 miles south of Charleston on the South Carolina coast. For the attack, Flag Officer Samuel F. Du Pont, an aristocratic 59-year-old veteran officer who would later command the first big naval assault on Charleston, assembled a far more formidable fleet—17 warships and 25 supply vessels plus 25 transports—to carry a force of 12,000 Federal troops under Brigadier General Thomas W. Sherman.

Du Pont's armada was blown all over the ocean by a ferocious storm while rounding Cape Hatteras on November 1, and two ships were sunk. But Du Pont continued southward, collected his fleet, and launched his attack on November 7. The main targets were two bastions, Fort Walker on the tip of Hilton Head Island and Fort Beauregard on Bay Point, that between them bracketed the entrance to Port Royal Sound.

The combative Du Pont wasted little time. His ships entered the sound and attacked immediately, concentrating their fire on Fort Walker. The fleet's 155 guns fired at almost point-blank range. The rain of shells pulverized the Confederate works, dismounting guns and blasting apart the sand revetments. In hours the bloodied survivors of Fort Walker's garrison gave up and fled inland. They were followed that night by the occupants of

Fort Beauregard, who had realized that their situation was hopeless. The officer in charge of a Federal landing party hoisted the U.S. flag and proclaimed proudly he was the "first to take possession, in the majesty of the United States, of the rebel soil of South Carolina."

The swift capture of Port Royal Sound gave the Federal navy a strategic anchorage for its blockading squadron and a base from which it could mount further attacks on Rebel coastal strongholds. General Sherman's troops promptly occupied Hilton Head, which had been abandoned by its white plantation owners, and were soon happily feasting on the turkeys, chickens, and pigs left behind. Within months, army work details had turned Hilton Head into a superb supply-and-repair base complete with a new long dock; a narrow-gauge railway; and warehouses packed with rations, cannon and shot, and engineering equipment. The navy filled the harbor with hosts of receiving ships—for use as barracks, warehouses, and offices—as well as coaling vessels and even an elaborate floating machine shop. Engineers built a desalinization plant to purify seawater for use in the boilers of the navy's growing fleet of steam-powered frigates and sloops.

Profoundly alarmed by the Union advances, Confederate president Jefferson Davis dispatched an unproved general named Robert E. Lee to bring some order to the Confederate defenses, putting him in charge of a newly created Department of South Carolina, Georgia, and Florida. It was an enormous area, and Lee had little with which to protect it—at most 14,000 men—but as he was to do again and again in future years he set up the best defense he could.

Lee first established his headquarters at Coosawhatchie, a small town on the Charles-ton & Savannah Railroad about 20 miles inland from Port Royal. Then, knowing the Confederate batteries situated on outer barrier islands had proved easy pickings for the Federal navy, he pulled the men and guns from these isolated posts and relocated them along the rivers and creeks that led to the interior. Next he organized a small mobile force that could move up or down the rail line to concentrate at any threatened point. At the same time he reinforced the harbor defenses of Charleston and Savannah.

Still Lee was deeply worried. Most of South Carolina's regiments had long since been shipped north to face the Union army in Virginia. His men had lost a great deal of equipment at Hilton Head, and despite receiving a small number of reinforcements dispatched by Richmond, he feared that the Carolina Coast was poorly defended. The Federals, he wired the Confederate War Department, had "complete possession of the water and inland navigation, commands all the islands on this coast and threatens both Savannah and Charleston." The enemy's strength, Lee summed up, "exceeds the whole force we have in the state" and could be "thrown with great celerity against any point."

The situation looked dangerous. Had the Federals landed a substantial army led by a daring general, it could have pushed ashore at any of a dozen places on Port Royal Sound, sliced through Lee's thin defenses, and marched inland almost at will, destroying rail lines and possibly investing Charleston from the rear, or landward, side.

Fortunately for Lee and the Confederate cause, the Union's General Sherman on Hilton Head had only his small force of about 12,000 men, who were scattered on the sea islands around Port Royal and Saint Helena Sounds. Although he had orders to press the Southerners, Sherman was dependent on the navy for transportation and support, and without Du Pont's approval he could do little. Further demands were made on Sherman's forces by the navy's decision to occupy Beaufort, South Carolina, and Fernandina, Florida. In addition to his military obligations, Sherman's forces were ultimately responsible for more than 10,000 slaves abandoned when their masters fled at the Federal approach.

The easy capture of the big prize of Port Royal took the Union high command and everyone else by surprise, including General Sherman, who later confessed that "we had no idea, in preparing the expedition, of such immense success." His small army, as one of Sherman's staff officers acidly complained, "did practically nothing but sit down and hold the sea islands which the navy had captured for it."

With the opportunity gone begging and no other plans afoot, the navy would use the Port Royal bases as originally intended—to help it tighten the blockade of the Southern ports. Then when all was ready Du Pont and his sailors, backed by the army when needed, would settle the North's account with the loathed city of Charleston.

Charleston, in fact, soon suffered a catastrophe, but through no effort of the Federals. On December 11, 1861, an accidental fire roared through the old central part of the city, destroying 540 acres of buildings, including both St. Andrews Hall, where secession had been debated, and the Institute Hall, where the Ordinance of Secession had been signed. But the blaze had little effect on the waterfront and its docks, which continued busily loading and unloading the city's many blockade-running ships.

Southern ships running in and out of

Charleston, Savannah, and other ports continued to evade the reinforced Federal blockading squadrons with astonishing ease. The nights were dark, and Southern captains and their pilots were uncannily adept at slipping unseen through the coast's innumerable sounds and bays that gave access to the sea. In 1861, by some estimates, 9 out of 10 incoming blockade runners reached port safely.

These daring, clandestine efforts were growing more numerous and sophisticated. Enterprising Southern businessmen had been busy enlarging and fine-tuning their operations, often forming syndicates with profit-hungry English entrepreneurs.

By late 1861 Southern-British combines had acquired numbers of merchantmen—the best were the fast Clyde steamers from Glasgow—and other vessels suitable for conversion to blockade runners. Eventually they launched long, low, steam-powered blockade runners—seagoing greyhounds with names like *Fox* and *Banshee* that could outspeed even the fastest Federal frigates and gunboats. The largest of the blockade-running companies, Charleston's Fraser, Trenholm & Company, which also had offices in Liverpool, owned more than 50 ships.

The syndicates also set up a superbly efficient shuttle system. The blockade runners, loaded to the gunwales with 700 or more bales of cotton, would slip through the Federal cordon and speed for the port of St. George on Bermuda, or for the Bahamas or Cuba.

Once moored in one of these neutral havens, the blockade runners were safe from the U.S. Navy, because the United States was officially at peace with both Great Britain and Spain. The runners then off-loaded their cotton for transshipment in foreign-flag freighters to Liverpool and Britain's textile mills.

In exchange, the Southern ships loaded up with rifles, cannon, gunpowder, and other supplies. In a single trip in 1861 a blockade runner called the *Fingal* brought in a cargo of 13,000 Enfield rifles, 400 barrels of powder, artillery pieces, and untold bales of British-made Confederate uniforms. Even later in the war, with many ports closed, dozens of blockade runners still eluded the Federal pickets. In one month in 1863 Southern ships unloaded a total of 110,000 British and Austrian rifles, 21,000 British muskets, and 129 cannon from Bermuda alone.

Eager to cut back the traffic, the Federals in Port Royal Sound decided in early 1862 to try to close up Savannah and its busy port. The key target was Fort Pulaski, which guarded the mouth of the Savannah River. The fort appeared all but impregnable, but a determined army engineer, Captain Quincy Adams Gillmore—who would, like Flag Officer Du Pont, figure largely in the siege of Charleston—decided it could be taken.

Sailing to Tybee Island, a mile across the water from Fort Pulaski, a contingent of troops under Gillmore managed in late February and early March 1862 to hoist 36 siege guns, some weighing eight and a half tons each, onto the island's rugged shores. Working by night and concealing their progress with marsh grass and brush, the troops spent more than a month positioning the guns on Tybee's north shore. Then at 8:15 on the morning of April 10, Gillmore opened fire, his new rifled cannon flinging dozens of high-speed conical shells.

Within minutes Colonel Charles Olmstead, Fort Pulaski's commander, found "shots were shrieking through the air in every direction." By noon the next day, Union guns had destroyed 16 of the fort's 20 guns and had opened huge

gaps in the seven-foot-thick masonry walls.

The Federal fire had also blasted holes in a casemate that shielded Pulaski's magazine, which was crammed with 400 kegs of black powder. Rather than be annihilated by the relentless shelling or a catastrophic explosion of the exposed magazine, the fort's 385-man garrison surrendered. In all, Gillmore and his cannoneers had fired 110,643 pounds of shot and shell, and with the capture of the fort had sealed off the channel into Savannah's harbor.

Gillmore and his heavy artillery had succeeded brilliantly in smashing Savannah's main fortress, but a similar artillery assault on Charleston was, for the moment anyway, out of the question. First of all there was no undefended piece of land where the Federals could sneak in to place batteries of big guns. Such a toehold would have to be conquered. Second, Charleston's harbor defenses were far too formidable for Du Pont and his ships to sail in—as they had done elsewhere—and knock them out with a few broadsides.

Charleston was in fact an exceedingly tough nut to crack. The city itself lies on a peninsula jutting into the harbor between the Ashley and Cooper Rivers. To the south is the marsh-rimmed James Island, and off it two sandy barriers facing the Atlantic called Folly and Morris Islands. The northern tip of Morris Island forms the southern entrance to Charleston Harbor. There and on James Island the Confederates had several formidable strongholds, including Battery Gregg and Battery Wagner, all bristling with heavy guns.

Across the harbor mouth to the north, less than two miles away, lies Sullivan's Island, where sat powerful Fort Moultrie, a bastion of masonry reinforced with earth-covered palmetto logs, as well as other fortified batteries. Out in the water, blocking the harbor mouth, sat massive Fort Sumter itself with its thick walls and batteries of cannon. By the time Major General John C. Pemberton took over the city's defenses from General Lee in March 1862, more than 75 heavy guns could pour fire on the main ship channel. The U.S. Navy declined that year to risk its ships in an attack on the ring of forts protecting Charleston Harbor. The place was a "circle of fire," one navy officer said, or a "porcupine's quills turned outside in." In time, when the Federal navy did make attempts to blast its way through, the results were largely lost and battered ships, and tarnished naval reputations.

The first effort to gain a foothold on Charleston's perimeter came in the form of a flanking movement aimed at capturing some of the Confederate batteries from the rear. This opening move of the fighting for Charleston would have the odd if perhaps fitting name of the Battle of Secessionville. It would give warning of just how tough the long, agonizing siege of the city would be.

The job of trying to smash a hole in the city's defenses fell to the 12,000-man Union army based at Hilton Head Island. Unfortunately for the troops and the Union cause, the small army was led by green officers who had virtually no combat experience—and who generally lacked the confidence of their subordinates as well. The new head of the force was Major General David Hunter, an ambitious West Pointer sent in April 1862 to replace General Thomas Sherman because, the Union high command thought, Sherman had not been aggressive enough. Commanding a division under Hunter was Brigadier General Henry W. Benham, also a West Pointer whose only experience was as a military engineer. Both men, in the view of veteran regimental commander Isaac Stevens, an

acerbic New Yorker, were plainly "imbeciles," and Benham was worse: "an ass—a dreadful man, of no earthly use except as a nuisance and an obstruction."

Benham was impressively bluff and hearty, however, and Hunter gave him the job of planning and then leading the attack. Benham's scheme was to land two divisions totaling 6,500 men on the lower end of James Island south of Charleston. Once ashore, the troops, supported by fire from Federal gunboats lying in the nearby Stono River, would march up the island and rout the few defenders before they could be reinforced. The troops would then capture the Confederate batteries on the island's northern tip and turn the big guns on Charleston itself. This, Benham grandiosely announced, would force the city to surrender.

Plausible on paper, the plan turned out to be a recipe for disaster. The Federals lost the element of surprise as soon as the first gunboats began to probe up the Stono River in late May 1862. Guessing what was coming, General Pemberton—who had replaced General Lee as Confederate commander in Charleston—immediately rushed every spare unit he had to James Island. To take charge of the defense Pemberton dispatched Brigadier General Nathan G. "Shanks" Evans, already famous for his brilliant holding action the previous year at the Battle of First Manassas. Nicknamed for his skinny bowlegs, Evans was also famous as a drinker—he was said to have an orderly follow him everywhere with a gallon container of whiskey—and for being, as one staff officer put it, the "most eloquent swearer" and "magnificent bragger" in the entire Confederate army. But Evans was also an able and exceedingly combative general who never backed away from a fight.

Quickly organizing the James Island defenders, Evans set the troops to work building a breastwork across the Federal line of march just south of the tiny village of Secessionville—so named because some years before, a group of local planters had seceded from a cooperative venture with another group. Taking advantage of the terrain, the earthwork stretched across the neck of a long, narrow cotton field hemmed in on both sides by impassable marshes. By the time Benham had gotten his troops in motion, the unfinished stronghold was packed with about 500 Confederate infantry under Colonel Thomas G. Lamar, along with several guns of the 2d South Carolina Artillery.

Apparently Benham had been ordered by his superior, General Hunter, not to attack until he had received reinforcements. But eager for glory, Benham hurried his dozen regiments northeast across the island and at dawn on June 16 ordered the attack. Trouble began immediately. The 8th Michigan, leading the assault, was blown apart by sheets of Rebel musket fire and blasts from the guns. Then the confused Benham, unaware that the cotton field was only 125 yards wide, ordered his second wave, the 7th Connecticut and 28th Massachusetts, to attack in line of battle. With hardly enough room for a single regiment to deploy, the troops became hopelessly jumbled together. Into the tangled chaos the Confederate gunners hurled grapeshot, scything down the Federal center. Still, the surviving attackers charged ahead through what one Union officer later described as a "storm of grape, canister, nails, broken glass and pieces of chain which swept every foot of ground." Then the Union front shattered and the Connecticut and Massachusetts troops tumbled backward, sweeping with them the

46th New York of Benham's second brigade that was trying to move up. Worse, shells from the Union gunboats began to fall short, killing more of the charging troops. Worse still, Colonel Johnson Hagood, commanding the Confederate right flank, shortly sent the 4th Louisiana Battalion and other troops moving up to enfilade the Federals from across a marsh.

Yet despite the dogged defense, the succeeding waves of Union troops somehow gained ground and after half an hour of furious fighting reached the yellowish brown earthen sides of the enemy fort. With fresh brigades ready to go in, the Federals seemed on the point of victory. At this critical moment, Benham suddenly and unaccountably ordered a retreat. The frustrated Federal units fell back, leaving 683 dead and wounded strewn across the battlefield. The 8th Michigan had lost a third of its men and 13 of 22 officers; in the 79th New York, 110 of the 484 men engaged were casualties. Evans' defenders had lost at most 200. The murderous fiasco, called the "culmination of obstinacy and folly" by one Union soldier, caused dismay in the North. Benham was placed under arrest for attacking contrary to orders and for failure of generalship, and he was stripped of his commission by President Lincoln. Later reinstated, he was never again given command of troops in combat. To compound Benham's failure, General Hunter withdrew all Federal troops from James Island, abandoning a valuable foothold that might have been used later for another attack. For the Confederacy, the victory at Secessionville came as an enormous relief. Shanks Evans was lionized as the savior of Charleston and of the South. The city had passed its first trial by fire, but many others, bigger and more bloody, were to come.

CHRONOLOGY

1861

April	14	*Fort Sumter surrenders to the Rebels*
August	28	*Forts Hatteras and Clark at Cape Hatteras fall to Union forces*
November	7	*Federals seize Forts Walker and Beauregard on Port Royal Sound*

1862

| April | 11 | *Confederates surrender Fort Pulaski on the Savannah River* |
| June | 16 | *Battle of Secessionville on James Island* |

1863

January	31	*Rebel ironclads Chicora and Palmetto State attack Federal blockaders*
March	28	*Federals occupy Cole's and Folly Islands*
April	7	*U.S. Navy ironclad fleet bombards Fort Sumter*
July	10	*Union forces land on Morris Island*
July	18	*Battle of Battery Wagner on Morris Island*
August		*Federals lay siege to Fort Sumter*
August	21	*First Federal shells explode in the city of Charleston*
September	6	*Confederates evacuate Battery Wagner and Battery Gregg*
September	9	*Fort Sumter turns back a Federal amphibious assault*
October	5	*Confederate torpedo boat David strikes Federal ironclad New Ironsides*

1864

| January | | *Siege of Charleston city continues* |
| February | 17 | *Rebel submarine H. L. Hunley sinks Union ship Housatonic* |

1865

| February | 17 | *Charleston falls to Union forces* |

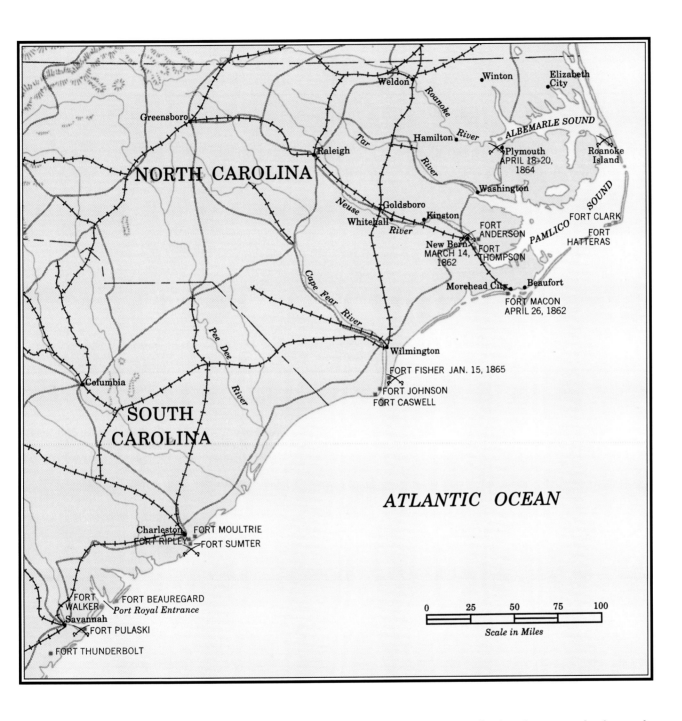

Early in the war the Federal government laid plans to seize strategic areas of the Southern coastline in order to strengthen its naval blockade of the Confederacy and to provide bases for incursions inland. By the spring of 1862, combined army-navy operations had won control of the North Carolina sounds and sealed off the harbor of Savannah. The seizure of Port Royal Sound in November 1861 gave the Federals a base from which to launch attacks against the port of Charleston, the most important—and elusive—prize of all.

COLONEL EDWIN METCALF
3D RHODE ISLAND INFANTRY

Metcalf and the 3d Rhode Island were part of the expeditionary force under General Thomas Sherman that occupied Hilton Head Island and environs in South Carolina in the fall of 1861. Metcalf served as post commander on the island and later as commander of Fort Pulaski outside Savannah, Georgia. Recalling his tenure on Hilton Head, Metcalf had kind words for his superior, General Sherman, a fellow Rhode Islander.

I have sometimes thought that full justice has not been done to General Thomas W. Sherman. His name is overshadowed by that of his great namesake. He did not possess the qualities or exhibit the manners which easily command popularity. In fact, he often seemed to prefer an ill-natured criticism to a flattering compliment from a newspaper correspondent. A long and perhaps hard experience in the army, had taught him to yield obedience, absolute and unhesitating, and when put in power, he rigorously exacted such obedience from others. The immediate result was, of course, unlimited grumbling from volunteers, as yet wholly unacquainted with discipline. But he was an admirable soldier, familiar with every detail of a soldier's duty, and capable of instructing others in the discharge of their duty, however important or however trivial, and such instruction he never failed to give to any who had the sense to seek and to accept it. Vigorous in enforcing regard for authority, he never overlooked preparation for the care and comfort of his men, nor spared the officer who neglected those under his command. His staff, with the single exception of his medical director, I believe, was composed of very young men. Undoubtedly, he taxed their activity and energy to the utmost, and made small allowance for their inexperience. Many a story can be told of him to illustrate this. But the result was that his work was all well done, and no headquarters throughout the army, probably, had a higher or better deserved reputation for ability and efficiency. It hardly needs to be added that under the training of such a commander, raw recruits rapidly attained proficiency in drill and something of that discipline which distinguishes soldiers from militia. And yet, General Sherman had won no great success on the southern coast. In co-operation with the navy, he took possession of all the islands and held the approaches to all the available harbors south of Charleston; but for this a force of five thousand ought to have been as effective as fifteen thousand. Charleston was what we wanted, and I thought when we landed on Hilton Head, that the men we had, could march into Charleston. I think so now. I suppose General Sherman thought so, and never doubted he would have been in Charleston before Christmas, 1861, if his superior at the head of the Army of the Potomac, or at the War Office, had consented.

Sharing a surname with an army general of greater fame and accomplishment, Brigadier General Thomas W. Sherman was relieved of command of the Expeditionary Corps, some 12,000 troops deployed along the Carolina coast, for being ineffectual, and transferred to the western theater. Sherman lost a leg at Port Hudson, Louisiana, and was later breveted for his war service.

PRIVATE ELIAS A. BRYANT
4TH NEW HAMPSHIRE INFANTRY

Steaming to Port Royal Sound on board the Baltic, a side-wheel steamer towing the disabled Ocean Express, Bryant, a recruit from Francestown, New Hampshire, passed the empty hours at sea on deck with his mates, braving rough weather and trying unsuccessfully to stay dry. The Federal fleet under the command of Flag Officer Samuel F. Du Pont lost four of its 66 ships to gale-force winds.

Saturday, Nov. 2, 1861.
During the night weather was squally. While lying in our bunks we could hear the surging and splashing of the water, so we didn't sleep much. The water poured in through the little port-holes at times. This morning it was very squally and the wind blew like a hurricane. Hundreds were seasick, swearing that they would never go home by sea; if they could not go any other way, they would go on foot through the rebel states. The men were sitting about in groups of twos, threes, and fours, playing cards, etc. I was sitting just forward of the paddle-wheel house on the stalls, playing euchre in a group of four, while others sat about watching us. I noticed the spray dash over the bows and often wetting the men standing there to watch it. I watched the waves as the boat ploughed deeper and deeper into them, causing the men in the front to retreat farther and farther. I excused myself from the game for a moment and went below and got my rubber blanket, which had a hole in the middle, so that it could be put over the head and drop all about me. With this nicely adjusted, I continued the game. No one took the hint, and in the course of the next fifteen or twenty minutes a huge wave broke over our high seat, giving us a good ducking.

Between the force of the waves, which constantly dashed over it, and the pitching of the vessel, it was difficult to get about. In the gale, during the night, we lost one of our best horses overboard. Several times the hawser of the "Ocean Express" broke, and she finally got clear of us entirely.

Confederate guns of Fort Beauregard at Bay Point, South Carolina, remain trained on Port Royal Sound in this sketch by Alfred R. Waud. On November 7, 1861, Union warships forced the evacuation of Forts Walker and Beauregard and secured Port Royal as a Federal base.

CAPTAIN JOHN S. BARNES
U.S.S. Wabash

An 1854 graduate of the U.S. Naval Academy, Barnes spent five years in the navy before taking up law. At the outbreak of the war, the New York native and son of a West Point instructor reenlisted and was assigned to the steam frigate Wabash. Barnes saw action in the seizure of the Cape Hatteras forts in August 1861. Three months later he participated in the fight to subdue Fort Walker at Port Royal Sound and witnessed the aftermath of that battle.

Passing slowly down the coastline of Hilton Head Island, sounding regularly as though entering harbor, we approached the battery. Stretching out of the port I could plainly see the outline of the fort clear-cut against the sky. Every gun and every man at them were in bold relief. Our distance when abreast, going as we were then pointed, could not be more than 600 yards, and with a conscious certainty of receiving much damage to life and to our noble vessel, I pointed out the fort to the captains of guns, adjusted their sights and exhorted them to coolness and promptness. Never did men behave better.

Some time before our broadside guns would bear, although turned sharp forward, the fort opened fire upon us and shot and shell flew and burst ahead, astern, over, and beneath us. Soon we opened and the [preceding] painful silence and inactivity, broken only by the whistling of the enemy's shot and the bursting of their shell, was changed for the deafening roars of our own guns, the rapid shouting of orders, the drifting smoke, and an occasional crash succeeded by showers of splinters. The gun deck was a scene of intense interest. The men had, many of them, stripped to their waists and with brawny chests and arms exposed worked and hove at the guns like demons. Dense clouds of smoke drifted in through the ports over which could be dimly seen the heads of

the men a few ports off, while all more distant were obscured as the firing grew more rapid. For 25 minutes did we remain right abreast the fort, the engines barely turning over so as to keep the ship in command as she headed the strong flood tide. The fire of the enemy gradually slackened and finally ceased as we drove them from their guns into their "bomb proof," utterly unable to withstand the tremendous fire poured into them by the *Wabash* and *Susquehanna,* which last ship with her powerful battery nobly sustained us, her jib-boom being over our taffrail from the beginning to the end. . . .

A few well-aimed shot from the fort came plunging and screaming at us, doing us slight damage as we approached, but suddenly their fire ceased. . . . At the same time one of our vessels to the southward of the fort signalled: "The enemy are deserting the fort!" Quickly passing down the line, we were soon abreast and fired one single gun, but elicited no reply. Going aloft, with my glass I could see the men running for dear life, scattered in every direction, some with arms, most of them without, carrying many wounded. Informing the Como. of the state of affairs, a boat was lowered and, with a flag of truce flying at the bow, Capt. Rodgers, an officious passenger, was sent on shore.

I was at the same time ordered to get my battalion on shore in the tug Mercury as soon as possible and take possession of the fort and surroundings. Soon reaching the beach, with Robertson, we formed and marched straight to the fort down the ditch and up the ramparts with a cheer. *We were first inside.* Posting sentinels upon each face, I detailed a guard of 25 men as pickets and posted them about one-half mile from the fort towards the woods where the enemy were last seen retreating. The scene inside baffles all description. Five guns were dismounted and lying in a heap of fragments about their respective positions in battery. Near each, one or two dead, horribly mangled, were lying, crushed out of all semblance to the human form divine, a

The U.S.S. Wabash survived 30 hits from Confederate batteries during the battle for Port Royal.

Federal troops patrol the waterfront earthworks of South Carolina's Fort Walker, later renamed Fort Welles for Gideon Welles, Lincoln's secretary of the navy. The simultaneous seizure of Forts Walker and Beauregard gave the Federals control of a strategic anchorage midway between the cities of Charleston and Savannah.

mere miserable, dusty heap of gory clothes and flesh. In the bomb proof, stripped of his clothing, for the purpose probably of dressing his wounds, but carefully rolled in blankets, was lying the dead body of an officer, both legs shot away close to the body, which was not uninjured. Poor fellow, he survived the mutilation but a few moments, but the frightful contortion of his features revealed his last agonies.

Collecting, with my men, the bodies left lying about, for burial, at the suggestion of Capt. Rodgers (Raymond), our chaplain was sent for and at sundown we buried the victims of South Carolina's madness in one deep trench. "Consigning our deceased brothers to the mercy of their Creator." *"Plunder"* was lying about begging us to pick it up and *our men* did. I could have got any quantity of trophies. My men brought me things continually. I took a sword and sash of some high officer, a very pretty fan, and several little things which were strewed about. Everything betokened the greatest haste: swords, pistols, sashes, watches, money, ladies' paraphernalia, jewels, etc., dinners half cooked, pots still boiling with their contents overdone. Such a sight as this deserted fort and camp presented brought forcibly to the mind the affrightened condition of its late occupants.

T. H. SPANN

RESIDENT OF BEAUFORT, SOUTH CAROLINA

On November 5, 1861, a Federal reconnaissance flotilla commanded by Flag Captain John Rodgers steamed into Port Royal Sound and was met by a ramshackle collection of Confederate vessels led by Flag Officer Josiah Tattnall, a Georgia native and U.S. Navy veteran. The two fleets immediately exchanged fire, sending several steamers carrying civilian onlookers hurrying for cover. In a letter to family members, Spann, of nearby Beaufort, tries to assess the threat to his town and make arrangements for his loved ones.

Beaufort 5th Nov 1861

The cannons commenced at Bay Point this morning about sunrise and continued until between 9 & 10 o'clock when it ceased. The last dispatch is that we disabled two of their ships and they retired. What is the cause of the long silence we do not know but the presumption is that the fleet has retired out of range of our shot, I suppose to make another attack soon. It is not known whether any one was hurt on our side or not, as we can get no news from the Island. God grant that all are safe. The town is nearly destitute of ladies nearly all have left. It was a source of much relief to me when I was assured that all I cared for was over the ferry. It is my earnest desire that if things should assume a more alarming appearance that you go to Charleston and board for a few days and then should it be unsafe there to go to my brother and James Jennings. Teresa will be delighted to have any of you. Wife Martha I suppose will remain in Charleston. I did think I would come out this evening and spend the night but have concluded it was best not to leave. The best is not to go to Bay Point but to remain and guard the town. God grant that we will all meet again in safety. If Lawrence wishes to come to Beaufort in the morning, he can do so as I think it will be safe. Littleton can come with him and bring my [clothes].

With the fervent prayer that the Almighty will protect us and our cause, I remain to all affectionately

T. H. Spann

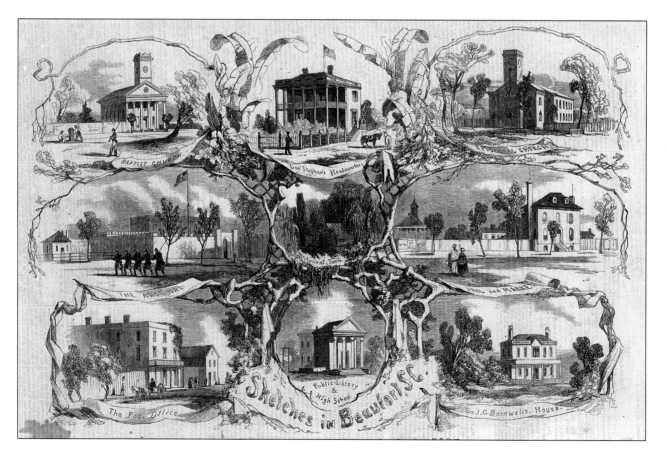

An engraving from Frank Leslie's Illustrated Newspaper depicts idyllic scenes of occupied Beaufort. An elegant summer haven for wealthy plantation owners, Beaufort saw its beautiful gardens and sweeping grounds transformed into an army camp by the Yankees in General Isaac Stevens' command. On his arrival Stevens halted all looting in the virtually abandoned town and set about restoring some of the buildings ravaged by the occupying troops.

"On the Monday following we left for Charleston, the plantation being considered unsafe for ladies."

Yankee soldiers congregate in front of John S. Fyler's dry goods store and the post office in downtown Beaufort in this picture by Samuel A. Cooley, a local photographer contracted by the Federals. Cooley, who also operated a general store, was one of many local merchants who found themselves doing a brisk business with the Federal occupying forces.

ANN BARNWELL
RESIDENT OF BEAUFORT, SOUTH CAROLINA

As the Federal fleet steamed toward Port Royal Sound and news of imminent hostilities reached Beaufort, residents hastily packed up their families and headed inland, seeking refuge from the fighting. Ann Barnwell, daughter of a prominent South Carolina family, moved to her uncle's plantation near Charleston; years later she would write of the toll the war took on her family.

Late in the day our cousin, Miss Eliza Barnwell (afterwards librarian of the South Carolina College) called. She told us that her father said that we should leave the town as early as possible and take refuge in one of his plantation houses on the mainland; our own plantation being on Beaufort Island was no safer than the town. We sent to our plantation for carts to take such things as we thought best to carry—not much, for we expected soon to return—and rose early Monday, packed and had the house put in order before leaving it.

At twelve o'clock the church bell rang. My mother, her five daughters, three sons (the other four being with the armies), and our neighbor, Mrs. Edward Cuthbert, with her two little boys, assembled. We united for the last time in that house in prayer.

That afternoon we reached the plantation, where we spent one week in anxiety among strange negroes. They and the men servants who had accompanied us went into the town every night, bringing back with them such "prog" as they could "tote." One offered my mother doylies her father had taken from the stores. Our old coachman brought my mother a discarded "bombazine bonnet" which he had found in her

"In a few weeks after our arrival the 'minges' made their appearance, and tormented us nigh unto death."

room. The negroes did not at that time realize that we were not to return soon, and that they could easily have deserted us and crossed over to "Old Laurel Bay," to which those who survived the war returned.

My brother, Edward H. Barnwell, went, with a few others, into the town one night before the Yankees had taken possession. It was as still as death. They met no one, and he even entered our house, which headed the bay. Looking from the window of the fourth story, he saw the gunboats of the enemy not far away.

In a few days our forts were abandoned and our soldiers made their way to the mainland, but my brother, Stephen E. Barnwell (afterwards acting adjutant-general to Gen. Stephen Elliott during his defence of Fort Sumter), was missing from the ranks, having tarried to assist the wounded.

It was, to us, the first of many pangs we suffered during the war, Stephen missing! What did that mean? Our suspense was only of a few hours' duration, but who can ever measure anxiety by time? Is it not degree? That night we heard Maum Nancy's voice, "Missus, Mass Steben come, Mass Steben come." Out we rushed to meet him. We saw the old woman trying to bring him in as she had done when a boy.

On the Monday following we left for Charleston, the plantation being considered unsafe for ladies. Upon arriving there we found my brother, William H. Barnwell, lying mortally wounded at my uncle's house. He had been accidentally shot by a friend. He was lieutenant of Regiment C. S. A., and lacked one week of his twenty-first birthday. It was a fearful grief. It seemed so terrible that he should have fallen so uselessly; but when we passed through the disappointment of the surrender and the fiery ordeal of Reconstruction, we felt that he had been spared *much,* for *his* was an uncommonly high-spirited, imperious nature, and he would have suffered more than most.

SERGEANT EUGENE BEAUGE
45TH PENNSYLVANIA INFANTRY

After Port Royal Sound was secured, some 12,000 Federal troops spread out and occupied the southeastern sea islands from just south of Charleston to Ossabaw Sound on the Georgia coast. For Beauge and his mates, duty on Otter Island included building a wharf, commissary, guardhouse, and hospital. Hard labor notwithstanding, the Pennsylvanian discovered that the island offered much more than the fighting man's customary rations.

Otter Island in St. Helena Sound on the coast of South Carolina, where Companies B, F, G, H and K, with Colonel Welsh in command, landed December 11th, 1861, was a barren sandbar six or seven miles in circumference. No part of the island was cultivated, and except here and there a group of stunted palmetto trees and a few tufts of wild grass, nothing would grow there, any way. At one end of the island was a swamp with a lot of frogs and a few alligators in it. . . .

The coast between Port Royal and Charleston seemed to be made up of islands and islets, around and through which wound in eccentric courses numerous rivers and creeks.

The islands, however, were not all barren by any means. There is probably no better soil anywhere in South Carolina than on Fenwick, Lady's and Coosaw Islands. They were good places to go foraging. It didn't take us long to find that out. Crossing the water in row boats, details from the different companies would go to one or the other of these islands one day and come back the next with a load of plunder, such as beef, mutton, poultry, sweet potatoes, peanuts, milk, honey, canned fruit, dishes and other needful commodities. One day the boys found a case of long-necked bottles filled with rare sparkling wine. Negroes frequently went along to act as guides and make themselves useful generally. Once our fellows tore down a house on Fenwick Island and brought back a lot of second hand lumber that came in handy to make floors, benches, tables, shelves, etc., in the tents.

PRIVATE DANIEL ELDREDGE
3D NEW HAMPSHIRE INFANTRY

For the many thousands of Federals who landed on the Carolina shores in November 1861, the new duty seemed to promise an exotic vacation of balmy weather and abundant foraging. But as Eldredge, who saw light clerical duty owing to ill health, later recalled, their tenure on Edisto Island involved combat with a ubiquitous and indefatigable enemy.

The picket duty there was the most tedious we had in South Carolina. In a few weeks after our arrival the "minges" made their appearance, and tormented us nigh unto death. Mosquito netting (technically "mosquito bars") was issued as a measure of relief; but the meshes were so large that the minges easily passed through. Our quarters were the old negro huts (cabins), which were inhabited by fleas on our arrival. As we were determined to occupy the same quarters, many and hot were the battles between us, and in which more or less blood was shed.

The reader will perceive that our nights were disagreeable, whether on picket or in quarters. The abandoned cotton fields, not having a cultivator, brought forth blackberries spontaneously. They were so plenty, some of us ate but little else. The pickers for sale got ten cents a quart readily.

Boat loads of negroes, of both sexes, old and young, came over from "de main" nearly every night, and in such numbers that provision could scarcely be made for them. They were shipped to Hilton Head and St. Helena Islands as fast as possible.

At one time a sort of mania for gambling seized the men, many of them, and it took the particular form called a "sweat board." Daily and hourly, while the fever lasted, men could be seen singly, in pairs and by squads, silently stealing away into the bushes to ply their favorite game. Much money changed hands. In vain the officers attempted to stop it. They only succeeded in reducing its proportions. This mania suddenly disappeared, without leaving a trace behind, save in the minds and pockets of those who had been fleeced.

PRIVATE ELIAS A. BRYANT
4TH NEW HAMPSHIRE INFANTRY

By the end of 1861, the strategic Hilton Head Island had been transformed into a bustling Yankee community with its own hospital, church, bakery, and theater. Bryant, who played in the regimental band, described his routine: "Every morning there is a detail of about twenty men to go shoveling, or to work on the wharf. I feel a great deal better when I have shoveled all day than I do to stay here and drill." As he would also recall, special excursions made the hard work worthwhile.

Tuesday, Dec. 10, 1861

About twenty of us went over to Bull Island foraging, taking two boats and landing at a wharf built for large vessels. We found a large number of negroes digging potatoes on a very large plantation. It belonged to a wealthy gentleman, Colonel Seabrook, who had left it to the care, or otherwise, of the negroes. Whenever we found houses or plantations deserted we were permitted to take freely of provisions, whatever might be wanted, but were ordered not to molest dwellings. Whenever premises were occupied by Union or those representing themselves as such, they were protected even to placing guard over their property, if requested.

Upon this island were great numbers of sheep, cattle, and fowl. Here we found some of the most splendid roses I ever saw. Turkey buzzards are as plenty here as flocks of blackbirds in New England. I saw here a big rosebush full of large red blossoms, almost purple, and they were the most beautiful I ever saw, they were so dark a red.

Midges, black flies, and mosquitoes were a great annoyance to us here, as in camp.

We killed beef cattle and sheep, and ducks and chickens, and had sweet potatoes in plenty. We had trouble in getting our poultry, the negroes considering that it belonged to them, and showed such determined fight for their rights that we were obliged to give it up for that day. Dodge found castor-oil plants and obtained some beans.

CHAPLAIN FREDERIC R. DENISON
1ST RHODE ISLAND HEAVY ARTILLERY

Denison, a minister from Pawtucket, Rhode Island, became chaplain of the 1st Rhode Island Heavy Artillery in 1861 and accompanied the regiment to the Carolina coast in the fall of that year. From the base at Hilton Head, detachments of his regiment fanned out to take control of surrounding islands and waterways. Writing after the war, Denison described how the men found plantations abandoned by their owners and jubilant, newly liberated slaves.

Company H that had been thrown across the harbor with Company I to hold the islands around Fort Beauregard, was sent out in detachments, early in January, to different points. Captain Rogers held a part with his head-quarters at Coffin's Point, on the north end of St. Helena Island, opposite Otter Island. Lieutenant Brayton had a portion of the company at Brickyard Point, on Lady's Island. Squads under Sergeants Burroughs and Hiepe were sent across St. Helena Island to St. Helena village—quite a hamlet of near fifty houses of all sorts—and quite a summer resort for southern gentility. As the rebels had stampeded, everything was in the hands of the negroes, who received our men with delight, and furnished them with a good supper. Says Sergeant Burroughs, "We were the first Yankee troops they had seen. We found the men clothed in suits made from Brussells and tapestry carpets, and from cloth cut from the covering of old massa's furniture. They were helping themselves to everything, even tearing down their old masters' residences to build up their own huts." Sergeant Hiepe was left with a squad in charge of this village.

Sergeant Burroughs, with ten men and a boat's crew of negroes, passed over to Coosaw Island, in the Coosaw River, and was joyfully welcomed by the "contrabands." Here he found the abandoned plantation of General Barnwell, with a quantity of cotton that the flying rebels had failed to burn. The Sergeant immediately detailed the negroes on the fatigue service of baling this "King" of South Carolina, while he took up military head-quarters in the Barnwell mansion. This was a war-picture, and we wish a photographer had been present to seize it. The sergeant said he had a plenty of fresh meat, sweet-potatoes, Johnny-cakes, and milk. So General Barnwell's secession tables were turned.

The Sergeant was a true, administrative genius, and equal to his times. We see him sitting up to his live-oak fire in the Barnwell castle, in this part of South Carolina, with his men rubbing up their rifles, and his detail of happy negroes strapping up "King Cotton" for a Yankee market. Meanwhile he counted the probabilities of his situation. Apprehensive that no exasperated chivalry might venture to attack him, having only ten men in full mail, he concluded to enlist a number of the negroes, who had old shot-guns, used in bringing down game for Massa Barnwell. The "contrabands" were ready, and he supplied them with ammunition. So they gladly stood guard and gloried in their new dignity. These, we are sure, were the first colored troops in the Department of the South.

Apropos to the Sergeant's Johnny-cakes; the corn was ground by the negro women, in little hand-mills, the only sort used on the Sea Islands, rather the pattern of the ancient (old Hebrew) mills—"two shall be grinding at a mill,"—the two mill-stones, about the size of No. 1 Northern cheeses, mounted on a bench or block of live-oak, the upper stone revolved by a stick inserted in a hole near its margin. One person attended to the revolving of the stone, while the other fed in the grain; and both usually singing some easy and cheering refrain.

Situated near Fort Walker on Hilton Head Island, the William Pope house served as the Federals' main signal station during the occupation. As seen here, siege gun carriages litter the mansion's front lawn, and a tower, built to increase signaling range, tops its roof. Countless messages passed through this station between the warships at sea and the Federal army headquarters nearby.

"In June, rains will come in South Carolina and when they come, men's plans always fail if they won't stand drowning."

COLONEL EDWIN METCALF
3D RHODE ISLAND INFANTRY

Ordered to march east across Johns Island in the approach to Charleston, newly appointed battalion commander Metcalf and his untried men found themselves slogging through some six miles of mud. He wrote: "I saw the hardiest in my command sit down and cry like children while they cut off their shoes, then dragged themselves along to shelter. Nor was it possible for them to move again until three days of nursing and new shoes put them once more in marching order."

Instructed to await reinforcements before launching an assault on Secessionville, Brigadier General Henry W. Benham single-handedly created a Federal fiasco when he disobeyed orders and sent his men into a bloodbath. Benham was court-martialed, but on a presidential reprieve he was reassigned to the Corps of Engineers.

If I could only describe that midnight march! You all see that that is the effective incident I am so anxious to bring out into full view, and have no words to do it with. You understand that it had been timed so that the column should reach the landing, be ferried over to James Island, effect a junction with other troops arriving by water, and before daybreak advance upon the works of an enemy surprised and unable to resist. Then, a short, victorious march to Charleston, and the whole sea coast is ours! How simple, easy, natural—how well contrived, how impossible to fail! Alas! no; success was very certain—if it should not rain, and it did rain. In June, rains will come in South Carolina and when they come, men's plans always fail if they won't stand drowning. My horse did not drown, perhaps because he was born to be shot. I stand a good deal of drowning myself, having tried it in early childhood and made a failure of it even then, and my men would have been ashamed to do anything but follow me that night. How the water did pour! how the road deepened and lengthened, until a march that would without fatigue have ended long before daybreak, was not over at nine o'clock in the morning. And when it was over, and we all snugly quartered in the church, houses and barns of a deserted village, the failure of the well contrived plan of operations was the last thing we thought of. Indeed, that was not a matter of the slightest importance to us just then.

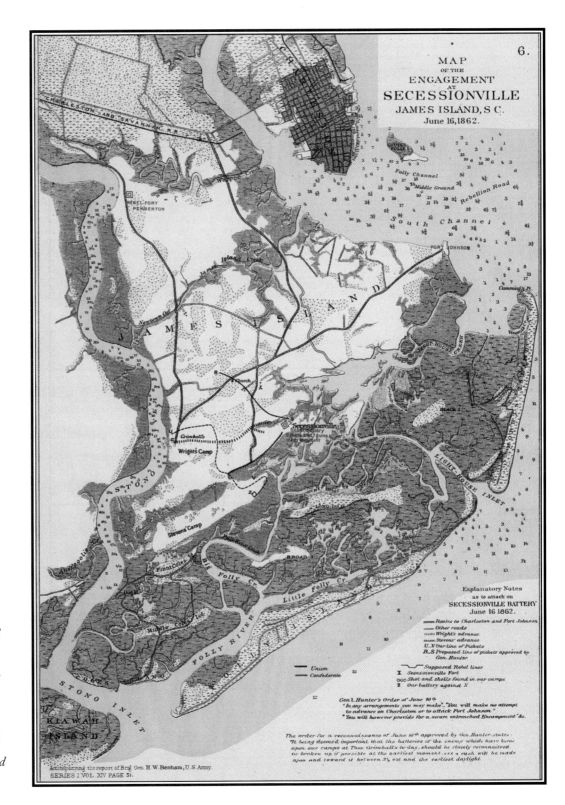

Early in June 1862 Federal forces under Generals Benham, Wright, and Stevens came ashore at Grimball's Landing on the Stono River with the intent of seizing James Island and advancing on Charleston. At dawn on the 16th, supported by gunboats on the Stono, the Federal troops attacked a dominating Confederate stronghold near the hamlet of Secessionville. Although the Federals far outnumbered their foe, the entrenched Rebels held their position in bloody fighting and repelled the Union charge. The retreating Federals left behind 683 dead, wounded, and missing, and James Island remained in Confederate hands.

PRIVATE PHILIP W. COLEMAN

8TH MICHIGAN INFANTRY

Stricken with a series of illnesses, Coleman spent his first two months in South Carolina in the hospital. Rejoining his regiment in January 1862, the Vernon, Michigan, native was in the first line of battle when his regiment charged the Rebel works at Secessionville, and he was cut down by enemy fire. In a memoir Coleman recounted his near superhuman struggle to survive.

On the morning of the 16th of June the regiment being in front advanced across the first cotton field on the Yates plantation. The regiment was deployed to the right and left, passing through a hedge fence across the first cotton field, then through an opening in another hedge into the second cotton field, formed in line of battle about half a mile from Fort Johnson at just daylight. The order was to charge with unloaded guns and fixed bayonets. The charge was made and at the third volley from the enemy's guns I was among those who fell having been wounded by a cannister shot in the left arm, left side, and a bullet went in the top of the head, and right thigh, the left arm hanging by the muscles at its back. The question came like a flash through my mind, how was I to save my life, mother having told me the morning I left home that I was to return but that there was to be a change, but what that change was she was not privileged to know. After the first charge the regiment fell back to the first cotton field to await re-inforcements. They were re-inforced by the second brigade in which was the 79th Highlanders. A second charge was made passing by those who were dead and wounded. After the second charge the enemy having been re-inforced, our men were repulsed and ordered to fall back, the Colonel informing those on the field who were wounded but able to retreat to do so or they would be taken prisoners. Being hampered with my

haversack, my blanket and cartridge box and belt the question was how to relieve myself of this burden in order to enable me to escape. With my knife I cut myself loose from all this burden, saving only my canteen. Then the question arose in retreating whether I would have sufficient vitality to get off the field. In order to save my life, the veins and arteries in my arm having been severed by the cannister shot, I held the artery of my left arm with the thumb of my right hand and retreated off the first field. On reaching the hedge I sat down with my feet hanging in a ditch. The Captain of Co. A of the 8th Maine seeing me come off the field remarked that any man brave enough to come under that storm was entitled to proper care and he immediately detailed four men of his company who put me on a blanket and carried me to my regimental field hospital which was in a negro shanty in which were some 12 or 15 other wounded men, some crying, others groaning and some cursing their fate. One man in particular more noisy than the rest created considerable of a disturbance. I inquired of him how badly he was wounded. He said he had two flesh wounds. I told him of my condition and then informed him that I didn't want to hear anything more from him and that if he made any more noise I with my Colts revolver would be compelled to break a bone for him so he would have something to cry about. There was no more noise in that hut. The surgeon soon came around and I asked him to have me moved out into the sun as I was cold and weak and felt that I needed sunlight to warm me up. The surgeon examined me, shook his head and said to me, "Coleman, your case is desperate." I asked him if he would not have me sent to the camp by the first ambulance, and here I want to speak a good word for one of the despised Jews who was our ambulance driver known by all the boys as "Little Jake." The surgeon true to his promise I was the first man to be sent to the regimental hospital in the ambulance. And such a journey! It was a ride of about two miles, one half mile of it being over a corduroy road. I leave it to you to judge of what must have been that ride in my condition. My constant plea to Little Jake was— "Jakey, please drive slower." His answer always was: "The mule scarcely moves."

"I told him … that if he made any more noise I with my Colts revolver would be compelled to break a bone for him so he would have something to cry about."

Private Thomas C. Shepherd of the 1st South Carolina Infantry survived the fierce fighting at the Secessionville earthworks, but he succumbed to disease only months later in November 1862.

LIEUTENANT IREDELL JONES
1st South Carolina (Regulars) Infantry

In the defense of Secessionville, Lieutenant Jones and fellow infantrymen of the 1st South Carolina were called upon to change roles and join the artillery batteries in the Rebel bastion. Jones recalled his comrades' valiant efforts to repel the Federal onslaught at daybreak on June 16. While mourning the Confederate losses, he professed admiration for the Federals' courageous attempts to gain the fort in the face of deadly fire.

The battery was contested on the ramparts in a hand to hand fight, and a log was rolled from the top to sweep the enemy from the sides of the breastwork. All praise is due to the Charleston battalion and Lamar's two companies of artillery, as well as Smith's battalion, and had it not been for the desperate fighting of these commands, while reinforcements were being sent for, the important point at Secessionville would have been lost. But while we give all credit to our own troops, let us never again disparage our enemy and call them cowards, for nothing was ever more glorious than their three charges in the face of a raking fire of grape and canister, and then at last, as if to do or die, they broke into two columns and rushed against our right and left flanks, which movement would have gained the day, had not our reinforcements arrived. We were emphatically surprised, but could not have been otherwise expected, when we recollect that the three commands before mentioned, which were at Secessionville, had been under fire of the enemy's battery for the past two weeks, being shelled day and night, and thereby almost exhausted from want of sleep. The lamented Captain Reed had been manning our battery for ten days with his company. Many of our finest men were killed, and all the friends or relations of some of the officers in the Fort, and a general gloom is spread over the countenances of all here now.

MAJOR JOHN G. PRESSLEY
25TH SOUTH CAROLINA INFANTRY

On June 16 Pressley and his comrades were in the woods on the Confederate left, east of the main earthworks at Secessionville. The first Federal assault was driven back, and when a second column of Union troops attacked, the men of the 25th held their fire, believing the troops were friendly. When the order to fire was finally given, the regiment fought admirably, as Pressley later recalled.

From the time we took our position and for a long time afterwards, in fact, till after the enemy retired from the field in front of Secessionville, we were under a heavy artillery fire from the enemy's fleet of gunboats in the Stono and from their land batteries. No damage was done us by the artillery. Quite a number of Congreve rockets were flying over and around us in very eccentric directions. When we got into position, the men were ordered to lie down for better protection, and were lying down when the fight commenced. The field and staff-officers were in rear of Company B. After the enemy began to come out of the woods, and Company B commenced firing, I passed along the line to communicate with Colonel Stevens, who was in the rear of our right, endeavoring to prevent the men firing, still believing that the men in the woods belonged to his regiment. As I passed along, one of the enemy fired at me over our men from behind a stump. The ball struck the ground near my feet. I pointed him out, and after the battle he was found with three or four balls through his body. After assuring Colonel Stevens that the enemy and not his men were in our front, and causing the companies on the right to commence firing, I returned to my place. The battalion behaved splendidly. I saw but two men during the day who were not acting like heroes. Sergeant-Major Samuel W. Dibble drove one from his hiding place behind a tree about four inches in diameter, which he supposed in his fright covered his whole body. Colonel Hagood stopped the other, who was making his way to the rear and brought him back. No captain would claim either of them. Every one was ashamed to acknowledge that they belonged to his company, and I am not sure that either of them were of the Eutaws. They probably belonged to some other command. May have been some of the demoralized pickets who had been driven in. One company of Colonel Stevens' regiment had fallen in with us and behaved very well. Both Stevens and Hagood acted very coolly. The former was not at all to blame for causing us to hold our fire so long, though this circumstance was unfortunate, as, had the whole battalion commenced firing as soon as it got into position, the enemy's fire would not have been concentrated on one of our companies, nor would we have fought at such close quarters.

> "Quick as thought, I dropped flat on the ground and let the iron hail pass over me, and when I rose it was to see the gound strewn with Roundheads dying, dead, and wounded."

Though outnumbered by the Yankees nearly 4 to 1, Brigadier General Nathan G. Evans succeeded in retaining James Island and blocking the Federals' route to Charleston. Evans had earlier distinguished himself on the battlefield at First Manassas.

Henry H. Williams, a fiddle-toting member of the Confederacy's Washington Light Infantry, and his mates relax outside a tent grandly dubbed Music Hall on Cole's Island in the spring of 1862. Lieutenant Richard W. Greer, seated at right, was killed fighting at Secessionville.

Quick as thought, I dropped flat on the ground and let the iron hail pass over me, and when I rose it was to see the ground strewn with Roundheads dying, dead, and wounded, in all sorts of mangled horrid forms, and the Regiment cut in two, just as the other had been. . . . Meanwhile the right of the Highlanders and part of the Roundhead Regiment got on the parapet and fired into the fort at the gunners, but two rifle pits filled with men and a couple of Howitzers on the opposite side of the fort opened fire on them, and either killed or wounded most of them and drove the others back.

By this time Major Lecky with about two companies of the Roundheads came up to their support, but before he reached them somebody gave the order to fall back, which they did, accompanied by all of the 8th Michigan and the Highlanders that were able to go with them.

I now turned my attention to retrieving the mistakes of the day. . . . panic and disaster were imminent every minute, for if my Brigade fell back in disorder, the enemy would make a sortie and cut us to pieces. During all the time the storm of grape hissed over the ground and every discharge did fearful execution.

By this time one of my mounted orderlies (I had four) had ridden his horse down, carrying my orders, and went for a fresh horse, two of them were wounded and carried off the field, and the fourth had his horse shot from under him, while listening to my orders to be carried to Gen'l Stevens in the rear. . . . A cannon ball had struck his horse fair in the forehead and buried itself in his heart and on rising from the ground, the poor fellow was covered with hairs and blood of his horse and was not quite sure whether he was killed or his horse or both.

COLONEL DANIEL LEASURE

100TH PENNSYLVANIA INFANTRY (ROUNDHEADS)

Leasure led the 100th Pennsylvania as that regiment advanced with the 79th New York Highlanders to support the battered men of the 8th Michigan. After the retreat, Leasure, a surgeon before the war, worked tirelessly to save the men mangled by the storm of grape and canister that cut through the Federal ranks.

I advanced with the left flank of the Highlanders, cheering them to the charge, till when within about one hundred yards of the works three immense guns bellowed out a perfect cloud of grape, canister, old chains, empty porter bottles, nails, and even brickets, and just cut the regiment in two leaving one half to go [to] the right and the other to the left. Still the two portions passed on till when about thirty paces from the parapet, the rifles and musketry opened on us, and in less than two minutes I was the only man left on his feet.

Within fifty yards of me . . . I saw a whole regiment, the 28th Massachusetts, lying in the bushes behind a kind of bank that led up to the left of the fort. I had barely time to see this . . . when again the storm of missiles from the huge guns leaped out with tongues of fire, darkening all the air with the projectiles with which they had been crammed to the muzzle.

"General Benham disobeyed these positive orders and clear instructions, and the result, I deeply regret to say, has been a disastrous repulse."

Flanked by his staff at Beaufort, South Carolina, Brigadier General Isaac I. Stevens sat for this photograph in the spring of 1862. After the Federal rout at Secessionville in June, Stevens was reassigned to Virginia where, on the field at Chantilly, his son, Captain Hazard Stevens (third from left) was wounded, and the general was killed.

BRIGADIER GENERAL DAVID HUNTER

COMMANDER, DEPARTMENT OF THE SOUTH

By June 2, 1862, Hunter had nearly 7,500 troops on James Island, poised to make a move on Charleston. Stalling when he thought himself outnumbered, he returned to Hilton Head and left Benham in command, ordering him to await reinforcements. After Benham disobeyed, at great cost to the Federals, Hunter had him arrested and sent him to Washington bearing the letter below.

Headquarters Department of the South
Hilton Head, Port Royal, S.C., June 23, 1862.
Sir: On the 13th Instant I had the honor of informing you that we had occupied the southwestern portion of James Island, on the Stono River, within 5 or 6 miles of Charleston, intending to make a rush for the reduction of that city as soon as re-enforcements should arrive. As we failed in being able to make a *coup de main* on Charleston, in consequence of our transportation not having been returned to us from the North, the enemy had time to throw strong re-enforcements on James Island, rendering an advance with our existing force extremely hazardous. I therefore determined to make no forward movement, having satisfied myself by reconnaissances of the increase of the enemy's strength; and on leaving the Stono to return to this point, where matters affecting the safety of the command in other portions of the department called for my presence, I gave positive orders to General Benham that no advance should be made until further explicit orders had been received from these headquarters. General Benham disobeyed these positive orders and clear instructions, and the result, I deeply regret to say, has been a disastrous repulse, only redeemed by the brilliant conduct of the troops while engaged in the assault and their steadiness and patient courage when compelled to retire. . . .

In view of these circumstances and the serious consequences which have arisen from his disobedience, I have felt it my duty to arrest General Benham and order him North by steamer conveying this letter.

Modeled on a proposed national color recommended by the Charleston Mercury in March 1862, the flag of the 27th South Carolina Infantry boasts a shield in its center bearing the battle honor "Secessionville," in remembrance of the battle of June 16, 1862. The initials stand for the regiment's former designation as the Charleston Light Infantry.

The Threat of the Ironclads

Well before the Union army's bloody setback at Secessionville, the navy high command in Washington had begun cooking up its own scheme for a purely naval attack on Charleston and its bristling ring of forts. Essential to the plan would be a flotilla of those new and revolutionary marvels the ironclad warships, such as the *Monitor,* which had slugged it out with the Confederates' heavily gunned *Virginia* in a historic battle off Virginia's Hampton Roads in March 1862. The *Monitor* alone, boasted Gustavus Fox, combative aide to navy secretary Gideon Welles, could attack with impunity at Charleston Harbor. Given a fleet of the armored vessels, the navy could blast its way past the enemy forts and bring Charleston to its knees in a day.

Through late 1862, Union shipyards were busy riveting together more ironclads. By the

The shot-dented turret of the monitor Passaic shows some of the damage inflicted by Confederate guns during the Federal naval attack at Charleston Harbor on April 7, 1863. The Passaic was hit no fewer than 35 times during the engagement—a dismal failure for Admiral Du Pont's Union flotilla.

early spring of 1863 the first of seven new monitor-style vessels was being towed southward by a navy steamer—the low-slung ironclads were not seaworthy enough to make an ocean voyage on their own. At the end of the journey they joined the South Atlantic Fleet commanded by Samuel Du Pont, who had been promoted to rear admiral for his capture of the superb anchorage of Port Royal Sound in 1861. Du Pont's orders were to steam into Charleston Harbor with the new ships and seize the hated city.

Du Pont, a veteran saltwater sailor, was exceedingly dubious about the tactical plan. The monitors' armor plate might be impervious to enemy shot and shell, but the ships were painfully slow, with a top speed of six knots, and difficult to maneuver. Worse, each monitor carried only two cannons, hardly enough for a punishing broadside. The guns were big and powerful—usually 11-inch and 15-inch smoothbores—but they were so slow firing that, as one wag put it, a man could smoke a cigar between shots.

Determined to thwart Du Pont was the new commander in Charleston, the flamboyant Pierre Gustave Toutant Beauregard. Beauregard's career as a field general was in temporary eclipse. President Jefferson Davis had relieved him of command of the main Confederate army in the West after his retreat from Corinth, Mississippi, following the Battle of Shiloh.

Beauregard, however, was a first-rate military engineer. He quickly beefed up Charleston's defenses, placing new big guns in Fort Sumter and Fort Moultrie and adding new defenses on Morris Island at the harbor entrance. Made aware by Northern newspaper reports that the ironclads were coming, he anchored buoys at measured distances from the forts, giving the gunners precise ranges, salted the channels with mines, and sank all manner of obstructions and torpedos calculated to foul the propellers or crush the hulls of attacking ships. By the spring of 1863 Charleston had become, said Captain Percival Drayton of the monitor *Passaic*, "almost the strongest place by sea in the world."

Beauregard also decided to knock the Federal blockaders off balance before the monitors arrived. On the morning of January 31, 1863, he sent two armored Confederate rams, the *Chicora* and the *Palmetto State*, steaming out of Charleston Harbor. Attacking in the misty dawn, the rams badly damaged two Federal vessels in short, sharp actions and hit several other blockaders before returning safely back into the harbor. The exploit, much celebrated in the South, was only a temporary embarrassment to the North, but it augured ill for the forthcoming big attack.

Admiral Du Pont's own experiment with his monitors provided no cause for optimism. He dispatched one of the first vessels to reach Port Royal, the *Montauk,* to bombard Fort McAllister, a small Confederate earthwork on the Georgia coast. The *Montauk* shelled the fort twice but did little damage.

Du Pont then sent three more monitors, the *Passaic, Patapsco*, and *Nahant,* on the same mission. The ironclads were hit repeatedly by the fort's guns but suffered little damage. Yet neither could the vessels do much harm to the forts.

Glumly reporting that the ships' "offensive powers" were "feeble in dealing with forts," Du Pont protested to Washington that the only effective way to attack Charleston was with a combined land-sea operation. Secretary Welles would have none of it. To him, Du Pont lacked the will to fight; he was "a man with a reputation to preserve instead of one to make." In early March, Welles sent Du Pont three more monitors and a sharp letter suggesting he act, and soon. Finally on April 6 the admiral ordered his fleet of flat-decked little warships with their "cheese-box" turrets into action.

A storm frustrated the first attempt, but shortly after noon the next day, April 7, the seven monitors steamed in a line up the deepwater channel heading for Fort Sumter accompanied by the *Keokuk,* a lightly armored experimental ironclad, and Du Pont's flagship, the *New Ironsides,* a ponderous 3,500-ton armored steam frigate with 16 big guns. In all, the Union fleet had 36 guns to face 80 guns in Fort Sumter, as well as additional Rebel firepower from the various coastal batteries. As the ironclads approached, Sumter's commander, Colonel Alfred M. Rhett, defiantly raised the fort's flags, fired a salute, and ordered the band to strike up "Dixie."

The Federal line almost immediately came to a dead halt as the leading monitor, the *Weehawken,* got its anchor chain tangled with a large raft it was pushing ahead as a minesweeper. The deep-hulled *New Ironsides,* in the center of the line, also stopped

for fear of going aground. Shortly Du Pont ordered the three monitors in line behind the flagship to steam around it, and the other ironclads also made headway. The *Keokuk's* commander, convinced that his poorly armored ship could not withstand Sumter's heavy guns, chose to prove his convictions by steaming as close to the fort as possible.

Finally, about 2:50 p.m. the Federal ships fired the first shots at Fort Sumter. The fort's gunners immediately blasted back, first with thunderous salvos, then with better-aimed rapid-fire shots. Scores of shells screamed across the channel. Near misses threw up enormous waterspouts around the ironclads while dozens of hits clanged and banged off their turrets. Soon large, angry-looking gray clouds of powder smoke were drifting over the water, engulfing the ironclads. "It seemed," said one eyewitness, "as if all the fires of hell were turned upon the Union fleet."

The ear-splitting cannonade continued for nearly two hours with the guns in Fort Moultrie and the shore batteries joining Sumter to catch the monitors in a hair-raising cross fire. The Union return fire was slow and sporadic. The deep-drafted *New Ironsides,* plagued by steering problems, ran aground and remained too far away to help, firing only a single broadside. The monitors managed to hit Sumter 55 times. Some of their huge 440-pound shot shook the fort to its bedrock and blasted eight-foot craters in the ramparts. But the walls held and the explosions did little damage to the fort's batteries. In all, the Union ships fired 139 shells while the Confederate guns got off a staggering 2,200. Of these about 300 hit the ironclads.

Du Pont, seeing that the attack was getting nowhere, ordered a withdrawal about 5:00 p.m.

The admiral intended to try again the next day, but that night his captains reported crucial damage. Only one sailor, miraculously, had been killed, but enemy shells had jammed turret mechanisms, damaged gunports, and put guns out of action. The *Weehawken* had been hit 53 times, the *Nantucket* 51, the *Patapsco* 47, the *Nahant* 36, the *Passaic* 35, the *Catskill* 20, and the *Montauk* 14. As for the *Keokuk,* it had been shot into a sieve by 90 hits and would sink early the next morning in shallow water off Morris Island.

Reluctantly, Du Pont canceled the attack. "We have met with a sad repulse," he told his captains. "I shall not turn it into a great disaster." The retreat of the ironclads caused wild rejoicing in Charleston and the South. In the North there was dismay and outrage. Welles and Fox, unable to comprehend what had occurred, bitterly blamed Du Pont. Welles sneered, "A fight of 30 minutes and the loss of one man satisfied the admiral."

In a last, sad humiliation for Du Pont, Rebel salvage experts managed to recover the 11-inch guns from the sunken *Keokuk* and added them to Charleston's batteries. On June 3 the admiral was relieved of his command. Once more it would be up to the army to hammer a wedge into the city's defenses.

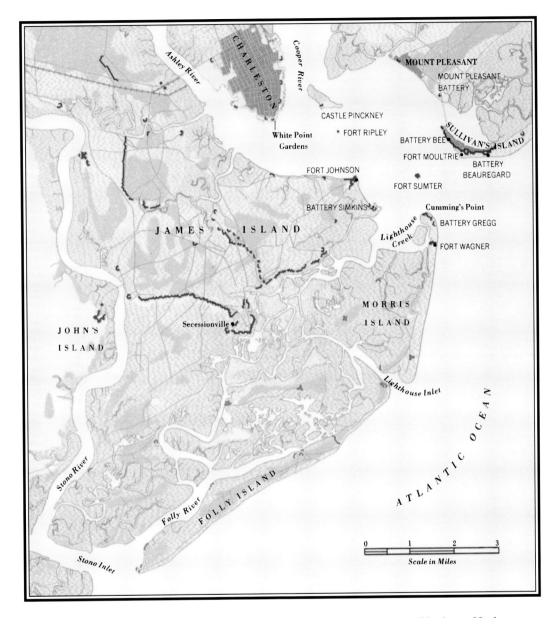

When Admiral Du Pont's fleet of ironclads and wooden steamers crossed the bar at Charleston Harbor on April 7, 1863, they entered what one U.S. Navy officer described as "a cul-de-sac, a circle of fire." The Confederate defensive ring included batteries on Morris and James Islands to the south and Sullivan's Island on the north—all anchored by Fort Sumter in the middle of the harbor. The Rebel guns joined together to weave a curtain of crossing fire that overwhelmed and repelled the Federal attackers.

PRIVATE ARTHUR P. FORD

Buist's Battery, South Carolina Artillery

Arthur Ford was only 17 years old when he volunteered for the Confederate service in April 1861. Shortly after helping capture the U.S.S. Isaac P. Smith in the clash described here, his battery in Buist's company increased its mobility by exchanging its massive eight-inch howitzers for lighter 12-pounder Napoleons.

At this time the Federal gunboats were very annoying in Stono River, coming as high up as possible daily, and shelling our pickets, and it was determined to make a diversion. Therefore, in January, 1863, our battery with Capt. Smith's and other troops were sent over to John's Island, and ambushed at Legare's point place to cooperate with two companies of Lucas' battalion and some other troops on James Island. The design was to capture the *Isaac P. Smith.* This vessel was an iron screw steamer of 453 tons, and carried eight 8-inch navy guns, or sixty-four pounders, and a 7-inch thirty-pounder Parrott gun. She was commanded at the time by Capt. F. S. Conover; and her crew consisted of 11 officers and 105 men.

The affair was completely successful. The gunboat in her daily ascent was taken by surprise, and after a short fight at only 75 or 100 yards distance, as she ran trying to escape, had her steam drum torn by a shell, and had to surrender. She had twenty-three men killed and wounded, while we lost one man killed. My howitzer was at a sharp bend in the river, and as the gunboat ran past, her stern was directly about 100 yards in front of the gun I served. It put one 8-inch shrapnel shell into her stern port, and I learned afterwards that the shell knocked a gun off its trunnions and killed or wounded eight men. A prize crew was put on board immediately and the vessel towed by a tug up the river, and later on to the city. While the prisoners were being landed, the U.S.S. *Commodore McDonough* steamed up the river and

opened fire on us, but a few well-directed shots from our batteries soon made her desist and drop back down the river. At nightfall, our command returned to Charleston.

COMMANDER CHARLES STEEDMAN

U.S.S. Paul Jones

On October 21, 1862, Steedman, a veteran with more than 30 years of service in the navy, shepherded a combined army-navy small-boat raid up the Coosawhatchie and Pocotaligo Rivers. The operation was intended to harass Confederate pickets and artillery batteries guarding the water approaches to the Charleston & Savannah Railroad. Promoted to captain in December 1862, Steedman served in the navy until 1873, when he retired with the rank of rear admiral.

At sunset, by signal from the *Vermont,* I got underway and proceeded up the mouth of Broad River, where I came to anchor, the other vessels following and taking their stations in line. After anchoring General Brannan called on board for the purpose of consultation, and at his request the three launches of the *Wabash* and one from this vessel were dispatched up the river in tow of a small tug carrying 100 men of General Terry's command for the purpose of surprising the picket guards of the enemy at Mackay's Point and Cuthbert's Landing. The orders were that the tug should proceed up within 2 miles of these points, when the troops were to be taken on board the launches and continue up cautiously to effect the object in view. I will here inform you that owing to the ignorance of the contraband guide who accompanied the *Wabash*'s launches the party failed in their object of capturing the picket guard at Mackay's Point; the party in the *Paul Jones*'s launch, in charge of Acting Master Ormond, being more fortunate in having a good guide, was successful in every respect.

At 12:30 a.m. of the 22d, the signal for getting underway was made, and allowing thirty minutes for the rest of the vessels to get ready, this vessel weighed and stood up the river, following a tug in charge of Lieutenant Preston, who was kind to show the way above the flats. . . . The *Ben De Ford,* with General Brannan on board, followed closely. Proceeding slowly up the river (making but six revolutions), I arrived and anchored just above Mackay's Point at 4:30 a.m., accompanied only by the *Ben De Ford.* I regret to say that at daylight not a vessel of the expedition was in sight, nor did they make their appearance until some time after sunrise; the cause of this can be explained by their respective commanders. I have since learned from Commander Werden, of the *Conemaugh,* that the signal for getting underway was not seen by him, and when he moved, owing to his having no copy of the order of sailing and directions for passing the lights, his vessel grounded by passing on the wrong side of one of them. The *Conemaugh,* the third vessel in line, in not getting underway, and then grounding, I am satisfied was the principal cause of the disarrangement and delay of the other vessels, with the exception of the *Marblehead* and *Water Witch,* which ran afoul of each other, got out of line, and did not leave the anchorage until daylight. Upon anchoring the disembarkation of troops was at once commenced from the *Ben De Ford* and continued from the other vessels as they came up. . . . By 10 o'clock a.m. the whole force was landed and moved on to meet the enemy. . . . The three howitzers of the *Wabash,* in charge of Lieutenant Phoenix and Ensigns Wallace, Pearson, and Adams, by request of General Brannan, were landed and placed under his orders. The good services rendered by these guns and the gallantry and skill of the officers and men in handling them are, as I am informed by the general, beyond praise.

Confederate artillerymen enjoy a game of cards at a picket post on Cole's Island on the Stono River in 1862. At left, four black servants prepare a meal in a kettle.

The U.S.S. Paul Jones participated in numerous raids along the South Carolina coast and in the attacks on Battery Wagner in Charleston Harbor in July 1863.

"One shot from these fifteen-inch guns weighed more than the entire metal discharged by a single broadside of the whole fleet of Commodore Perry."

COLONEL ALVIN C. VORIS
67TH OHIO INFANTRY

Voris' regiment sailed from Norfolk, Virginia, on New Year's Day, 1863. He characterized the army-navy assault on Charleston as an "untried experiment with new and almost untried instrumentalities against new and almost untried defensive works, and constructed of material capable of resisting the force of the largest guns."

SEAMAN OSCAR W. FARENHOLT
U.S.S. CATSKILL

The Catskill was one of a new class of ironclads patterned after the original Monitor designed by John Ericsson. While on duty in the pilot house on August 17, 1863, Farenholt narrowly escaped death when a Confederate shell hit the ship, killing the two men standing beside him. He remained in the navy for more than 30 years, rising to the rank of rear admiral—one of the few ordinary seamen to do so.

This fleet embraced every class of structure known to modern warfare—the old ship of the line, of 100 guns, a very sea fortress of the old school; the steam frigate, the most beautiful craft ever launched, models of which the United States gave to the world; the iron-clad frigate; the impregnable monitors; together with every other kind of watercraft, from a double-ender and a ferry-boat to the harbor tug; and armed with rifled guns of immense range and penetrating force, and smooth bores of every caliber up to fifteen inches, capable of discharging shot varying from 10 to 500 pounds in weight; and exhibited in connection with the blockading squadron and auxiliaries every thing the merchant marine could sell, from an old square-rigged ship to a dumping scow, a fishing smack to a splendid pleasure yacht. The steam frigate "New Ironsides" carried twenty eleven-inch guns, and a 200 pound pivot rifle on her fore deck. These enabled her to command great respect in the operations before Charleston, as she could discharge a broadside of ten guns at short range every three minutes, while the heavy guns of the monitors occupied about seven minutes between fire. Each monitor was armed with two guns, usually a fifteen-inch smooth bore, and a heavy rifle. One shot from these fifteen-inch guns weighed more than the entire metal discharged by a single broadside of the whole fleet of Commodore Perry, which decided the supremacy of the United States on the upper lakes in the war of 1812 with Great Britain.

The ship left New York for Port Royal, S.C., in tow of the "Bienville," a converted side wheel merchant steamer of eleven guns. Bad weather was experienced the first night out, compelling the ship to cast off from the tow, the latter "standing by." The "Catskill" leaked through the deck, through the sides; the gun turret and gaskets worked loose and tons of water poured below; the bilges fouled, the pumps could not free the ship and bucket parties passed the water up through the turret. For four days no one on board had dry clothing or bedding, and little cooking could be done. Officers and men, unused to the peculiar and untried craft, were glad when they arrived at Port Royal and found there the other monitors, all of which had had similar experiences while coming from the North.

A temporary wheel had been placed for this sea trip on the turret forward of the pilot house. Wheel ropes, from a very small tiller on deck, led amidships up to the turret and to the wheel; there was no purchase, it was like "a rope yarn over several nails"! After a try out of all the deck force, Captain Rodgers selected three men (of whom I was one) and they steered the ship during the entire voyage. Standing exposed in wet clothing to wind, snow and rain, seas breaking over the turret, vessel steering heavy and wild, a four hours' trick at the wheel, severe pain in a weak arm—it was only pride that kept one to this hard and exhausting work.

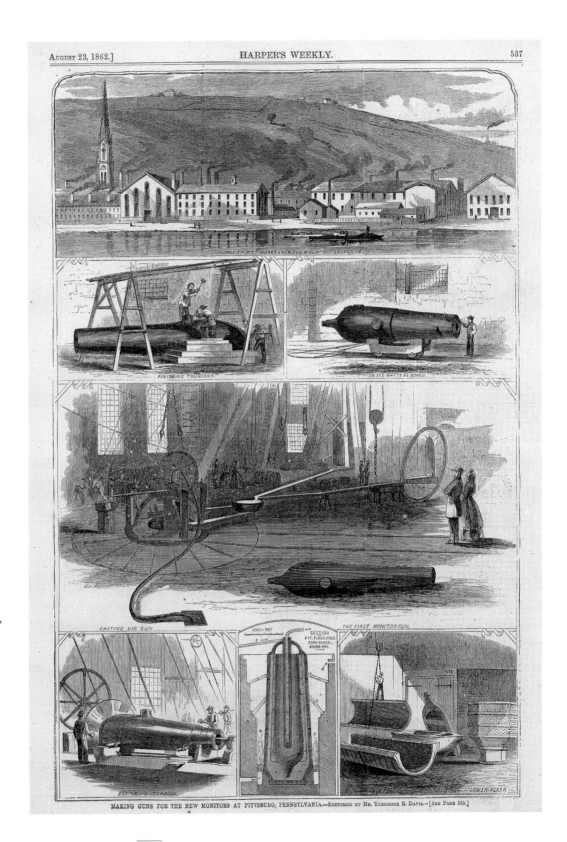

MAKING GUNS FOR THE NEW MONITORS AT PITTSBURG, PENNSYLVANIA.—SKETCHED BY MR. THEODORE R. DAVIS.—[SEE PAGE 535.]

Convinced that a new flotilla of ironclad monitors was just the weapon to bring Charleston to its knees, Secretary of the Navy Gideon Welles launched an ambitious building program in the summer of 1862. This page from Harper's Weekly illustrates the construction of guns for the new class of warships.

"In the ward-room the surgeon was preparing his instruments on the large mess-table."

LIEUTENANT WILLIAM H. PARKER
C.S.S. PALMETTO STATE

Born in New York City, Parker graduated first in his class from the U.S. Naval Academy in 1848 after serving with a naval battery in the Mexican War. Unlike his brother, who joined the Federal forces, Parker resigned his commission to join the Confederate navy in 1861. Several months after his ship's attack on the Mercedita, described below, he organized the Confederate Naval Academy and became its first superintendent.

Both vessels were painted a pale blue or bluish-grey, the blockade runners having demonstrated that it was the most difficult to be distinguished. Before going into action we greased the shield with slush, as the *Merrimac* had done at Hampton Roads. Our officers in the *Palmetto State* were: Captain John Rutledge; Lieutenants Parker, Porcher, Shryock and Bowen; Surgeon Lynah; Paymaster Banks; Engineer Campbell; Master Chew; Midshipmen Cary, Sevier and Hamilton. We had a good boatswain and gunner, and a crew of about 120 men. . . .

About 10 P.M., January 30th, Commodore Ingraham came on board the *Palmetto State,* and at 11:30 the two vessels quietly cast off their fasts and got underweigh. There was no demonstration on shore, and I believe few of the citizens knew of the projected attack. Charleston was full of spies at this time, and everything was carried to the enemy. It was nearly calm, and a bright moonlight night,—the moon being 11 days old. We went down very slowly, wishing to reach the bar of the main ship channel, 11 miles from Charleston, about 4 in the morning, when it would be high water there. Commander Hartstene (an Arctic man who rescued Kane and his companions), was to have followed us with several unarmed steamers and 50 soldiers to take possession of the prizes; but, for some reasons they did not cross the bar. We steamed slowly down the harbor and, knowing we had a long night before us, I ordered the hammocks piped down. The men declined to take them, and I found they had gotten up an impromptu Ethiopian entertain-

ment. As there was no necessity for preserving quiet at this time the captain let them enjoy themselves in their own way. No men ever exhibited a better spirit before going into action; and the short, manly speech of our captain convinced us that we were to be well commanded under any circumstances. We passed between Forts Sumter and Moultrie—the former with its yellow sides looming up and reflecting the moon's rays—and turned down the channel along Morris Island. I presume all hands were up in the forts and batteries watching us, but no word was spoken. After midnight the men began to drop off by twos and threes, and in a short time the silence of death prevailed.

I was much impressed with the appearance of the ship at this time. Visiting the lower deck, forward, I found it covered with men sleeping in their pea-jackets peacefully and calmly; on the gun-deck a few of the more thoughtful seamen were pacing quietly to and fro, with folded arms; in the pilot-house stood the Commodore and Captain, with the two pilots; the midshipmen were quiet in their quarters (for a wonder), and aft I found the lieutenants smoking their pipes, but not conversing. In the ward-room the surgeon was preparing his instruments on the large mess-table; and the paymaster was, as he told me, "lending him a hand."

As we approached the bar, about 4 A.M., we saw the steamer *Mercedita* lying at anchor a short distance outside it. I had no fear of her seeing our hull; but we were burning soft coal, and the night being very clear, with nearly a full moon, it did seem to me that our smoke, which trailed after us like a huge black serpent, *must* be visible several miles off. We went silently to quarters, and our main-deck then presented a scene that will always live in my memory. We went to quarters an hour before crossing the bar, and the men stood silently at their guns. The port-shutters were closed, not a light could be seen from the outside, and the few battle-lanterns lit cast a pale, weird light on the gun-deck. My friend Phil Porcher, who commanded the bow-gun, was equipped with a pair of white kid gloves, and had in his mouth an unlighted cigar. As we stood at our stations, not even whispering, the silence became more and more intense. Just at my side I noticed the little powder-boy of the broadside guns sitting on a match-tub, with his powder-pouch slung over his shoulder, fast asleep, and he was in this condition when we rammed the *Mercedita*. We crossed the bar and steered directly for the *Mercedita*. They did not see us until we were very near. Her captain then hailed us, and ordered us to keep off or he would fire. We did not reply, and he called out, "You will be into me." Just then we struck him on the starboard quarter, and dropping the forward port-shutter, fired the bow gun.

A native South Carolinian, arctic explorer, and former U.S. naval officer, Commander Henry J. Hartstene directed a small flotilla of three steamers that were intended to support the sortie by the Rebel ironclad rams. But his ships were unable to cross the Charleston Harbor bar because of a falling tide.

CAPTAIN HENRY S. STELLWAGEN
U.S.S. MERCEDITA

Stellwagen had retired to his cabin to sleep about half an hour before the Palmetto State rammed his ship. In concluding his official report, he noted that "everything was done the circumstances permitted in a proper manner—the signal books thrown overboard, and all the officers and crew generally behaved very well. The result, though unhappy, only shows the immense advantage ironclads have over other vessels."

Lieutenant-Commander Abbot was on deck, giving orders to Acting Master Dwyer about recovering the anchor, when they saw a smoke and faint appearance of a vessel close at hand. I heard them exclaim, "She has black smoke. Watch, man the guns, spring the rattle, call all hands to quarters!" Mr. Dwyer came to the cabin door, telling me a steamboat was close aboard. I was then in the act of getting my peajacket, and slipped it on as I followed him out; jumped to poop ladder, saw smoke and a low boat, apparently a tug, although I thought it might be a little propeller for the squadron. I sang out, "Train your guns right on him and be ready to fire as soon as I order." I hailed, "Steamer ahoy! Stand clear of us and heave to! What steamer is that?" Then ordered my men "Fire on him;" told him, "You will be into us! What steamer is that?" His answer to first or second hail was "Halloo!" the other replies were indistinct, either by intention or from being spoken inside of his mail armor, until in the act of striking us with his prow, when he said, "This is the Confederate States steam ram ———." I repeated the order to "Fire, fire!" but no gun could be trained on him, as he approached on the quarter. Struck us just abaft our aftermost 32-pounder gun and fired a heavy rifle

Federals abandon the Mercedita and take to lifeboats after the steamer was struck by the ironclad Palmetto State before dawn on January 31, 1863. In the background, the Palmetto State's sister ram, the Chicora, attacks the U.S.S. Keystone State.

through us, diagonally penetrating the starboard side, through our Normandy condenser, the steam drum of port boiler, and exploding against port side of ship, blowing a hole in its exit some 4 or 5 feet square. The vessel was instantly filled and enveloped with steam. Reports were brought to me, "Shot through both boilers," "Fires put out by steam and water," "Gunner and one man killed." "Number of men fatally scalded," "Water over fire-room floor," "Vessel sinking fast. The ram has cut us through at and below water line on one side, and the shell has burst on the other about at the water's edge."

After the ram struck she swung around under our starboard counter, her prow touching, and hailed, "Surrender, or I'll sink you!" "Do you surrender?" After receiving reports I answered, "I can make no resistance; my boiler is destroyed." "Then do you surrender?" I said, "Yes," having found my moving power destroyed, and that I could bring nothing to bear but muskets against his shot-proof coating.

CAPTAIN DUNCAN N. INGRAHAM
Commander, Charleston Naval Station

Born into a family of sea captains in 1802, Ingraham became a midshipman at the tender age of nine and saw action in the War of 1812. By the time of the Civil War, he had achieved the rank of commander and was serving as chief of the Bureau of Ordnance—the same post he assumed for the Confederate navy in 1861.

I then inquired if he surrendered, and was answered in the affirmative. I then directed him to send a boat on board, which was done. After some delay Lieutenant-Commander Abbot came on board and informed me that the vessel was the U.S.S. *Mercedita*, Commander Stellwagen, and that she was in a sinking condition and had a crew of 158, all told, and wished to be relieved; that all his boats were lowered without the plugs being in and were full of water.

At this time the *Chicora* was engaged with the enemy and the alarm was given. I knew our only opportunity was to take the enemy unawares, as the moment he was underway, from his superior speed, we could not close with him. I then directed Lieutenant Rutledge, commanding, to require from Lieutenant-Commander Abbot his word of honor for his commander, officers, and crew that they would not serve against the Confederate States until regularly exchanged, when he was directed to return with his boat to his vessel to render what assistance he could. I then stood to the northward and eastward, and soon after made another steamer getting underway. We stood for her and fired several shots at her, but as we had to fight the vessel in a circle to bring the different guns to bear, she was soon out of our range. In this way we engaged several vessels, they keeping at long range and steering to the southward. Just as the day broke we made a large steamer (supposed to be the *Powhatan*) on starboard bow, with another steamer in company, which had just got underway. They stood to the southward under full steam and opened their batteries upon the *Chicora*, which was some distance astern of us. I then turned and stood to the southward to support the *Chicora*, if necessary, but the enemy kept on his course to the southward.

ASSISTANT ENGINEER JAMES H. TOMB
C.S.S. Chicora

A Floridian by birth, Tomb rejected an appointment to the U.S. Navy in 1861 to join the Confederate navy. The following year, while serving on a steamer operating out of New Orleans, he was captured and imprisoned for three months at Fort Warren, Massachusetts. After being paroled in Virginia, Tomb returned to active duty at Charleston, where he earned the notice of President Jefferson Davis for "gallant and meritorious conduct."

*W*e fired into the *Keystone State,* and they evidently were not prepared for us. From what we could learn below, she was heading away from us when a shot from our bow gun, under the command of Lieutenant W. T. Glassell, struck her steam pipe or drum and another her wheel. At this time she was within close range, and our shots told on her. The *Keystone State* hauled down her flag and did not change her course any. Her engines were working right along. The signal was made to us to stop our engine. Chief Engineer Clark took my station in the engine room, and I was ordered to take my crew of fire-

"They say we raised the blockade, but we all felt we would have rather raised h——l and sunk the ships."

men and, along with the officer who was to take charge of the *Keystone State* as a prize, to take charge of the engine department. When we got ready to take the second cutter to go aboard the *Keystone State,* Lieutenant Glassell requested permission to fire on her again, as she was passing out of range. Captain Tucker said, "No; she has lowered her flag and surrendered." Shortly after this, realizing that she was only getting away and had no intention of surrendering, Captain Tucker gave orders to run the cutter up and for Lieutenant Glassell to open on her

again; but she had got well down to the southeast and well out of range.

The upshot of the engagement was a good bit of glory, but not a prize or ship destroyed, and when we passed back over the bar and back to Charleston we all felt disappointed at the night's work. We did not accomplish as much as our sister ship, the *Palmetto State.* They say we raised the blockade, but we all felt we would have rather raised h——l and sunk the ships. There was quite a heavy fog at the time we went out, but cleared up at the time we came into the harbor and anchored.

The ironclad ram C.S.S. Chicora guards Charleston Harbor. Its sides were protected by iron plating four inches thick backed by 22 inches of oak and pine, with two-inch armor at its ends. The longboat in the foreground is probably from a British or French warship; both nations sent observers to Charleston.

PRIVATE E. A. LABAY
U.S. Marine Corps

Labay was part of a 13-man marine guard aboard the Keystone State when the side-wheeler was attacked by the Chicora at about 4:25 a.m. on January 31, 1863. Roused from a deep sleep, Labay had just jumped down from his hammock when a shell exploded on the berth deck, wounding him slightly near the left shoulder. His fellow marines were not so fortunate; eight of them died from the blast.

We had been on blockade off Charleston for several months, and it was nothing unusual to hear a shot fired at night by some vessel on the blockade. There were no signals by the Mercedita, and only that one shot heard, so it was not thought that there could be anything very serious up. But the first thing we knew the Chicora was alongside of us. Commander Le Roy hailed the Chicora, but the answer he got was a shot. The order to call all hands and slip anchor was given in short order. Just as we got under way another shot struck us. Both these shells exploded on the berthdeck and made sad havoc of things down there. The forehold was set on fire. Fire quarters was sounded and we had to run out to sea.

In about half an hour the fire was put out, the deck cleared and everything made ready for action. We put about to look up the Chicora. We had not long to look, and soon began to bang away at one another. Now that we were under way, the shots did not seem to do us any harm. It was getting daylight, and the vessels on the blockade were under way.

About this time a shot from the Chicora struck us amidship and glanced downward into the steam drums. At that time I was on the quarter-deck helping the sailors at the guns. Instantly the ship was enveloped with steam, and for a few minutes it was difficult to see anything on deck.

The sailors made attempts to go down on the berthdeck, but were driven back by hot steam. It was several minutes before any one was able to go below on the berthdeck, and when they did get there it was too late to render any assistance to any one, for all had been scalded to death. Not one man escaped. The Surgeon and Steward were below attending to the wounded and met their death at their post of duty.

The Keystone State was disabled and things looked rather gloomy for a while. Commander Le Roy did order the Flag hauled down. I was on the quarter-deck, but a few feet away from Commander Le Roy and Lieut. Eastman, when this was done. The Flag had hardly touched the deck when Commander Le Roy ordered the Flag to be run up again, and at the same time exclaimed: "We will sink before we surrender."

By this time the gunboats were getting nearer and nearer to us, and I could see the Housatonic under full steam hurrying to meet the Chicora, and the sailors standing at their big pivot gun hurling shot after shot at the ram. The Housatonic did not get in close range of the Chicora, and she put back into Charleston.

When the gunboats reached us we were hailed by the Memphis, asking if she could render any assistance. Commander Le Roy replied:

"Send your Surgeon on board, as our Surgeon has been killed, and you will have to take us in tow, as we are disabled."

We reached Port Royal about sunset and buried our dead at Bay Point the next day. Commodore Du Pont was the first officer to board us when we reached Port Royal. He dispatched the New Ironsides, which had just arrived from Philadelphia, to Charleston that same evening. The rams never came out of Charleston again.

This sketch by an officer aboard the Keystone State depicts the shell burst that blew apart the ship's boilers, enveloping the vessel in steam and scalding 20 men to death.

'Both sides of the harbour for several miles appear to bristle with forts mounting heavy guns."

COLONEL ARTHUR J. L. FREMANTLE
BRITISH MILITARY OBSERVER

Fremantle was a British army officer 28 years old when he arranged for a six-month furlough and set off for America to witness the Civil War. To maintain his status as a neutral, he entered the Confederacy from Mexico, thus avoiding the Federal blockade. The visiting Englishman was warmly welcomed by the Confederates. "The fact of being an officer in the Queen's service," he wrote, "was sufficient introduction to any South gentleman."

From the summit of Fort Sumter a good general view is obtained of the harbour, and of the fortifications commanding the approach to Charleston.

Castle Pinckney and Fort Sumter are two old masonry works built on islands—Pinckney being much closer to the city than Sumter. Between them is Fort Ripley, which mounts —— heavy guns.

Moultrieville, with its numerous forts, called Battery Bee, Fort Moultrie, Fort Beauregard, &c., is on Sullivan's Island, one mile distant from Fort Sumter. There are excellent arrangements of ——, and other contrivances, to foul the screw of a vessel between Sumter and Moultrie.

On the other side of Fort Sumter is Fort Johnson on James Island, Fort Cummins Point, and Fort Wagner on Morris Island. In fact, both sides of the harbour for several miles appear to bristle with forts mounting heavy guns.

The bar, beyond which we counted thirteen blockaders, is nine miles from the city. Sumter is three and a half miles from the city. Two or three thousand Yankees are now supposed to be on Folly Island, which is next beyond Morris Island, and in a day or two they are to be shelled from the Confederate batteries on Morris Island. The new Confederate flag, which bears a strong resemblance to the British white ensign, was flying from most of the forts.

This view of Charleston Harbor was drawn from James Island by Frank Vizetelly of the Illustrated London News. At right a Confederate supply ship steams past Fort Sumter. Battery Bee and Fort Moultrie are visible at left on Sullivan's Island.

*A Confederate soldier standing beside a palmetto tree scans the horizon at a
"Quaker" battery made of logs painted black. The Southerners emplaced the fake
guns to make their fortifications appear more formidable than they actually
were. The scene was painted by Conrad Wise Chapman, a soldier-artist commissioned by General Beauregard to document Charleston's heroic resistance.*

"He has filled an old boiler with powder, 10,000 lbs. and is to sink it in the channel."

HARRIOTT MIDDLETON
RESIDENT OF CHARLESTON

The daughter of a wealthy and well-connected Charleston landowner, Harriott Middleton was a cousin of the wife of Brigadier General Ripley (right), commander of the 1st Military District of South Carolina, which included Charleston. She passed on the rumor about a huge mine beneath Charleston Harbor in a letter dated March 13, 1863, to another one of her cousins, Susan Matilda Middleton. The mine—actually only 3,000 pounds—failed to detonate.

I hear of an "infernal machine" of Ripley's contrivance which ought to do mischief to the monitors even. He has filled an old boiler with powder, 10,000 lbs. and is to sink it in the channel—a wire cable, which has been a year on its way from New York, leads from this sunken boiler to Fort Sumter, and, at the right moment, it is to be fired by an electric spark blowing whatever is passing above to atoms. One lady thinks the safety of the Fort will be endangered by such an explosion—and would not be surprised if half of old Charleston is knocked down by the shock! Mrs. Izard thinks Col. Chestnut's arrival in town quite ominous, as he has always said he would certainly not miss the attack, and as he is the President's Aide, and supposed to be a good deal in his confidence, and has been for months quietly in Richmond, her idea is that the Government have advices of the enemy's movements which he has been sent on to communicate to Beauregard!

Brigadier General Roswell S. Ripley's spirited defense of Charleston won plaudits from his superior, General Beauregard, but Ripley's disputatious nature soon sullied their relationship. "He complains of every commanding officer he has served under," Beauregard angrily noted, "and has quarreled with almost every one of his immediate subordinate commanders."

FRANK VIZETELLY
Correspondent,
Illustrated London News

Vizetelly filed this colorful account of the opening phase of the Union naval attack on Fort Sumter, April 7, 1863. Descended from an Italian family that had immigrated to England in the 17th century, Vizetelly was an inveterate war correspondent who covered civil conflicts in Italy, Spain, and Egypt as well as in America.

Scarcely had I entered General Ripley's apartment when an aide, stepping quietly from an adjacent room, placed a slip of paper in his chief's hand. As the latter read it, his face flushed. It was a telegraphic dispatch from Colonel Rhett, commanding at Fort Sumter, stating that the Ironsides and nine Monitors had crossed the bar, and were steaming slowly towards the batteries. Turning to me, the general said: "Thank God, we shall soon know the issue of this fight." And then he immediately forwarded instructions to the various forts to prepare for action.

Yes, sure enough, there they came, their turrets whirling in a waltz of death. Cautiously they worked their way up the ship channel, and, as I watched their approach through my glass, I could almost hear the thumping of my heart against my ribs.

It is now between two and three in the afternoon, and as yet not a single shot has been fired on either side, but suddenly the southeastern parapet of Sumter is enveloped in smoke. Boom! comes the report over the quiet waters of the bay, and we see at once that it is nothing more than a salute to the State flags as they are unfurled by Colonel Rhett, in defiance to the foe. At intervals we catch the strains of the garrison band, as a favorable current of air wafts the notes to the city. And throughout that city the news has been flashed that the hour is at hand. Every house is pouring out its inmates, eager to witness the engage-

ment: ladies, in almost gala costume, are hastening to the battery promenade, from whence an unobstructed view of the harbor and forts, and of the enemy's fleet, can be obtained. There is no terror expressed in any of those countenances—all are calm and collected; they are going to witness the bravery of their defenders.

The non-fighting population of Charleston fall into their places, young girls with their negro nurses—a piebald medley of black and white but all apparently sharing an unbounded confidence. Ominously the Northern fleet approaches, working its way towards the forts in single file, led by the "Passaic." Scarcely a word is spoken by any of the staff as they stand grouped upon the wharf, waiting for the general, whose boat is preparing to take him to Battery Bee on Sullivan's Island. All have their eyes fixed on the leading Monitor, watching eagerly for the moment that will bring her in range of the iron-throated mastiffs that lie couched in the sand.

At length a spiral column of smoke rises gracefully in the still atmosphere from Moultrie (Sullivan's Island), and a jet of spray close on the "Passaic's" quarter tells us that the first shot has been fired. Round swings the "Monitor's" turret, an iron shutter glides aside, disclosing a dark port, which, in a few seconds, vomits forth a cloud succeeded by a crash that shakes the very ground we stand on. That further puff and deafening report shows where the shell has burst—to old Moultrie the first honor of the challenge, and to old Moultrie the first reply. Again a pause of some minutes and the fleet draws nearer in: they are all now within the circle commanded by the forts, but no shot must be thrown away. At three o'clock, Fort Sumter, having the range, opens her batteries, and almost simultaneously the white smoke-puffs from the low sand-hills on Morris and Sullivan's Island indicate that Battery Beauregard and Fort Moultrie on the left, and Battery Wagner and Cumming's Point on the right, have become thoroughly engaged. The ironclads, forming in line of battle in front of Fort Sumter, maintain a rapid return fire, occasionally hurling their fifteen-inch shot and shell at Moultrie and the minor batteries, but all chiefly directing their efforts against the eastern face of Sumter's gray volcano.

CAPTAIN CHARLES INGLESBY
1ST SOUTH CAROLINA ARTILLERY

This dramatic account of the opening moments of the naval bombardment was included by Inglesby in his regimental history, published in 1896. "Fort Sumter," he claimed, "by reason of its commanding position and heavy armament, bore the brunt of the attack."

On the 7th of April, at about 2 o'clock P.M., it was seen that the fleet were in motion and approaching. Immediately Col. Rhett had the long-roll sounded, the officers and men went to battery, the band was assembled on the terreplein and played "Dixie." As the flags, the Confederate garrison flag on the main flag staff and the State and regimental flags on the two other flag staffs were run up, with signal flags as decorations, from the main flags at the head of each staff down to the base, a salute of thirteen guns was fired, and the fort, decked as for a holiday and gala occasion, waited for their friends, the enemy. The writer understood at the time, and still believes, that this salute was for Commodore Dupont, and was an exhibition of the chivalric spirit which in olden times prompted foeman to gracefully salute each other before crossing swords.

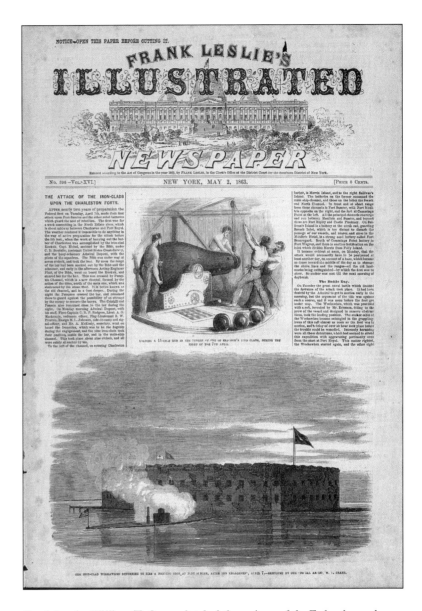

Colonel Alfred Rhett commanded the Confederate artillerists defending Fort Sumter against the Federal ironclad fleet. He and his gunners remained at the fort until September 1863, when they were replaced by an infantry garrison.

Special artist William T. Crane sketched these views of the Federal naval attack on Fort Sumter for Frank Leslie's Illustrated Newspaper. Crane, a native of New Hampshire, was widely admired for the accuracy of his work. He died in Washington, D.C., of disease in July 1865.

CAPTAIN PERCIVAL DRAYTON
U.S.S. Passaic

One of the ablest officers in the U.S. Navy, Percival Drayton was the scion of a distinguished South Carolina family. He defied the wishes of his relatives by siding with the North in the Civil War; as a consequence, the South Carolina legislature denounced him as an outlaw and declared him "infamous."

When opposite the center fort we came pretty close to some obstructions which seemed to extend the whole way from Fort Moultrie across. Here I stopped as the *Weehawken* had done just before. At the fourth shot from the XI-inch gun I was struck in quick succession on the lower part of the turret by two heavy shot, which bulged in its plate and beams, and, forcing together the rails on which the XI-inch carriage worked, rendered it wholly useless for the remainder of the action, several hours being necessary to put it again in working order. Soon after it was discovered that there was something the matter with the turret itself, which could not be moved, and on examination it was found that a part of the brass ring underneath it had been broken off and being forced inboard had jammed; on clearing this, the turret could again be moved, but for some time irregularly.

A little after a very heavy rifle shot struck the upper edge of the turret, broke all of its eleven plates, and then glancing upward took the pilot house, yet with such force as to make an indentation of 2 1/2 inches, extending nearly the whole length of the shot. The blow was so severe as to considerably mash in the pilot house, bend it over, open the plates, and squeeze out the top, so that on one side it was lifted up, 3 inches above the top on which it rested, exposing the inside of the pilot house and rendering it likely that the next shot would take off the top itself entirely.

Seated on the deck, the crew of the U.S.S. Passaic, a single-turreted, coastal monitor, observe Sunday services off Port Royal, South Carolina, in 1863.

The ship's officers occupy the chairs behind the chaplain and his pulpit, which is decorated with the Stars and Stripes.

BRIGADIER GENERAL JAMES H. TRAPIER
COMMANDER, SULLIVAN'S ISLAND

Trapier was offended when Ripley refused him a combat command after he had helped drive off the Federal fleet. In passing along the complaint to Beauregard, Ripley acidly noted that Trapier would be better served by "obeying orders rather than caviling and criticizing those orders in language which appears to me to be unmilitary and disrespectful." Beauregard sided with Ripley.

At 3 o'clock Colonel William Butler, commanding in the fort, reported to me that the leading ship was in range. I ordered him immediately to open his batteries upon her, which was done promptly and the action began. Fearing that the range was rather long for effective work, the firing after a few rounds was suspended for a short time, but finding the enemy refused close quarters, there was no alternative but to engage him at long range or not at all. We decided upon the former, and Fort Moultrie again opened her batteries. Batteries Bee and Beauregard had, also, by this time opened fire, and the action had become general. It soon became obvious that the enemy's intentions were to fight and not to run by, and orders were given to train on vessels nearest in, and to fire by battery. Volley after volley was delivered in this way, but although it was plain that our shot repeatedly took effect, their impact against the iron casing of the enemy being distinctly heard and seen, yet we could not discover but that the foe was indeed invulnerable.

"We were within 500 yards of Fort Sumter, unmanageable, and under the concentrated fire of, I think, 100 guns at short range."

CAPTAIN JOHN JOHNSON
C.S. ENGINEERS, FORT SUMTER

A native South Carolinian, Johnson was in charge of Fort Sumter's defenses. The fort absorbed no fewer than 55 hits from the ironclads that cratered her ramparts but failed to impair her fighting capacity. In a memoir Johnson wrote the following dramatic description of war on the water.

COMMANDER JOHN DOWNES JR.
CAPTAIN, U.S.S. NAHANT

Downes' forebears were military heroes. His grandfather was an officer in the American Revolution, and his father served in the War of 1812. During the April 7 attack on Fort Sumter, Downes' life may have been saved when the steering wheel of the Nahant deflected a piece of shrapnel headed for his vital parts into his foot. Downes ignored the painful wound, refusing even to mention it in his official battle report.

Now, for the first time since the fight began, did the whole of the squadron become engaged. The forts and batteries also were firing with more steadiness and combined effect than they had hitherto attained. Upward of one hundred of the heaviest cannon of all descriptions were flashing and thundering together, shooting their balls, their shells, and fiery bolts with deafening sound and shocks of powerful impact that surpassed all previous experience of war. The smoke of the battle, brightened by the sun into snowy clouds, seemed to the distant observer entirely to envelop the small objects on the water which were causing all the trouble. Only when the light breeze availed to lift or part and roll away slowly the heavy masses could a glimpse be had of the movements of the squadron. The water all around the fighting ships was seen on nearer view to be constantly cut, ploughed, and splashed with every form of disturbance, from the light dip of the ricochet shot to the plunge of the point-blank missile, from the pattering of broken pieces of solid shot falling back from the impenetrable turrets to the sudden spout of foam and jet of spray sent up by a chance mortar-shell exploding just beneath the surface of the water. Sometimes from the same cause a waterspout raised near the fort would reach to a great height and throw its shower of descending spray upon the guns frowning over the parapet or in the act of discharging their own messengers of defiance.

We soon began to suffer from the effects of the terrible and I believe almost unprecedented fire to which we were exposed, and at about 4:30 the turret refused to turn, having become jammed from the effects of three blows from heavy shot, two of them on the composition ring about the base of the pilot house (one of these breaking off a piece of iron weighing 78 pounds from the interior that assisted to keep the house square on its bearings, throwing it with such violence to the other side of the house, striking, bending, and disarranging steering gear in its course, that it bounded from the inside curtain and fell back into the center of the house) and the other on the outside of turret, bulging it in and driving off the 1 5/8-inch apron bolted onto the inside to keep in place the gun rails and down the main brace of turret. The boltheads flying from the inside of pilot house at the same time struck down the pilot, Mr. Sofield, twice struck and senseless, and the quartermaster, Edward Cobb, helmsman, fatally injuring with fractured skull, leaving me alone in the pilot house, the steering gear becoming at the same time disarranged. We were within 500 yards of Fort Sumter, unmanageable, and under the concentrated fire of, I think, 100 guns at short range, and the obstructions close aboard.

SURGEON CHARLES E. STEDMAN
U.S.S. NAHANT

Stedman, a Boston native and Harvard graduate, watched the opening of the attack from the Nahant's pilot house. When shells began churning up the water around the ship he retired to the ward room below, where he had laid out his surgical gear in readiness.

I could hear the faint reports of the enemies guns from my air tight den. Pretty soon a shot struck up, just over Severing's head in the engineers store room knocking him off his stool to his great delight, and after that the balls & shells & bolts rattled like hail upon us; every little while showers of water would fall upon us and down the turret, thrown up by shot striking alongside.

"Here comes a wounded man" cried one of the boys, & who should it be but the poor pilot. "Open the door for another" and the old Signal Quartermaster, was brought in with his head stove in. "Stand by boys, make room for McCallister—g——d— we're catching it now." I found that the pilot on recovering from his swoon was only severely bruised in the neck and shoulder, & McCallister was stunned only, but poor old Cobb, the quartermaster, who had been thirty years in the service was past surgery & died in the night.

Burly sailors on the berth deck of the Nahant wrestle 15-inch cannonballs onto a hoist to be lifted up to the ironclad's turret gun. The sketch of the action was made by Charles Stedman, the Nahant's surgeon.

SEAMAN OSCAR W. FARENHOLT
U.S.S. CATSKILL

Although the monitors took a terrible beating from the Confederate batteries on April 7, 1863 (the Confederates fired about 2,200 shots), casualties were light—one man killed and 22 wounded. The Confederates lost four dead and 10 wounded, all at Fort Sumter.

The tide seemed to set us nearer in shore than the other monitors. The gun sights were lowered to 600 yards, and pounding away at Sumter, one could not miss it. We were struck some thirty times but no serious damage was done to our ship. When a shot hit the turret, it sounded like the ringing of many bells. We were in action over two hours, withdrew, and anchored about three miles below Sumter.

Officers and men were astounded to see the injuries done to these supposed invulnerable ironclads! Several had their turrets jammed and could not use their guns. The "Passaic" had to be sent north. A large force of navy yard workmen from New York, were on hand, and made repairs on the spot, and at North Edisto. In several weeks the monitors were ready for another attack, and many officers believed it would prove to be successful, and should be made before the enemy could erect, as they did, other powerful batteries.

This panoramic view of the historic clash in Charleston Harbor was painted by an eyewitness—John R. Key, a relative of Francis Scott Key, who served as a draftsman with the Confederate engineers. Fort Johnson is in the foreground with Battery Simpkins at far right; Fort Sumter is in the middle distance. The other Confederate defenses on the horizon are (left to right): Mount Pleasant Battery, Battery Bee, and Fort Moultrie on Sullivan's Island, and Battery Gregg on Morris Island.

FRANK VIZETELLY
CORRESPONDENT, ILLUSTRATED LONDON NEWS

Frank Vizetelly wrote some of the most graphic descriptions of the April 7 fighting. After the Federal flotilla withdrew, he and General Ripley took a boat out to Fort Sumter, where Vizetelly found the garrison "elated, confident, and eager for another brush."

The bay, lately so calm and peaceful, is now like a seething cauldron. Huge spiral columns of water leap into the air around the ironclads, the thud of the bolts as they strike the enemy can be heard above the universal crash, the fifteen-inch shell of the Monitors are bursting in bouquets over the parapet of Sumter and the other forts. Vlau! a cloud of sand is scattered over our party, followed by a howling screech above, which makes us all instinctively incline our heads. A deafening report, a lurid glare, and a rattle of falling bricks, sufficiently indicate what has happened. "Anybody hurt?" cries the general, and the answer, "No," makes everyone draw a deep and thankful breath. This shell is succeeded by another and another, but all too high, thank goodness, to injure those within our battery, doing no further harm than destroying some wooden shanties in the rear. Now the leading Monitor staggers and reels like a drunken man, the water churning and foaming around her from the hail of shot with which she is greeted. She must be disabled, for she is turning feebly from the fight. Next, the "Ironsides," withdraws out of range, driven back by the concentrated fire of Sumter's heavy batteries; but there is one double-turreted ship that still stands boldly in, the "Keokuk." The gallant commander of this vessel, relying upon the reputation she had achieved theoretically, places her within seven hundred yards of the forts, and, being the post of honor, it is made the post of danger. Dearly she pays for her temerity; her boats are shot away, her smokestack riddled, and a portion of her bow smashed in; at five o'clock she follows the example of the "Ironsides," and withdraws, evidently seriously crippled. The action now perceptibly slackens on the part of the enemy, but still the forts pour in destructive broadsides, firing by battery. The southeastern face of Sumter shows a novel speckled appearance, from the impact of the shot; and the bricks that are flying from the parapet denote that the Northern missiles are doing mischief. Fortunately, Battery Bee and the other sand-works are comparatively uninjured, the shot and shell mostly striking the slopes and embedding themselves, or else going completely over, to waste their power beyond.

REAR ADMIRAL SAMUEL F. DU PONT
COMMANDER, SOUTH ATLANTIC BLOCKADING SQUADRON

Secretary of the Navy Gideon Welles, the recipient of this report from Admiral Du Pont, was scarcely satisfied with Du Pont's explanations for the Union failure. "After all our outlay and great preparations," Welles scornfully wrote, "giving him all our force, and a large portion of our best officers, a fight of 30 minutes and the loss of one man satisfied him."

Flagship New Ironsides
Inside Charleston Bar, April 8, 1863.

Sir: I yesterday moved up with eight ironclads and this ship and attacked Fort Sumter, intending to pass it and commence action on its northwest face, in accordance with my order of battle.

The heavy fire we received from it and Fort Moultrie and the nature of the obstructions compelled the attack from the outside. It was fierce and obstinate, and the gallantry of the officers and men of the vessels engaged was conspicuous.

This vessel could not be brought into such close action as I endeavored to get her. Owing to the narrow channel and rapid current she became partly unmanageable, and was twice forced to anchor to prevent her going ashore, once owing to her having come into collision with two of the monitors. She could not get nearer than 1,000 yards.

Owing to the condition of the tide and an unavoidable accident, I had been compelled to delay the action until late in the afternoon, and toward evening, finding no impression made upon the fort, I made the signal to withdraw the ships, intending to renew the attack this morning. But the commanders of the monitors came on board and reported verbally the injuries to their vessels, when, without hesitation or consultation (for I never hold councils of war),

I determined not to renew the attack, for, in my judgment, it would have converted a failure into a disaster, and I will only add that Charleston can not be taken by a purely naval attack, and the army could give me no cooperation.

CAPTAIN CHARLES INGLESBY
1ST SOUTH CAROLINA ARTILLERY

The anecdote Inglesby relates here occurred just after a Federal shell passed through brickworks of the upper tier of casemates on Fort Sumter, exploding in the barracks on the eastern side of the fort. No one was injured either by the enemy shell or by the bursting Confederate gun.

The writer, who was Officer of the Day, returned to the parapet by way of the turret stairs at the northeast angle. As he stepped from the turret to the terreplein, the gunner of the first gun saluted him and gravely said: "Mr. Officer of the Day, have you seen an eight-inch Columbiad running around anywhere that you have been?" In reply to the question, "Are you crazy or drunk my man; what do you mean?" he pointed to his gun carriage, which was empty, and said, "We fired our gun just now, but when we started to sponge her for a new load we saw that she had gone!" The gun had burst, the chase going over the parapet and landing on the berme of the fort, the breach going clear over the quarters and falling into the parade.

Rear Admiral Samuel F. Du Pont (second from left) meets with his staff on board the frigate Wabash. Du Pont's officers unanimously supported his decision not to renew the attack of April 7.

CORPORAL AUGUSTINE T. SMYTHE
C.S. Signal Corps

Corporal Smythe made the following observations in a letter to his aunt written about two weeks after the battle. In Fort Sumter during the fighting, he spent his time decoding the signals between Du Pont's flagship New Ironsides and the ironclads. According to Smythe, the Confederates had learned the Federal codes from a captured Union signalman.

To us in the city it seemed but a skirmish, but the walls of Sumter as well as her garrison bear testimony to the terrible conflict in which they were engaged. It lasted for only two hours, but entre nous, if they could have stood it for two hours longer the whole east, or seaface of Sumter would have been cracked & perhaps beaten down. As it is it has been severely damaged, several of the solid 15 in. shot penetrating three or four feet into the solid brick-wall. These have been mended of course & the wall really strengthened by removing the guns from the lower tier of casemates, & filling them up with sand. These guns were only smooth bore thirty-two pounders & were of no use against the Monitors. Thus the wall is really stronger than before. The guns on the parapet have also been changed, & several heavy ones on the inner face have been moved to the other side, so that if they return they will meet, from the same battery, a much heavier fire. The men & officers are both confident of their ability to cope with & drive off the Monitors when ever they come back. The Yankee report is very incorrect. The closest that they came was about 900 yards & they did not receive our heaviest fire as they were at no time directly between Sumter & Sullivan's Island. True Battery Bee did fire; but only at the "Keokuk" & one other & then at long range. Our gun boats did not fire a shot but waited quietly for them near Fort Johnson. As to their being able to shell the city, it may be so, but they were farther off than Sumter a good deal. Then as to their being hit by torpedos, as is said of the "Keokuk" it is untrue. They did come up boldly to the fight, but had to give it up. Their 15in shot & shell are awful projectiles. The officers say that they could be distinctly seen flying thro' the air & almost "dodged." The authorities are hard at work trying to raise the "Keokuk" on account of her guns, boilers, iron &c. & they hope to succeed.

The Federals fabricated engine parts and repaired armor plating for the ironclads at floating machine shops like this one, located off Port Royal, South Carolina, the staging area for the advance on Charleston.

"Never did morning dawn upon lighter spirits as they saw themselves free at last to return to the city with their well-earned trophy."

A tugboat steams to the aid of the shell-riddled U.S.S. Keokuk, sinking in choppy waters off Morris Island. The scene was painted by Xanthus Smith, an officer with the Federal fleet at Charleston. Secretary Welles accused Du Pont of negligence for failing to destroy the disabled ironclad and allowing its guns to fall into Rebel hands.

CAPTAIN JOHN JOHNSON
C.S. ENGINEERS, FORT SUMTER

Laboring at night and at low tide Confederate riggers working under Adolphus W. La Coste, a civilian engineer, succeeded in salvaging the Keokuk's 11-inch guns. They mounted one of them at Fort Sumter and the other on Sullivan's Island. Captain Johnson later described the exceedingly dangerous, herculean task of removing the weapons.

The first thing to be done was to convey the workmen to the wreck with their tools, then push off and stand guard some distance out and down the channel in the small boat or boats provided. . . . With slippery footing on the tops or roofing of the turrets, constantly awash with the swell of the ocean breaking over them, their scant clothing kept wet with the salt spray, and no light allowed them, the mechanics bend themselves to the work. The first turret is attacked with sledge and chisel, wrench and crowbar, for nothing less than the removal of a large section of the roof will satisfy them, sufficient to allow the lifting and free passage of a gun thirteen feet five inches long, nearly three feet in diameter at the breech, and weighing sixteen thousand pounds.

Two thicknesses of inch or inch and a half iron, held up by girders of the same material set close together, and [sealed] on the under side with one thickness of iron plate, constituted the first obstacles to be overcome. Besides the upper and lower plating, three of the heavy girders had to be cut through, each in two places, and removed. Then the gun . . . mostly under water, could not be made ready for lifting until two massive cap-squares of brass confining it to the carriage were cut and wrenched out of place. The elevating screw, removed from the cascabel, gives place to a strong rope of hawser passed through the cascabel and wrapped around the breech of the gun with lashings sufficient to sling it to the hoisting tackle.

LaCoste had all now in readiness for the crowning act. The gun had been prepared for him by the artificers, who labored at first a whole week in cutting through the roof, and were further delayed by the difficulties encountered within the turret. Altogether, more than two weeks were consumed in cutting through both turrets and in getting the first gun ready to be hoisted out of its watery bed. . . .

. . . When the final preparations for the removal of the first gun were completed, a favorable night in the early part of May was chosen, and a carefully-planned expedition to the wreck set out from the city, stopping at Fort Sumter on its way down the harbor.

An old but solid hulk, a lightship formerly in use at Rattlesnake Shoal, north of the harbor, was made ready for the hoisting and transporting of the guns to the city. From the bow projected two outriggers of timber fourteen inches square and twenty feet long, arranged with blocks, stays, and tackle ready for the work, while, to suit the necessity of a lift from the low level of the submerged guns in the wreck, the bow was weighted down with fifteen hundred sandbags, destined to play, subsequently, a yet more important part in the execution of the plan. . . .

Secrecy and dispatch were never more the requisites of success than at this juncture. The Union fleet lay outside, and even some of their small boats on picket-duty could be descried from the deck of the Etiwan. But so lulled into confidence were they that no interruption whatever occurred from this quarter. The background of the sandhills of Morris Island must have obscured and favored the movements of the Confederates.

On reaching the wreck the hulk of the lightship was made fast to the nearly submerged turret, and then began the earnest work of the night. Lieutenants Boylston and Rhett were there in command of the detail from their regiment, but they all accorded to LaCoste the directing of the delicate operations, and vied with each other in encouraging their men to render him obedience with a good will and a pull all together. With the slinging of the gun safely effected came the order to hoist away, the men on the lightship responding cheerily, though with the hush of caution, to their comrades waist-deep in water within the iron turret. The strain begins, the stout ropes tighten, the block slowly rises; then the massive breech of the gun appears, inch by inch, above the level of the roofing, the muzzle yet hanging far down below it and splashed by the swell of seawater. The same swell outside the turret was making everything on board the hulk unsteady, save the earnest, lively pull of the men and the dauntless spirit of their leaders. Stick to it as they did, the task was a heavy one, the progress slow, the operation very delicate.

The muzzle of the gun, as was said, was hanging down within the turret, while the heavy breech, hoisted out and clear, was at this stage swaying and swinging freely with the roll of the lightship. Had the contrivance been higher above the water, the capacity of its blocks and tackle would have been sufficient for all purposes; but already the two blocks were nearly touching each other, and the falls could do no more toward pulling the muzzle free of the turret. There it sloped down to the water, grating and grinding upon the edge of the iron roofing, but refusing to be dislodged by any further application of muscular strength. Equal to the emergency, LaCoste was not to be thwarted, but, looking a moment to the bow of the hulk, weighted down with sandbags in order to reach the lowest level of the hoist, he resorted to what he hoped would give him instant success.

"Shift the deck-load, boys! Handle those sandbags! Pass them to the stern!" were orders uttered with earnestness and obeyed with alacrity. The men made fast their rope, and sprang to the bow, where the bags of sand, piled up by hundreds, awaited their removal. As they were taken off, the bow, heaving with the tide and becoming more buoyant every minute, gradually responded to the lightening of its load and the lifting force now exerted by the weighting down of the opposite end of the boat. The gun is plainly rising: it is almost clear; another minute and it promises to swing free from the restraining edge of Keokuk's turret. But no, not yet! The last bag of sand has been transferred from bow to stern, and human ingenuity can do no more. . . .

. . . Adding to the embarrassment of the enterprise, the first streaking of the eastern sky with the early dawn was now discovered. The Confederate gunboat was now coming in. The transport Etiwan hailed to know if all was ready. Still the great gun was swaying in its sling from side to side, but with the tip of its long muzzle lodged upon the turret, as if resisting to the last its own capture by the enemy.

Not a moment was to be lost. Who would give the order to cut loose the prize? Every one shrank from it. Yet what else remained to be done?

Suddenly, to their relief, there came at this instant a friendly wave from the ocean, swelling landward and lifting the hulk higher than before, lifting the spars and blocks, lifting the muzzle of the gun free from its detaining lodgment, and lifting the hearts of all those waiting men from the depths of painful suspense to joy and satisfaction. They could give no cheers in such close proximity to the enemy, but loud murmurs of glad congratulation passed from one to another. Never did morning dawn upon lighter spirits as they saw themselves free at last to return to the city with their well-earned trophy.

GENERAL P. G. T. BEAUREGARD
COMMANDER, DEPARTMENT OF SOUTH CAROLINA, GEORGIA, AND FLORIDA

One of the South's leading military engineers, Beauregard worked furiously to improve Charleston's defenses. Besides mounting power-ful new guns, he salted the harbor with various types of mines and placed buoys at measured distances to establish accurate firing ranges.

The torpedoes, as anchored, floated a few feet below the surface of the water at low tide, and were loaded with one hundred pounds of powder, arranged to explode by concussion—the automatic fuse employed being the invention of Captain Francis D. Lee, an intelligent young engineer officer of my general staff, and now a prominent architect in St. Louis. The fuse or firing apparatus consisted of a cylindrical lead tube with a hemispherical head, the metal in the head being thinner than at the sides. The tube was open at the lower extremity, where it was surrounded by a flange; and, when in place, it was protected against leakage by means of brass couplings and rubber washers. It was charged as follows: In its centre was a glass tube filled with sulphuric acid, and hermetically sealed. This was guarded by another glass tube, sealed in like manner, and both were retained in position by means of a peculiar pin at the open end of the leaden tube; the space between the latter and the glass tube was then filled with a composition of chlorate of potassa and powdered loaf sugar, with a quantity of rifle powder. The lower part of the tube was then closed with a piece of oiled paper. Great care had to be taken to ascertain that the leaden tube was perfectly water-tight under considerable pressure. The torpedo also had to undergo the most careful test. The firing of the tube was produced by bringing the thin head in contact with a hard object, as the side of a vessel; the indentation of the lead broke the glass tubes, which discharged the acid on the composition, firing it, and thereby igniting the charge in the torpedo. The charges used varied from sixty to one hundred pounds rifle powder, though other explosives might have been more advantageously used if they had been available to us. Generally, four of the fuses were attached to the head of each torpedo, so as to secure the discharge at any angle of attack. These firing tubes or fuses were afterward modified to avoid the great risk consequent upon screwing them in place, and of having them permanently attached to the charged torpedo.

LIEUTENANT WILLIAM H. PARKER
C.S.S. PALMETTO STATE

The torpedo described by Parker was attached to the Palmetto State with a device similar to the one shown below for the C.S.S. Charleston. After the war, Parker was the captain of a Pacific coast packet before becoming a college president and minister to Korea in 1886. He published his autobiography, "Recollections of a Naval Officer," in 1883.

During the months of February and March we remained in a state of comparative inactivity; but kept our men in perfect drill. We put a torpedo on our bow at this time. The staff projected some 20 feet from the stem; it worked on a hinge or gooseneck, and by means of an iron davit the staff could be raised so as to carry the torpedo out of water—when ready for use it was lowered so as to bring the torpedo about six feet under water. The torpedo was loaded with 60 pounds of rifle powder, and had screwed in it in different positions near the head seven sensitive chemical fuses. We kept it in the water ready for use, and about every two weeks would bring it on board, take out the fuses and examine the powder to see that it was dry. As executive officer I always attended to this with the gunner, and it was no joke to do it. In the first place we had to go out in a boat and take the torpedo off the staff, and in rough weather it was hard to keep the boat from striking it. As a moderate blow was sufficient to break the glass phials inside the fuses and cause an explosion, this in itself was not a pleasant occupation. Upon getting it on board we would take it on the after "fantail," (as we denominated the ends outside the shield) behind a screen, and I have passed many a *mauvais quart d'heure* while the gunner unscrewed with a wrench, and took out, all the fuses. I think it was about the most unpleasant duty I ever had to perform.

The flag of the Chicora was never captured. Confederates removed it from the ship in 1865 when they destroyed the ironclad rather than surrender it to the Federals.

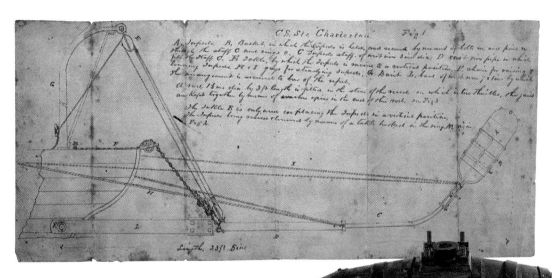

This diagram, drawn by an unknown Confederate engineer, shows how a spar torpedo was attached to a long boom on the bow of the Charleston, a 180-foot ironclad built largely with funds collected by the ladies of Charleston.

A common Confederate mine was made from a beer keg with wooden cones added at each end for stability. An anchor held it just beneath the water's surface.

Massacre on Morris Island

Following the failed attempts to take Charleston by land and by sea, the Federals in the summer of 1863 devised yet another scheme to capture the Rebel stronghold. The renewed effort was prefaced by a change in command. On June 11, 1863, Brigadier General Quincy Adams Gillmore took charge of the Department of the South, replacing the querulous and unpopular Major General David Hunter. Stocky and balding, the 38-year-old Gillmore graduated first in the West Point class of 1849, and in the decade preceding the war made a reputation as a talented officer of the Corps of Engineers. His successful siege of Fort Pulaski in April 1862 won Gillmore wide acclaim in the North and fueled his considerable ambition. To the Lincoln administration Gillmore seemed the ideal choice for commander of the Federal forces as they

tried once more to seize the elusive prize.

At his headquarters on Folly Island, Gillmore plotted a strategy for the reduction of Beauregard's defenses—a chain of events that would bring an ever increasing storm of naval and artillery fire over the city and its fortifications. Working in concert with Admiral John A. Dahlgren's fleet, Gillmore's troops would seize Morris Island, a low spit of sand that commanded the southern defenses of Charleston Harbor. From Cumming's Point on the island's northern tip, Federal batteries would pound the defiant garrison of Fort Sumter into submission. Once that threat was removed, Dahlgren's ironclads could draw closer to the defenses of the inner harbor, while the city itself would be open to Federal bombardment from sea and land. But in order to get to Cumming's Point, Gillmore's 11,000 troops first had to capture Battery Wagner and Battery Gregg, the Confederate earthworks that guarded the upper third of Morris Island.

The first part of Gillmore's strategy went entirely according to plan. In the early morning hours of July 10, Brigadier General George C. Strong's brigade set out in boats from Folly Island, crossed Lighthouse Inlet, and landed on the southern tip of Morris

Soldiers of the 54th Massachusetts Colored Infantry fight hand to hand with Confederates on the parapet of Battery Wagner on July 18, 1863. Of the tragic assault that day one of the regiment's officers declared, "The genius of Dante could but faintly portray the horrors of that hell."

In the attempt to capture Battery Wagner on Morris Island, Federal forces on Folly Island crossed Lighthouse Inlet on July 10, 1863, gained a foothold on the beach, and attacked the fort the next day, only to be turned back by the Confederate defenders. On July 18, following a massive bombardment by Union warships, Federal troops again charged the battery, with the 54th Massachusetts as the spearhead. Two successive waves of Federal troops—11 regiments in all—were repelled at the stronghold's parapet, with terrible losses. Some Federal troops managed to fight their way into the bastion, but they were ultimately forced to surrender after reinforcements failed to appear. At the end of the day Battery Wagner remained in Confederate hands.

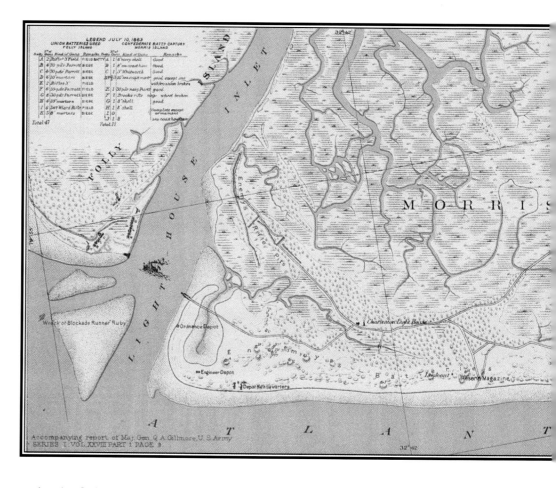

Island. With the young general leading the charge, the Federals routed the Rebel defenders, pushing them back up the beach to their stronghold at Battery Wagner. Strong's men took 150 prisoners, a dozen artillery pieces, and five flags. Had they stormed the fort that day, they may well have captured it; but they were exhausted, and Gillmore decided to call a halt.

This fateful pause permitted the Confederates to prepare for the inevitable Yankee assault, which came the next day, July 11. Despite General Strong's initiative and the gallantry of the 7th Connecticut—the only unit to reach the ramparts—the resolute Southern garrison succeeded in repulsing the

onslaught. Only 12 Confederates were killed or wounded, while the failed attack cost the Union 330 men. Gillmore shifted more troops to Morris Island and pondered his next move against the formidable Rebel bastion.

Originally constructed as a battery, Wagner by the summer of 1863 had been only partially strengthened and expanded. Named for Lieutenant Colonel Thomas M. Wagner of South Carolina, the work measured 250 by 100 yards and spanned the neck of Cumming's Point from the Atlantic on the east to an impassable swamp on the west. Its sloping sand and earthen parapets towered 30 feet above the level beach and were bolstered by palmetto logs and sandbags. Four-

teen cannons bristled from embrasures, the largest a 10-inch Columbiad that fired 128-pound shells. Battery Wagner's huge bomb-proof—its beamed ceiling topped with 10 feet of sand—was capable of sheltering nearly 1,000 of General William B. Taliaferro's 1,700-man garrison. The southern face of the fort, from which any Federal assault was bound to come, was screened by a water-filled ditch 10 feet wide and five feet deep. Buried land mines and razor-sharp palmetto stakes provided additional perils for an attacking force.

Gillmore had launched his initial attack on Battery Wagner without artillery support. Recognizing his mistake, the Union command-

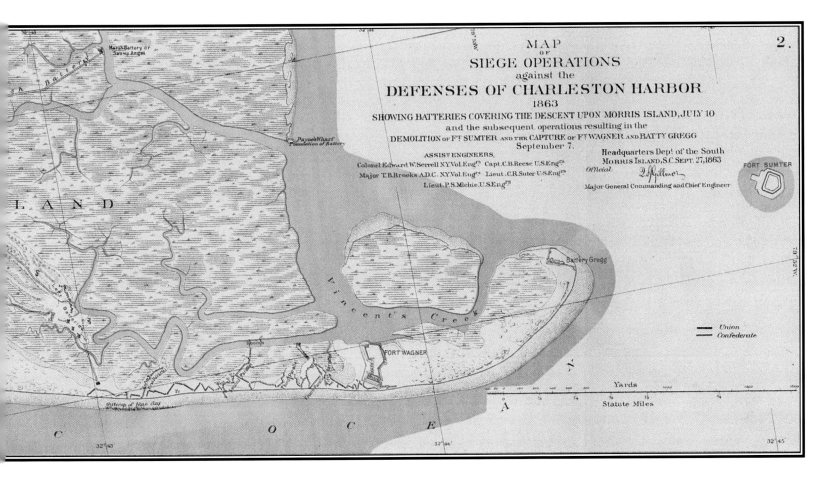

MAP
OF
SIEGE OPERATIONS
against the
DEFENSES OF CHARLESTON HARBOR
1863
SHOWING BATTERIES COVERING THE DESCENT UPON MORRIS ISLAND, JULY 10
and the subsequent operations resulting in the
DEMOLITION OF FT SUMTER AND THE CAPTURE OF FT WAGNER AND BATTY GREGG
September 7.

er chose to precede his second effort with one of the heaviest barrages of the war to date. At 8:15 a.m. on July 18, four Federal land batteries opened fire and soon were joined by the guns of a dozen vessels in Admiral Dahlgren's fleet. This formidable armada included the *New Ironsides,* a veritable floating gun platform, sheathed in iron.

The Confederates covered the fort's guns with sandbags in the hope of protecting the vulnerable ordnance from Yankee shellfire, and all but a handful of the garrison scurried for the shelter of Wagner's cavernous bombproof. General Taliaferro—a 40-year-old Virginian and battle-scarred veteran of Thomas J. "Stonewall" Jackson's campaigns—fully

expected the Yankees to follow up their barrage with another ground assault, and entrusted Lieutenant Colonel Peter C. Gaillard's Charleston Battalion with the perilous duty of manning the ramparts during the bombardment. The South Carolinians hunkered down to weather the iron storm as best they could.

As the day wore on, the tide rose, allowing the five smaller monitors to close within 300 yards of Battery Wagner. The ironclads were an awesome sight; to General Taliaferro they seemed "like huge water dogs, their black sides glistening in the sun." Naval shells weighing more than 400 pounds hurtled through the air with a roar that one Southern defender likened to "an ex-

press train." Some of the projectiles skipped across the waves, each smack on the water as loud as a cannon shot. One round exploded just offshore and showered the fort with a school of fish.

Dozens of shells burst over and within Battery Wagner's ramparts, dismounting a cannon and tearing wooden barracks and storerooms to splinters. Although most of the garrison was comparatively safe in the massive bombproof, the strain was intense as the structure trembled overhead. "Words cannot depict the thunder, the smoke, the lifted sand and the general havoc," Taliaferro wrote; "the whole island smoked like a furnace and trembled as from an earthquake."

At 2:00 p.m. the halyards of the fort's big garrison flag were severed and the banner fluttered to the ground. While four intrepid soldiers struggled to raise the fallen colors, Engineer Captain Robert Barnwell planted a regimental battle flag atop the parapet to show the Yankees that the defenders remained defiant. Afternoon gave way to evening and still the inferno raged. Shortly before sunset the Yankee fire rose to a crescendo. Shadowy forms could be seen massing on the open beach, and Taliaferro realized an enemy attack was imminent.

Eleven hours into the bombardment General Gillmore had every reason to expect that a determined land assault would carry the battered Rebel earthwork at the point of the bayonet. Gillmore's chief subordinate, division commander Truman Seymour, shared Gillmore's confidence. Two years earlier Seymour had been part of the Regular Army garrison that surrendered Fort Sumter, and he eagerly anticipated the day when Charleston would return to Federal control. General Strong, whose brigade would spearhead the attack, was won over by Seymour's zeal. But Colonel Haldimand S. Putnam, Strong's West Point classmate and fellow brigade commander, was less certain of success. "We are all going into Wagner like a flock of sheep," Putnam told his officers; "Seymour is a devil of a fellow for dash."

For the vanguard of the attack Strong chose the newly arrived 54th Massachusetts, the first regiment of black troops to be raised in the North. The regiment's youthful colonel, Robert Gould Shaw, was a slight, blond, 25-year-old Bostonian from a staunch abolitionist background. Shaw, happy for the chance to demonstrate the mettle of his regiment, deployed his 624 men in the forefront

of Strong's brigade. "His bearing was composed and graceful," Captain Luis Emilio recalled; "his cheek had somewhat paled, and the slight twitching of his mouth plainly showed that the whole cost was counted."

At 7:45 p.m. Shaw raised his sword, and the 54th Massachusetts started down the beach. At a point where the sand narrowed to a width of 100 yards between the ocean and swamp, the orderly ranks began to crowd together into a V-shape, Colonel Shaw at its apex. General Taliaferro's defenders scrambled to their posts, gunners ramming charges down the half-dozen cannon that had survived the shelling. The infantry leveled their muskets and when the Yankees were within 150 yards loosed a devastating volley. Dozens of Federals went down, but Shaw led his black soldiers through the vortex of fire, across the moat, and up the sloping walls of the fort. As he crested the flaming parapet, Shaw waved his sword, shouted, "Forward, 54th!" and then pitched headlong with three fatal wounds.

Unable to breach the defenses, many of the black soldiers began to retreat, while others fired across the rampart in a point-blank duel with the Charleston Battalion and the 51st North Carolina. One Southerner later recalled that he and his comrades were "maddened and infuriated at the sight of Negro troops," and little quarter was given on either side. One Rebel tore the white Massachusetts banner from its staff only to have it snatched back by a Yankee.

The 54th Massachusetts had been shattered before the five remaining regiments of Strong's brigade came charging up to the moat. Stumbling over the bodies of fallen comrades, soldiers of the 6th Connecticut followed their colorbearer onto the ramparts and

gained a foothold atop the bombproof and within the fort's southeast redoubt.

As the 31st North Carolina gave ground and General Taliaferro frantically rounded up more soldiers to fill the breach, Federals of the 48th New York joined the Connecticut men on the fort. But the remaining units of Strong's brigade faltered under a raking cross fire of canister from three howitzers that opened on their flanks. While urging on his men, General Strong was mortally wounded, and his devastated regiments collapsed in inextricable confusion.

It was 8:30 p.m.—more than half an hour after the attack began—before Colonel Putnam brought his four regiments forward to Strong's support. Shoving their way through the survivors of the first wave, several hundred attackers, most of them from the 7th New Hampshire, came to the aid of the embattled force on the bombproof and southeast bastion. But suddenly the situation was altered by a tragic error. In the gathering dusk, unable to tell friend from foe, the commander of the 100th New York ordered his men to fire a volley into the mass of troops silhouetted on the ramparts, felling Yankee and Rebel alike. The mistake compounded the chaos, and some enraged Federals fired back at the hapless New Yorkers.

As most of his troops retreated back down the corpse-strewn beach, Putnam took charge of the beleaguered Yankee contingent in the fort. He repeatedly sent messengers urging Seymour to commit his remaining brigade; but Seymour had been severely wounded, and reinforcements never arrived. Although several determined Rebel counterattacks had been beaten back, the Federals' ammunition was nearly exhausted. Colonel Putnam hoped to continue the stalled advance. "We had better get out of this," he said to Major Lewis Butler of the 67th Ohio, and an instant later Putnam fell with a bullet through his head. After a hasty consultation with the surviving officers, Butler ordered an evacuation. But many Federals never got the word and continued to fight on in the darkness.

Just as the Federal front collapsed, Taliaferro's garrison counterattacked, bolstered by fresh troops of the 32d Georgia, who had been ferried to Morris Island during the battle. The Confederates surged over the southeast bastion, killing or capturing every Yankee who remained. By 10:30 p.m. the desperate fight for Battery Wagner was over.

Daylight revealed the full extent of the Federal defeat. "In front of the fort the scene of carnage is indescribable," General Taliaferro wrote; "I have never seen so many dead in the same space." Numbers of Yankee wounded had drowned overnight when the moat was filled by the incoming tide, and others were smothered beneath the bodies of fallen comrades. For a loss of 36 killed and 145 wounded and missing, the Confederates had inflicted more than 2,000 casualties on their assailants. The gallant soldiers of the 54th Massachusetts had suffered the greatest regimental loss—281 men, of whom 102 were killed or never accounted for. The Southerners gathered up weapons and accouterments, stripped many of the slain of useful apparel, and piled the bodies into mass graves.

Shaken by the debacle, General Gillmore realized that Battery Wagner could not be taken by a head-on assault. The Federal commander decided to draw upon his engineering skills to work his guns and troops ever closer to the fort in an elaborate siege—tightening the noose until the Confederate garrison was forced to evacuate or surrender.

MORRIS ISLAND CAMPAIGN CASUALTIES

July 10, 1863

FEDERAL		CONFEDERATE	
Killed	15	Killed	17
Wounded	91	Wounded	112
Missing	-	Missing	67
Total	106	Total	196

July 11, 1863

FEDERAL		CONFEDERATE	
Killed	49	Killed	6
Wounded	184	Wounded	6
Missing	167	Missing	12
Total	400	Total	24

July 18, 1863

FEDERAL		CONFEDERATE	
Killed	246	Killed	-
Wounded	890	Wounded	-
Missing	391	Missing	-
Total	1,527	Total	222
Grand Total	2,033	Grand Total	442

LIEUTENANT GARTH W. JAMES

54TH MASSACHUSETTS INFANTRY

Known as "Wilkie" to his family, Garth Wilkinson James was the younger brother of famed novelist Henry James and the noted psychologist William James. In March 1863, while serving as sergeant in the 44th Massachusetts, James sought a commission in the newly formed 54th Massachusetts Colored Infantry and was appointed regimental adjutant.

Morris Island was a sandbar at the entrance to Charleston harbor. It was three miles and one-half long, and varied in width from twenty-five yards to nearly 1,000 yards. It was a mere mass of undulating sand heaps, rising from a long stretching beach to heights varying from three feet to perhaps forty feet above high water level. It was lashed on its eastern side by the rude seas of the Atlantic. On the south were the swampy courses of an inlet, known as Lighthouse Inlet, and to the west the marshy outflow of the Ashley River to the ocean. It protected the southern approach to Charleston harbor, while Sullivan Island on the north rendered the same service. Between these two formidable natural eathworks, and at the narrowest distance between each of them, stood Fort Sumter, the citadel of the Palmetto State, against which our land and naval forces concentrated. Near the northwestern extremity of Morris Island, and at a point where the ocean waters sprayed those of the bordering swamps, at the very narrowest expanse of the island, had been reared the most formidable sand earthwork known to modern warfare. Fort Wagner was a sand fortress, fashioned, in a measure, from the shape of the island at the point of its location. It was a towering mass of sand, utterly invulnerable to artillery, and pregnable only by a determined and heroic coup-de-main.

Battery Gregg—named for a Confederate general slain at Fredericksburg—guarded the wharf at Cumming's Point on the northern tip of Morris Island. Garrisoned by a scant 30 men of the 1st South Carolina Artillery, the earthwork was one of dozens of fortifications screening the approaches to Charleston Harbor.

"Fort Wagner . . . was a towering mass of sand, utterly invulnerable to artillery, and pregnable only by a determined and heroic coup-de-main."

PRIVATE JOHN D. MALLOY
14TH NORTH CAROLINA INFANTRY

Like many of Charleston's Confederate defenders, Private Malloy found service on James Island both dull and uncomfortable, as evidenced in a grumbling letter written to his cousin Kate Buie on March 24, 1863. A month later Malloy was promoted to lieutenant in the 51st North Carolina, one of several regiments dispatched to reinforce the garrison at Battery Wagner on Morris Island.

We are becoming more reconciled to this place than we were at first but on the whole there is nothing enticing here in S Carolina at least for the soldier. The boys have given James Island the name of *hungry-neck* inasmuch as they never draw half enough to eat. It would amuse you if you could hear the remarks made about S C by North Carolinians; one company this morning having drawn their rations of beef (for they draw no other kind of meat) and found it so poor that it was not fit to eat, they caried it off with all the solemnity of a funeral ocasion followed by a squad of men with spades and shovels reversed (which is the position in which funeral escorts carry their arms). Having reached the place of interment, they dug a grave— placed the quarter of beef in and having covered it up, they fired an old *pistol* over the grave, so they buried the beef with military honors! This Island is rather a disagreeable place to camp in. When the weather is fair, the dust raised by the wind which is generally blowing pretty lively, is almost insufferable—when it is calm, the gnats are always trying to form a new acquaintance with your ears, therefore rendering themselves a great source of annoyance and when it rains it rains two or three days at a time.

A wooden headboard bearing the palmetto tree emblem of South Carolina marked the James Island grave of John D. Gotjen, a sergeant in Company A of the German Artillery Battalion of Charleston. Gotjen died of yellow fever on January 22, 1863.

"He stood with his musket at full cock at the shoulder, and squinted along the barrel, taking dead aim at the General."

COLONEL CHARLES H. OLMSTEAD
1st Georgia Infantry

In early July 1863 the Confederate defenders of Morris Island were bolstered by a mixed force of 11 companies dispatched from Savannah under the command of Colonel Charles Olmstead. The colonel, who had spent seven months in Federal captivity following the capture of Fort Pulaski the previous year, put his soldiers to work burying deadly land mines—torpedoes as they were then known—in front of the southern approaches to Battery Wagner.

Now, at one point in our front, torpedoes had been planted the day before, and to prevent any of the garrison from treading upon them, a sentinel was placed to warn them off. At that time the man who held this post was private Donnolly, of Company G, First Georgia, a native of the Emerald Isle, as his name would indicate, and a true son of his mother. Of any knowledge of ordinary military manoeuvres he was calmly innocent. On one occasion a Lieutenant of the company asked him, impatiently:

"Donnolly, why *don't* you keep step? All the men are complaining about you." And received the reply:

"Faith, its divil a one of 'em can kape shtep wid me!"

Past this hero General Ripley spurred his horse, and was riding straight for the dangerous ground, when he was suddenly brought to a halt by a loud "Shtop!" uttered in the most emphatic tone, and the emphasis receiving additional point from Donnolly's attitude, as he stood with his musket at full cock at the shoulder, and squinted along the barrel, taking dead aim at the General. For a moment there was strong probability of a vacancy among the Brigadiers of the Confederate army, but an officer rushed forward, struck up the gun, and explained to General Ripley the reason for his being halted.

Subsequently, our sentinel was asked:

"Donnolly, what were you going to do?"

"I was going to shot him."

"And why?"

"To kape him from being blown up with the saltpaters, to be sure."

Artist Alfred Waud sketched Federal soldiers relaxing on the shore of Folly Island while vessels of Admiral Dahlgren's blockading fleet stand offshore. As the staging area for General Gillmore's drive on Charleston, Folly Island had received some 5,000 Union troops by early July 1863.

Sea Shore Folly Island S.C.

LIEUTENANT ELBRIDGE J. COPP
3D NEW HAMPSHIRE INFANTRY

Only 16 years old when he enlisted in 1861, Elbridge Copp—seen here in a postwar photograph—had risen through the ranks to become one of the youngest officers in Federal service. His regiment was one of five units in General George Strong's brigade, which was assigned the perilous task of spearheading the amphibious assault on Morris Island.

*I*n the afternoon of July 9, Adjutant Libby came into my tent and told me of the plan for the capture of Morris Island. Our brigade, he said, had been selected as the assaulting column. We were to make the attack in open boats; he seemed very much elated at the prospect of the glorious part we were to take as the "Forlorn Hope." I can't say that I shared his enthusiasm, on the contrary, to the best of my recollection, the cold shivers ran down my back, well knowing something of the horrors of facing a combined artillery and musketry fire under the most favorable circumstances, but to advance in open boats against the hail of grape and cannister, and a whirlwind of lead and exploding shell, called for the courage born either of a reckless disregard of life or a martyr's duty to his God and country.

1863

Blockading fleet off Charleston.

LIEUTENANT JAMES H. HAROLD
1ST NEW YORK ENGINEERS

In order to prepare the way for an attack on Morris Island, Gillmore's troops—including the 1st New York Engineers—worked under cover of darkness to erect an entrenched line of 47 cannons along the northern end of Folly Island. An English blockade runner ran aground at Lighthouse Inlet within sight of the Union position. But, as Harold recalled, Rebel salvagers failed to detect the nearby Yankees.

On the 3d or 4th of July a Confederate scout saw a long, low, rakish-looking vessel approach the south entrance of Lighthouse Inlet. She proved to be a blockade-runner, a steamer, called the Ruby, and, unfortunately, she got aground near Folly Island.

The toil-stained, weary, half-famished Confederates beheld plenty within their reach. Is it extraordinary that they should have left their labor on the batteries for awhile and engaged themselves in the business of "wrecking so nice a prize"?

Their absorbed eagerness was such, their nocturnal anxiety to secure some creature comforts so great, that they neither had eyes to see nor ears to hear what was progressing within 500 yards of their position. No glint flashed upon any man's mind of blue uniforms behind the trees, nor did a single ominous sound of hammer or saw stealthily applied reach any man's hearing. The enemy in that quarter was supposed to be at considerable distance. This delusion did not last long.

The morning of July 10, 1863, broke over the vicinity bright and tranquil, when a sudden and tremendous boom, the simultaneous discharge of 47 pieces of heavy artillery, saluted the astonished Confederates. The batteries on the north end of Folly Island had been unmasked, and aided by four monitors, delivered enfilading broadsides upon the Confederate works.

Under cover of this bombardment Gen. Strong, putting out in small boats from Folly Island, landed at Oyster Point.

Flanked by his staff, General Quincy A. Gillmore huddles over a map outside his headquarters tent on Folly Island. The bombardment of Morris Island was supervised by Colonel John W. Turner (standing, sixth from left), whose guns were placed in earthworks laid out by U.S. Engineer Lieutenant Peter S. Michie (seated at far right).

CAPTURE OF THE LOWER PORTION OF MORRIS ISLAND BY GEN. GILMORE.

BOMBARDEMENT OF FORTS ON THE LOWER PORTION OF MORRIS ISLAND

Engravings published in the popular New York journal Leslie's Illustrated depict the July 10 assault on Morris Island. Strong's brigade crosses Lighthouse Inlet and storms ashore (top), while the fleet shells Charleston's defenses (below).

LIEUTENANT ELBRIDGE J. COPP

3D NEW HAMPSHIRE INFANTRY

In the predawn darkness of July 10 four navy howitzer vessels escorted longboats bearing the 3d New Hampshire and the other units of General Strong's brigade to the starting point for their attack on Morris Island. At 5:00 a.m. the Union batteries on Folly Island opened a withering fire on the startled Confederate defenders, and two hours later Strong received orders to put his men ashore.

The enemy, all unconscious, are still sleeping in their camps on Morris island, less than a half mile away. The forest in front of our batteries falls as if by magic.

The signal gun booms out over the water, echoing and re-echoing from the waters to the clouds above. Then fifty guns and mortars shake the islands and pour a deadly shower of missiles into the camps of the enemy.

The guns of our ironclads in the harbor add to the din. The huge 15-inch shells from our monitor guns go crocheting over the water, striking the sand lands of the batteries upon the island, throwing cart loads high into the air, exploding with deadly effect and with the rumblings and vibrations of an earthquake.

The enemy although taken by surprise soon man their guns and heroically serve them with unerring aim; for two hours an incessant bombardment between our batteries and our warships in the harbor and the rebel guns upon Morris island is kept up. A signal has been given to General Strong to move his brigade up and assault the works.

A group of Federal infantrymen relax in a rowboat beached on the shore of Morris Island as the U.S.S. Commodore McDonough rides high in the shallow waters of Lighthouse Inlet. A converted ferryboat armed with six guns, the Commodore McDonough was among the vessels that provided covering fire for Strong's amphibious assault.

PRIVATE ROBERT D. KELLEY

6TH CONNECTICUT INFANTRY

While the main body of Strong's force rowed straight for the shoreline of Morris Island, the boats containing Colonel John Chatfield's 6th Connecticut continued to traverse the entire front of the Confederate line. Braving a heavy fire, Chatfield got his men ashore at the southeastern tip of the island and advanced parallel to Strong's column. Kelley, a drummer boy in Company I, recalled the daring feat.

We kept back in the stream under shelter of the island, out of sight of the enemy in case we would have to remain after daylight, and awaited with the patience we had left after two night vigils in leaky boats. . . . The day came clear and beautiful, and just as the sun's first beams were touching the tree tops above us the silence was broken by the roar of heavy guns, the firing being rapid and continuous, and almost immediately the orders "give way," "pull out," etc., were passed, and

we moved out into the inlet and turning rowed toward the ocean, as though racing. The lightest boats got ahead, and soon all semblance of the company formations which were intended to be kept was lost. The colonel stopped the boats in the stream opposite the landing place chosen, and under a rapid and well-directed fire from the heavy guns which the enemy had mounted on the [sand] hills of Morris Island got some of them into line and dashed for the shore. One boat was struck, but, being made with air-tight chambers at each end, sank only to the gunwales. The men jumped out into the water and held on to the boat outside until picked up. Two or three of them were nearly drowned and were caught hold of barely in time to save them. I was in the major's boat, and, it being lightly laden, was soon among those leading. The major ordered us to pull over under the shelter of the marshes of Morris Island, where he could control the rear boats without much exposure and could see almost everything that occurred. The line of boats formed in the stream soon touched the shore. The men jumped out and formed rapidly and charged.

pull striking the beach, out jump the men, some in water waist deep. All hastily forming upon the shore under the excited commands given by the officers they move on in the face of a deadly fire of infantry and artillery. "Charge bayonets!" is the command. With a wild yell, all along the line the enemy are routed from their rifle pits and earthworks upon the shore, pushing on and over their works we move, leaving a trail of the dead and wounded behind us in our advance, driving them back from battery to battery, through their camps, over the sand hills, back to Fort Wagner. . . .

Upon the approach of our boats to the shore, many of our men jumped too quick. General Strong was among the first to jump, went into the water all over, lost his boots in the mud, his hat floating off with the tide, and when I saw the general he was leading his brigade in the advance up the beach, bootless and hatless, mounted upon a diminutive mule or jack, captured in the camp of the enemy.

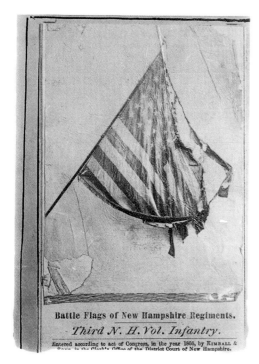

The bullet-torn colors of the 3d New Hampshire —one of General Strong's regiments—testifies to hard service in the battles for Charleston.

LIEUTENANT ELBRIDGE J. COPP
3D NEW HAMPSHIRE INFANTRY

Rowing for their lives through a blizzard of flying shells, Lieutenant Copp and his comrades were the third of Strong's units to hit the beach at Morris Island. Led by their zealous young general, the brigade captured the startled enemy pickets, overran rifle pits and gun emplacements, and chased the Rebels from encampments where breakfast was still simmering on the cookfires.

The boats are now fairly flying through the water. The rebel infantry are plainly seen upon the line of rifle pits upon the shore, and have opened fire. "Down, down men, and get what protection you can! Pull pull harder!" The zip and ping of the rebel bullets now sing about our ears, striking our boats, sometimes striking men. . . .

A shell explodes in the boat next to my own, killing and wounding many. The boat sinks, leaving a struggling mass of human forms in the water, reddened with the blood of the dead and wounded, but on, on we

Though new to command, George C. Strong won the trust of his soldiers. "The men are proud of their General," a reporter noted, "and will follow him anywhere."

"As the shot came bounding along the hard sand beach, Seymour would take off his hat and say, 'My compliments to you, gentlemen. We will give you something to talk about before night comes.'"

LIEUTENANT PETER S. MICHIE
U.S. CORPS OF ENGINEERS

A month after graduating second in the West Point class of 1863, Peter Michie found himself in the thick of the action on Morris Island; he was praised in General Seymour's official report for displaying "tireless zeal." Michie's wartime service won him promotion to brevet brigadier general. From 1871 to his death in 1901 he served as West Point's professor of physical and natural philosophy.

Inspired by the gallantry displayed by the troops, I sought and obtained permission to cross the inlet, and report for duty to Gen. Seymour, whom I found well up the beach in the vicinity of the Lighthouse. He was persistent in his efforts to get the troops ordered forward for the capture of Wagner, rightly reasoning that it was the golden opportunity while the enemy was demoralized with their present disaster.

But the troops were too much exhausted and fatigued with their long vigils, their severe exertions of the morning, and their hard march through the burning sands under the stifling heat of the sun, for it was an exceedingly oppressive day.

I shall never forget the impression made upon me by Seymour. He was a trim-built, soldierly-looking officer, with handsome, artistic features, something of a martinet in manner and speech. The enemy were firing grape down the beach at the group of officers and men, who found this the better traveling. At every discharge, as the shot came bounding along the hard sand beach, Seymour would take off his hat and say, "My compliments to you, gentlemen. We will give you something to talk about before night comes."

There was an old weatherbeaten boat half-buried in the sands, with its seams wide open, that attracted his attention.

"Michie," said he, "get that boat into the water, make your way out to the ironclads, and give the naval commander my compliments, and ask him if he will not move his vessels near to Wagner, so as to drive those fellows out."

I said the boat would not live in the water, as the seams were all open.

"Oh! it will hold you, and if it does sink a little you'll be able to paddle out there; they'll see you and send a boat for you."

Well, I had nothing more to say, but it appeared to me the most foolhardy thing that I ever heard of, and so I went up toward the sand-hills to get some men to launch the crazy thing.

But I was not more than 20 yards from the boat before a grapeshot came along and smashed the whole thing into smithereens; for which shot I mentally gave thanks to Providence and the rebels, for I was dreadfully afraid of sharks.

Division commander Truman Seymour had been an artillery captain assigned to Fort Sumter when the Federal garrison surrendered in April 1861.

COLONEL CHARLES H. OLMSTEAD

1ST GEORGIA INFANTRY

On July 10 the Confederate garrison of Battery Wagner—including Colonel Olmstead's Georgians—endured a heavy fire from the enemy ironclads working their way up the flank of Morris Island. Southern gunners scored 68 hits on the Yankee ships—60 of them striking Dahlgren's flagship, the Catskill. But the armored plating deflected most of the Rebel shells, and the Federal loss was slight.

I well remember the approach of the first monitor. How deliberate its movements; how insignificant its appearance; the deck almost level with the water, and the little black turret giving small promise of its hidden power for attack. My curiosity about the vessel was great, but was soon to be satisfied without stint. There was a slow revolving motion of the turret, a cloud of smoke, a deafening roar, and then, with the rush and noise of an express train, the huge fifteen inch shell, visible at every point of its trajectory, passed over head and burst far in the rear. The next shell exploded in the parapet, covering several of us with dirt. The introduction was complete. Thenceforward we held these singular looking craft in wholesome respect. The "Ironsides," however, was probably the most formidable ship of the fleet. She is said to have carried at bow and stern two hundred pound Parrott guns, and nine eleven inch Dahlgrens on a side. Her broadsides were not fired in volley, but gun after gun, in rapid succession, the effect upon those who were at the wrong end of the guns being exceedingly demoralizing. Whenever she commenced there was a painful uncertainty as to what might happen before she got through.

We had but one gun with which to fight the monitors—the ten-inch Columbiad located just over the sally-port. True, the thirty-twos were tried for a while, but they were so impotent to harm the heavy mail of the ships that their use was soon discontinued. This Columbiad was manned, I think, by the Matthew's Artillery, of South Carolina, and the gunner, Frazer Matthews, was as noble a soldier as the siege produced. In the midst of the hottest fire he would stand quietly on the chassis directing the aiming of the gun with all the coolness and precision of target practice. Never flurried, always intent upon the work before him, and never giving the signal to fire until the aim was taken to his entire satisfaction, the accuracy of his marksmanship was great. Again and again I saw the solid ten-inch shot strike upon the sides of the monitors, only to break into a thousand fragments, that would

splash into the sea like so much grapeshot.

At first we thought that no harm was done by our fire, but we learned afterwards that the concussion within the turret was tremendous, and that, among others, one very prominent officer had been killed by it.

Unfortunately, our Columbiad was soon dismounted, and although a new carriage was supplied, that too, was knocked to pieces in short order. Indeed, this experience was repeated half a dozen times.

. . . There was a constant strain upon all the faculties, that gave little time for anything save the stern duties of the hour, and yet there were humorous incidents ever occurring that even now will bring smiles to the lips of all who remember them.

Who can forget "Aquarius," the water bearer, as he was dubbed—

a simple-hearted fellow, from the backwoods of South Carolina, who devoted his time to bringing water to the wounded. Both heels of his shoes were carried away by a shell, and from that time he went barefooted—there was "danger in shoes," he said. And, then, the simple manner in which, on returning from one of his trips to the well, he held up one full jug and only the handle of another, saying, apologetically, "Oh, a shell took hit."

I can see in my mind's eye, too, the brilliant engineering feat of a member of the Oglethorpe Light Infantry, who while cooking a little dinner in the open parade, provided protection for himself by placing an empty flour barrel alongside of the fire, and gravely sticking his head into it whenever the scream of a shell warned him of approaching trouble.

"Both heels of his shoes were carried away by a shell, and from that time he went barefooted—there was 'danger in shoes,' he said."

The ironclad steamer New Ironsides was the most formidable ship in Dahlgren's fleet. Nearly 80 yards long, the vessel mounted 16 heavy guns. Its two-foot-thick hull made the New Ironsides virtually invulnerable to enemy fire.

PRIVATE JOHN WEIGEL
76TH PENNSYLVANIA INFANTRY

General Strong's amphibious operation netted 150 prisoners, five flags, and 11 pieces of artillery. The last of Strong's regiments to deploy, the 76th Pennsylvania Zouaves, scrambled into line and joined the victorious charge up Morris Island, stopping just short of Battery Wagner. Twenty-two-year-old John Weigel shared the general belief that Battery Wagner would have fallen if the attack had been permitted to continue.

Our fleet kept towing down the inlet to effect a landing, which was done under a severe fire from the rebels. One of the boats, I think of a Connecticut regiment, was cut in two by a cannon-ball, which took off the legs of one of the men; the others were soon seen struggling in the water, and all were rescued.

In making the landing we jumped into mud and water waist deep and waded to land, storming the Confederate rifle-pits and fort, capturing nine guns, camp equipage, and over 200 prisoners. Quite a number were killed and wounded. Any of the old comrades reading this will remember, when formed in line after disembarking, seeing Gen. Strong walking on one of the rifle-pits, with bare head, minus one boot, and in his shirt sleeves, pointing toward the rebel fort and shouting, "Come on boys, the day is ours!"

After capturing the fort, we were marched out on the beach toward Fort Wagner, on the north end of the island. Fort Sumter threw over into our midst solid shot, which caused every man to have his eyes fixed toward the fort, and it was really a grand sight to behold. As the balls came bounding among us the men would separate and the balls skip off into the Atlantic. The men would close up and march forward as steady as if nothing had happened. Not a man was injured, I believe.

LIEUTENANT ELBRIDGE J. COPP
3D NEW HAMPSHIRE INFANTRY

Contrary to Copp's assertion, Federal losses on July 10 in fact were remarkably light—15 killed and 91 wounded—while Confederate casualties totaled some 300. But the Union soldiers were exhausted by their exertions in the sweltering weather, and formations were disorganized by the chaotic assault. As Rebel shelling intensified, the Yankees hunkered down in the dunes and prepared for the next stage of Gillmore's offensive.

It was now 9 o'clock. The torrid heat of the sun upon the glaring sands, with the intense excitement of the morning, had added greatly to the casualties of battle. Many of our men were lying dead and wounded in front of the rifle pits and all along the line of march many were prostrated by the intense heat. Pickets were thrown out and the troops were glad to seek protection behind the sand hills of the islands and get needed rest and rations.

The firing from Wagner had now become continuous and occasional shots from Fort Sumter and from Fort Johnson on James Island came plowing along the broad beach and ricocheting over the sand hills down among our men. A group of officers, myself among the number, were sitting under the protection of one of those treacherous sand hills; a pail of butter, which had been found in a rebel tent was between us, and we were enjoying the luxury of hard-tack and butter, when a shell came plowing over the sands, bounding and striking within a few feet of us, nearly burying the whole party with dirt and demolishing our pail of butter, striking Colonel Bedel upon the leg as he sat upon the ground, wheeling him around and over and over like a tenpin.

The colonel was soon on his feet again, however, covered with dirt, his eyes, nose and mouth full of it, but yelling with a vigor characteristic of the man, and with language more forceful than elegant, "Where in H—— is our butter?" "Where's our butter?" the next instant picking up the shell a few rods away with the fuse still burning and throwing it down the beach into the water.

One of the few prewar structures on Morris Island, the Beacon House was the residence of the island's lighthouse keeper before being commandeered as Confederate headquarters. The building fell into Federal hands during Strong's assault and soon drew the fire of Battery Wagner's big guns.

Lieutenant Colonel Alonzo T. Dargan narrowly escaped capture when part of his regiment, the 21st South Carolina Infantry, was overrun during the Federal onslaught on the southern tip of Morris Island on July 10. Dargan, a lawyer from Darlington, South Carolina, survived the siege of Battery Wagner but was killed at Walthall Junction, Virginia, in May 1864.

EMMA E. HOLMES
RESIDENT OF CHARLESTON

With three brothers in Confederate service, 24-year-old Emma Holmes was a fervent Southern patriot whose wartime journal chronicled the pride and endurance of Charleston's population during the long siege. As a member of the city's monied aristocracy, she grieved over the deaths of several socially prominent officers during the Federal advance on Morris Island.

July 10. . . . This morning I was awakened about five o'clock by the dull boom of very heavy guns firing very rapidly from Folly I. evidently attacking Morris Island. We could see the shells bursting & occasionally hear their sharp whistle. As I expected to go to Carrie's tomorrow morning before breakfast, I quietly packed up my clothes. . . . Since breakfast the firing has only been at intervals. We went on the roof to look & saw our men had set fire to a house on Morris I. beach, preparing for an attack, that the enemy might not hide behind it. Everybody is in a state of uncertainty. Uncle James says he won't tell anyone they must go, but that we had better be prepared. I don't want to go at all & do not feel the slightest degree of alarm but do not like to be a burden or cause of anxiety to any of my friends. . . .

July 11 All day yesterday the cannonading was going on, but slower, and every deep boom of these tremendous guns seemed a death knell, so solemn was the feeling they produced, particularly when the reports of those killed & wounded commenced to come up. Poor Jamie Bee

This English-made pocketknife was a gift to Captain Langdon Cheves, a Confederate engineer, from his mother. Cheves, who had helped design Battery Wagner, was killed by a mortar shell on July 10.

"Every deep boom of these tremendous guns seemed a death knell, so solemn was the feeling they produced."

was the first whose death was announced, but Yankee prisoners taken today say he is not dead but desperately wounded. Rumors of every kind were rife, and the day passed slowly on, leaving almost everyone very quiet if not depressed. Beauregard had ordered no telegrams from the islands to be bulletined for fear of exciting the people, & most persons augured ill from that, particularly as we learned two or three of the batteries low down on Morris Island had been abandoned to the enemy. Thursday morning the Yankees cut down trees on Folly I. unmasking batteries of very heavy guns which together with Monitors and boat howitzers which flanked our little battery of nine guns concentrated a terrific fire of over fifty guns, under cover of which infantry was landed & the fighting became desperate, and hand to hand. Our men finally fell back to Battery Wagner, quite a strong fortification, & which, with Fort Sumter, kept up constant shelling to prevent the advance of the enemy. The papers say our loss is nearly 300 killed, wounded & missing, a number of wounded and exhausted men, & those who covered our retreat having been captured. The dead seem to be in small proportion, but most were left in the hands of the enemy & we cannot learn particulars except that Capt. Chas. Haskell & Capt. Langdon Cheves are both really killed. Both were fine officers & Capt. Cheves especially will be a severe loss to his family as well as his country.

Lieutenant John Stockton Bee of the 1st South Carolina Artillery, whose father was president of a blockade-running company, was shot down and captured while trying to stem the Yankee attack on July 10. He died in enemy hands.

COLONEL CHARLES H. OLMSTEAD
1ST GEORGIA INFANTRY

Gillmore's decision to delay his attack on Battery Wagner until the morning of July 11 allowed the Confederates time to reinforce the garrison with Colonel Olmstead's 460-man Georgia contingent, which filed into the defenses under cover of darkness. At dawn General Strong launched a headlong charge with three regiments, intending to take the fortress at bayonet point. But the Southern troops were ready and waiting.

At the first peep of dawn, on the 11th, we were wakened by a few straggling shots in our front, followed by a ringing cheer and three distinct volleys of musketry from our picket line. The anticipated assault was upon us. In an instant, the garrison was aroused, and as the men had slept in position they had only to spring to their feet, and we were ready. Now we could see our pickets, their duty having been faithfully performed, retiring rapidly towards our right, in accordance with the instructions they had received, so as to uncover the advancing columns of the enemy. And, then through the dim, gray light of the morning we could distinguish a dark, blue mass of men moving up the beach towards us, at the double quick, cheering as they came.

Then came the thunder of our first gun (what old soldier is there who does not recall *its* startling effect), then another and another, then the deafening rattle of small arms, mingled with yells and cheers, and we were fairly in the midst of battle. The issue was never doubtful for a moment. The attacking column attempted to deploy after passing the narrow neck in front, but entirely failed to do so; while the dense formation rendered it an easy mark for both infantry and artillery. Still it pressed gallantly on, and some few of the foremost men reached the scarp of the work, only to find themselves unsupported by their comrades, and with no alternative than to yield themselves prisoners. One brave fellow I saw, however, who had not the thought of yielding in him. Alone he reached the top of the parapet, immediately in front of a 32-pounder, double charged with grape shot. The officer in command (Lieutenant Gilchrist, of South Carolina, if memory serves me), struck by his bearing, called to him to come in before the gun was fired. His only reply was to put his musket to his shoulder, and a bullet whizzed by Gilchrist's head. The explosion of the gun followed, and a blue and mangled body, all that remained of a brave man and a good soldier, was hurled across the ditch.

Fort Wagner captured Sept 6 - 1863 Charleston

Set low against the horizon, Battery Wagner with its earth-and-sand walls was not a particularly imposing sight for the Federal assault force. But the Rebel bastion mounted 11 big guns, and the garrison had a clear field of fire down a narrow stretch of beach that forced the advancing Yankees into a compact column.

CORPORAL GILBERT EATON
7TH CONNECTICUT INFANTRY

General Strong allotted the perilous honor of spearheading the July 11 assault to four companies of the 7th Connecticut commanded by Major Daniel C. Rodman. Rodman's men managed to gain the outer slope of the fort but were forced to retreat when their supports failed to arrive. Corporal Eaton survived the debacle, but 103 of his comrades were killed, wounded, or captured.

At the order to forward the rebs opened fire with grape and canister, but our companies were so close to the fort it passed over our heads with but few exceptions, sweeping through the ranks of our support. On we went, down the ditch and up on to the fort, and began firing upon the gunners inside, but the fort being so large and our party so small we could not keep them from all of their guns, and they retained control of one ditch howitzer and one columbiad gun, with which they played upon our support. We had been on the fort but a few moments when Major Rodman gave orders to retreat, declaring that our support had broken and left us. At that time we could just see them in the far distance, scattering like sheep without a shepherd. At this I said to my captain, who had stood close by me on the fort, that I was one who would go; and his reply was that I never could get away, that I might as well surrender. I replied that I would obey an order to retreat as well as to advance. So down the ditch I went, and off the best I could, amid grape, canister, and musketry, escaping all.

SERGEANT THOMAS W. MORGAN
76TH PENNSYLVANIA INFANTRY

Strong planned for the 76th Pennsylvania and the 9th Maine to follow the 7th Connecticut into the fort. But the plan fell apart when the men of the 76th halted and lay prone to escape the fire savaging their ranks. By the time their officers got them to their feet, the Pennsylvanians were too demoralized to continue the assault. Wounded and captured, Sergeant Morgan spent five months in a Southern prison before being paroled.

We were called quietly and sent on our mission, and not a word was spoken till we came very near the fort. Then we received a salute from a few rebs who were just outside the fort, and then the secret was out, and the command was given to "forward, double-quick." So we had

just started when the fort opened on us, and it was a regular sheet of flame, but on we went till our line melted away. I was a file closer and I did not see a man trying to go to the rear before I was wounded, and I was within thirty yards of the fort. I did not hear any order to retreat given. . . .

. . . There were not many of the Seventy-sixth left to go back, for two-thirds of the Seventy-sixth were left dead and wounded around the fort.

Survivors of the attack on Battery Wagner, Corporal Solomon Miller (left) and Private Harry Baker sport the regalia of the 76th Pennsylvania, the Keystone Zouaves. At Deep Bottom, Virginia, in 1864, Baker was killed and Miller wounded carrying the regimental colors (inset).

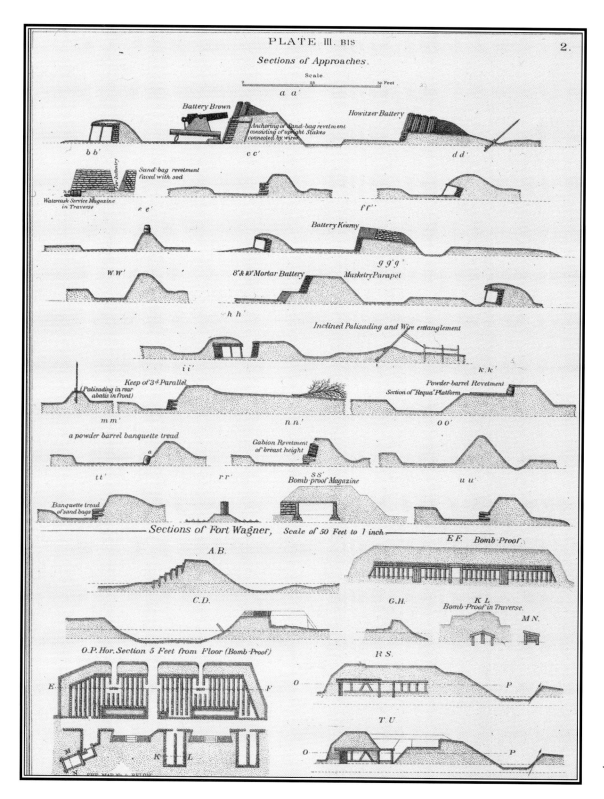

PLATE III. BIS

Sections of Approaches.

Scale

A page from General Gillmore's official report of his siege of Charleston includes a series of cross sections of Federal batteries (top) and of Battery Wagner (bottom). Before gaining Wagner's ramparts, attacking troops had to cross a water-filled ditch or moat fringed with a line of sharpened palmetto stakes (section CD). The Confederate defenders were able to shelter from the intense Yankee bombardment within a vast bombproof (section EF).

'It seemed as if there could be nothing alive in the shapeless heap of sand which we had been so persistently battering."

COLONEL
ALVIN C. VORIS
67TH OHIO INFANTRY

The 460 men of the 67th Ohio held the advanced outpost of the Union lines while Gillmore's soldiers dug their way closer to Battery Wagner. A prewar lawyer and judge from Akron, Voris commanded one of four regiments in Colonel Haldimand Putnam's brigade, which would follow Strong's troops in the second wave of the attack planned for dusk on July 18.

*A*ll through the night of the 17th, I lay with my men—the Sixty-seventh Ohio—within half-canister range of the fort; it was very dark, cloudy, enlivened by an occasional splash of rain and lightning, by which we could see sentinels on beat on the fort. It was an awfully anxious night for us, for the garrison must have known of our presence, as they could see us stretched out on the sand by the flicker of the lightning. We were wholly at the mercy of the caprice of the commandant of the fort. Just before break of day, we crawled quietly away, and took a good square breath of relief as we passed behind our first line of intrenchments. There we undertook to rest under a most scorching sun, and on burning white sand, which reflected back both light and heat rays with torturing rigor; at the same time, we had to keep one eye open, for we were supporting our working parties and batteries. We were compelled to work night and day, twelve hours on and twelve hours off, for two days; then one night on and two off; so that we had to be on active duty one full half of the time, all the while under shot and exploding shell from some quarter. When off duty, we tried to rest ourselves under the shelter of the low sand waves silently thrown up by the winds—always within easy range of Wagner, Gregg, and Sumter, and under the continual fire of

their guns, which at times poured upon us their death dealing contents with great fury, at all times at short recurring intervals, never of more than a few minutes duration. Our poor tired bodies became so exhausted under the great pressure upon us, that we would stretch out on the burning sands, even when under the greatest danger, and snatch a few hours of fitful, anxious sleep, that vainly struggled to refresh us, frequently to be awakened by the explosion of some great shell, louder than the report of a ten-pounder, scattering its fragments among the men, commissioned with dismay and death. The land and sea breezes, for about one-half the time each day, kept the air full of floating sand, which permeated every thing—clothing, eyes, ears, nostrils—and, at the height of the wind, would fly with such force as to make the face and hands sting with pain.

PAYMASTER
LUTHER G. BILLINGS
U.S.S. WATER WITCH

Paving the way for an infantry assault, Dahlgren's fleet opened a blizzard of fire at Battery Wagner at 12:30 p.m. on July 18. The Federal vessels closed to within 300 yards of the fort and expended some 1,700 shells, 810 of them from the New Ironsides. Through the offices of a friend, Billings volunteered for service aboard one of the monitors engaged in the bombardment.

*I*t was a magnificent sight to behold the black threatening hulls of the ships moving into position, to the thunder of hundreds of Rebel cannon, and still more stirring to hear the roar of the immense fifteen inch guns with which the monitors were armed, and to watch the huge missils go hurtling through the air until, burying themselves deep in the sand around the doomed fort they would explode and tear enormous pits. At first the Rebels attempted to reply, but soon the fire, particularly that of our splendid frigate "New Ironsides," became so hot that they retreated to their bombproofs. Our soldiers ran their trenches and traversed to some hundred yards of the fort with safety, but they could go no nearer because of our own fire. Still we kept it up, until it seemed as if there could be nothing alive in the shapeless heap of sand which we had been so persistently battering.

COLONEL ROBERT F. GRAHAM
21ST SOUTH CAROLINA INFANTRY

A respected lawyer from Marion, South Carolina, 29-year-old Robert Graham was the senior Confederate officer on Morris Island during the initial Federal assault. Despite his successful defense of Battery Wagner on July 11, many blamed Graham for his failure to prevent the preceding Federal amphibious landing. On July 14 General Taliaferro relieved Graham of command and took charge of the island's defenses. The following year Graham was wounded during the campaign for Petersburg, Virginia.

At the dawn of day, the pickets warned us of the approach of the enemy. Three volleys were fired into the approaching enemy, and the whole picket force retired into the fort without loss. The enemy advanced in two columns, one on the beach and the other on the island. I allowed them to get within a short distance of the works and gave the word "Fire." A few of the front line reached the parapet. The rest fled in confusion, and when the smoke cleared away they were out of sight. Those who reached the parapet never returned.

LIEUTENANT GARTH W. JAMES
54TH MASSACHUSETTS INFANTRY

Exhausted by three days of marching and skirmishing in the swamps of James Island, the black soldiers of the 54th Massachusetts joined General Strong's brigade on the beach facing Battery Wagner on the morning of July 18. When Strong tendered Colonel Shaw the fateful honor of leading the assault, the young abolitionist, eager to prove the valor of his men, readily accepted. Shaw's adjutant, Garth James, charged alongside his commander and was severely wounded.

Gen. Strong, mounted on a superb gray charger, in full dress, white gloves, a yellow bandana handkerchief coiled around his neck, approaches Col. Shaw to give the final orders for advance. He tells him that he desires to address a few words to his men. He stands before them and asks that the brave color bearers step out of the ranks. He takes the colors from the sergeants' hands and waves them aloft as a presage of a victory near at hand. To this signal of Gen. Strong respond the deafening cheers of this mighty host of men, about to plunge themselves into the fiery vortex of Hell. Strong asks them whether their bayonets are secure. The answer comes in tones of defiant affirmation. He tells them that these glorious colors must be planted on the fort, and that they must hold them planted there. After which the bugle sounds the advance.

As I turned to cheer the men, under the example of Col. Shaw, whose footsteps almost I followed, Fort Wagner made herself known to us in tones which left no doubt as to our proximity. We have now reached the first obstruction to our passage, the first chevaux-de-frise; this is the signal for her mightiest effort, and eighteen pieces of artillery, shotted with grape and canister, direct themselves into our melting line. To Shaw, in his boyish ardor, it undoubtedly seemed as if the worst had come and gone, and with the spectacle of a line fiercely broken there seemed no time for any other consideration save to urge on his men to swifter assault! After this mighty shock there followed perhaps five seconds of calm. It was the calm which precedes the reloading. To every soul in that surging column it must have seemed an eternity! A broken line, a mighty cheer! the flash of hand grenades and musketry from the parapets of Wagner, the renewed storm of grape and canister from her remorseless guns, and all individuality vanished from the line behind me! It was the moment for the final summons! the work had been swiftly done, the thunder was the funeral oration.

'The sand in front of the fort was so thickly strewn with blue that it seemed to be one solid color."

Though haunted by a premonition of death, Colonel Robert Gould Shaw wrote, "I want to get my men alongside of white troops, and into a good fight."

PAYMASTER LUTHER G. BILLINGS
U.S.S. WATER WITCH

The guns of the Federal fleet continued to pound Battery Wagner until the ground troops commenced their advance up the beach, around nightfall, when further bombardment would have been as dangerous to friend as to foe. The 54th Massachusetts led the charge down the narrow stretch of sand deployed in column by wing—two lines of battle, each five companies abreast—and as Paymaster Billings noted, Shaw's men bore the brunt of the first Confederate volleys.

Just about nightfall the fluttering of signal flags from the flagship called a halt, and running out of the grimy turrets we saw the head of the storming column under Shaw emerge from the trenches, and with lines as well dressed as if they were on parade, the colored troops rushed the fort. What a wonderful transformation scene! In the twinkling of an eye, as it were, the deserted hills of sand were drowned with grey and sheeted with flame, and I saw the whole front rank of the besieging troops lie down. I could not believe that they had all been killed. Still the survivors pressed on in their desperate run, until the partial protection of the side of the fort was reached, but alas, with what a sacrifice! The sand in front of the fort was so thickly strewn with blue that it seemed to be one solid color.

CAPTAIN JOHN W. M. APPLETON

54TH MASSACHUSETTS INFANTRY

A 31-year-old clerk from Boston, John Whittier Messer Appleton had been a zealous recruiter for the 54th and was the first officer commissioned in the regiment. As captain of Company A, he followed Colonel Shaw and the national colors across the moat and up the ramparts of Battery Wagner near the center of the Rebel earthwork.

At last we reached the moat of the fort. The sky had become black w/clouds & the thunder cracked & lightning flashed. As we reached the ditch someone gave an order, "By the right flank," & Co. B on my right, apparently filed off that way. My company preserved its alignment & the tier cannonade in the bastions at that instant were fired; the one on the right tearing the right of the company to pieces, killing Sgt. Benton & others & almost at the same instant, a like disaster fell upon the left of the company from the bastion on the left. I could hear the rattle of the volleys on the men & arms. I was in front of the company & leaped down into the water followed by all the men left standing on my left, the Col. w/the colors & the men of the companies on the left waded across abreast. With one we reached the base of the curtain & climbed up the parapet. Our second battalion right with us. On the top of the work we met the rebels & by the flashes of their guns we looked down into the fort. Apparently a sea of bayonets, some 8 or 10 ft. below us. The Col. planted the colors on the traverse, next the service magazine on the left of the curtain & the fighting was now hot about them. In the immediate front the enemy, were very brave & met us eagerly. Bayonets, musket butts, revolvers & swords & musket shots were all used, but our small number & our disadvantage in being up against the sky tolled heavily. The men rapidly thinning out around me. I rec'd a sword thrust through my blouse but it fortunately passed between my legs. About this time I saw our colors fall, rise again & go back through the water of the ditch, borne by someone. Finding it impossible to hold the crest of the parapet, we were so near the enemy as to be able almost to touch them & they were able to use cannon rammers & hand-pilers in the mélee.

SERGEANT WILLIAM H. CARNEY

54TH MASSACHUSETTS INFANTRY

When the 54th's color sergeant, John Wall, stumbled and fell at the base of the fort, Carney picked up the Stars and Stripes and carried the banner to the crest of the parapet. Though struck by several bullets, the 22-year-old sailor from New Bedford held onto the flag as he made his way to the rear. While recovering from his wounds, he was photographed with the flag he had saved.

Just after crossing the rifle-pit I found the National colors of my regiment unguarded; that is to say, that the Color-Sergeant had fallen into the rifle-pit, and as the regiment rushed on was trampled over, so far as I know. . . .

. . . I crossed the ditch with the flag and ascended the rising slope, which was of sand, until I came so near the tip that I could reach it with my flag, and at this time the shot—grape, canister, and hand-grenade— came in showers, and the columns were leveled. I found myself the only man struggling, and at this instant I halted on the slope, still holding the flag erect in my hand. In this position I remained quite a while, still thinking that there were more to come, and that we had captured the fort. While in this position I saw a company coming toward me on the ramparts of the fort, and I thought they were Federal troops and raised my flag and shouted to them at the top of my voice, but before they saw me I discovered, by the light of a discharged cannon, their flag to be that of the Confederates. Judge for yourself how close I must have been to them on that dark night. But they did not see me, and I rolled my flag around the staff, remaining still in the position that I had held for quite a while, and finding myself to be the only struggling man, as all around me, under me, and beside me, were dead or dying and wounded. This was after the retreat, for I did not hear the order to retreat.

I thought then I would try to get away, as I saw no one standing erect but myself. I descended the slope in the ditch over the dead and dying, and the ditch that was dry a half or three-quarters of an hour before, when I crossed it, now comes up to my waist in water; but, by the help of the Good Father, I struggled, and crossed the ditch, and crawled up the slope on my return. I still held the flag in my hand, and reached the top of the slope, going back. I had not been shot until I reached this place, where I received a bullet in the left hip. I was not prostrated, but continued struggling to the rear, seeing no living man but myself moving.

In 1900 William Carney was awarded the Congressional Medal of Honor (above) for his gallantry in the attack on Battery Wagner 37 years earlier.

The tattered state and national colors of the 54th Massachusetts testify to the carnage of the regiment's charge on Battery Wagner. While Sergeant Carney bore the U.S. flag safely through the battle, the Massachusetts banner (top) was torn from its staff after its bearer, Private Thomas Ampey, was killed atop the parapet. Confederate soldiers later found the flag under a pile of bodies at the base of the fort.

SERGEANT STEPHEN A. SWAILS

54TH MASSACHUSETTS INFANTRY

Swails took charge of a group of soldiers after Captains Russel and Simpkins were shot down on the slope of the fort. A former boatman from Elmira, New York, Swails was subsequently wounded at the Battle of Olustee, Florida, in February 1864, and the following month became one of the first black soldiers to attain an officer's rank—lieutenant—in the Union army.

Three days shy of his 19th birthday when he died at Battery Wagner, Cabot Jackson Russel had left his studies at Harvard to join the 54th as captain of Company H. Fellow officer Garth James called Russel "an enthusiast for freedom."

We had just arrived at No 2 when the rebel discovering us fired, the shot striking Capt Russel, I think in the shoulder or left breast as he twisted his head one side and fell back. Capt Simpkins then asked him if he should take him away and he answered "No" asking to be straightened out. Capt. Simpkins then asked me to help straighten Capt Russel out by taking hold of his (Capt Russel's) legs, which I did, my back towards the enemy, and Capt Simpkins had hold of his shoulders *facing* the enemy. Before we had time to effect this Capt Simpkins, who was on his knees, put his hand to breast and exclaiming "Oh I am shot!" fell over on his face and across the body of Capt. Russel. Capt. Simpkins did not move nor speak after he was shot. The rebel continued firing wounding one of the men. After snapping my own gun at him several times I threw it down and took the private's gun and fired. The rebel dropped and Capt Russel requesting that I should not fire any more as it would draw the fire of the rebels to that point I changed my position falling back to the first embrasure where I met Lieut. Emerson and Capt Appleton. There I remained some 20 feet from the first position till we all received the order to fall back it being madness to attempt anything further.

Captain William H. Simpkins of Company K was instantly killed while trying to assist his mortally wounded comrade, Captain Russel. A 23-year-old former clerk, Simpkins had earlier seen service as a sergeant in the 44th Massachusetts.

'The sand being our only protection, fortunately one shell would fill up the hole made by the last, or we would have been annihilated."

LIEUTENANT AUGUSTUS A. MCKETHAN
51ST NORTH CAROLINA INFANTRY

Among Rebel reinforcements shifted to Morris Island a week before the second Yankee attack, the 550 men of the 51st North Carolina emerged from Battery Wagner's bombproof and took position at the center parapet in time to confront the Federal onslaught. Although the 31st North Carolina gave way on their left, the men of the 51st held their ground. Though not present in the fight, McKethan, the regimental historian, compiled his account from interviews with survivors.

The sand being our only protection, fortunately one shell would fill up the hole made by the last, or we would have been annihilated. Our only guns that could reach the enemy had been dismounted by their fire, and our smaller ones we had been compelled to dismount in order to protect, so that we might use them when the assault should be made. During the day the garrison was protected as much as possible by the bomb-proofs, only those necessary to guard and work the guns being required to remain exposed. . . .

The enemy advanced in column of regiments, led by Shaw's Fifty-fourth Massachusetts, a picked negro regiment, between sunset and dusk with empty guns and orders to use their bayonets. Time had not been given us to mount our guns, which as before stated, we had dismounted for protection, so that the assault was met solely by our infantry, not a cannon being fired; but so murderous was our fire that the advancing columns broke and rushed to the rear through the ranks of their own support, causing confusion and delay.

This double-breasted frock coat was worn by Samuel Tupper Hyde, a private in Company D of the Charleston Battalion. Private Hyde was killed during the defense of Battery Wagner's seaward salient.

LIEUTENANT DANIEL J. WEST
6TH CONNECTICUT INFANTRY

The soldiers of Colonel John Chatfield's 6th Connecticut followed the 54th Massachusetts down the corpse-strewn beach with Strong's other regiments close behind. Lieutenant West, the commander of Company I, had been wounded in action at Pocotaligo, South Carolina, the previous October. He was among a group of Connecticut men who fought their way across Wagner's moat and gained a lodgment atop the southeast bastion and the adjoining bombproof.

I think it must have been one mile up that beach to the fort, as level as a floor, without the least possibility of any cover. As soon as the cannonading stopped the slopes of Fort Wagner were swarming with soldiers. We charged in company front. The peninsula was narrow, and at high tide Fort Wagner was an island. The water flowed over in low places between the main island and Wagner. Some of the wounded who could not crawl away were drowned after the charge.

I had been in several battles before in Virginia and in operations around Charleston and Savannah, but nothing in my experience compared with the slaughter in front and in Fort Wagner that night.

Charging in company front and crowded on the narrow beach, the darkness threw our formation into confusion, but the impetus we gained carried us into the fort over the guns, rebels and other obstructions, on to the top of the bombproof in rear of the guns. By this time it was pitch dark.

Forts Sumter and Gregg, and even Moultrie on the opposite side of the harbor, gave us a severe shelling as soon as we started up the beach. We were crowded in an angle of the fort on the side, and on top of the bombproof.

I recollect seeing Col. Chatfield in the angle of the fort where we were, and that in the darkness there it did not seem to be 10 feet between the muzzles of the rifles of our men and the rebels. The flash from the guns in the darkness lit up the faces of the men.

I recollect seeing our colorbearer, a tall, fine-looking young German, with the Flag near the top of the fort. Some one called out to him to plant the colors on top. Just then he was shot down and some one else picked up the Flag.

The front page of the popular weekly Leslie's Illustrated carried an engraving of the second assault on Battery Wagner a month after the fight. Based on an eyewitness sketch by an officer of the 7th New Hampshire, the engraving shows Strong's and Putnam's troops fighting their way up the southeastern bastion. The accompanying text notes the death of General Strong, who was felled by a canister shot and succumbed to tetanus 12 days later.

PRIVATE JOSEPH C. HIBSON
48TH NEW YORK INFANTRY

Although serving as a musician and not required to fight, British-born Hibson accompanied his comrades as they advanced with Strong's brigade. Hibson risked his life to stop the 100th New York from firing into the backs of Union soldiers atop Wagner's parapet, then returned to the fight and saved his regiment's flag—deeds for which he received the Medal of Honor.

We crossed the moat and engaged in a hand-to-hand fight with the Thirty-first North Carolina in their outer works. They soon weakened, and we drove them from the southeast bastion, which we held under a terrible cross fire. Re-enforcements were sent to our support, but by some blunder, they mistook us for the enemy and poured a destructive volley into us. We could not live under the three fires, and something had to be done to stop the fire in our rear. I ran down into the moat and told our men there of the terrible blunder they were making and on this errand was shot in the elbow.

Having stopped the fire in our rear, I returned to the crest of the fort to find Color-Sergeant George G. Sparks, severely wounded, the color staff shot in two, and all the color-guard either killed or wounded. I picked up the colors with my uninjured hand, but just at that moment the Confederates made a determined assault on us. We managed to repulse the assault, but I received two additional wounds; the bone of my left forearm was completely shattered, and I was wounded in the head by pieces of a shell that burst near me. My scalp was torn and the blood was running into my eyes.

Second Lieutenant Jacob Calvin Williams served at Battery Wagner with Company C of the 31st North Carolina, a regiment General Taliaferro accused of "disgraceful conduct" for failing to join a counterattack on the Yankees clustered atop the bombproof. Williams' younger brother George—a private in his company—had died of disease at Charleston two months earlier.

SERGEANT HENRY F. W. LITTLE
7th New Hampshire Infantry

Colonel Putnam deployed his former unit, the 7th New Hampshire, in the front rank as his brigade moved to support Strong's soldiers. Little, a sergeant in Company D, had been working as a typesetter when he obtained his parents' permission to enlist. He later served as adjutant of the 29th U.S. Colored Troops, and in 1896 he recalled the charge on Wagner in his history of the 7th New Hampshire.

For a moment the brigade was halted, at the moment that the regiment under Shaw, and the First Brigade struck the enemy's picket line—which time the writer of this occupied in placing a tourniquet upon one of the men in Company D, Hinckley D. Harris, by name, whose right leg was badly shattered at the knee by a grapeshot, and we had barely time to affix the instrument, the grape and canister in the meantime splashing the water into our faces; for the left of the regiment then stood in the edge of the marsh on the left of the narrow neck of land, and water was a foot deep or more where we stood—when we heard the ringing command, "Forward," from Colonel Putnam, who was ever on the alert to have his brigade on time; besides which we distinctly remember the order given by Lieutenant-Colonel Abbott, which was, "Seventh New Hampshire, keep closed on the colors." Springing to their feet the line pushed on into a storm of shot that seemed to fill the air like the drops of a summer shower. After that it was hard to know or hear any command, as there was such a noise from the shells and guns, together with the shrieks and cries of the wounded. All this time it was growing darker, and upon nearing the coveted works we went in on the double-quick. We passed their outer works and opened to let the remnant of the First Brigade with Shaw's broken battalion pass through on their way to the rear, for they had nobly borne the first shock, their onset being so fierce and heavy that they were badly shattered, and the Second Brigade had the front.

Closing up as well as possible the regiment reached the ditch, a trench with sloping sides, some fifty feet in width, five in depth; and for the whole length of the south front waist deep in water and soft mud, though at the southeast angle and along the sea front it was dry. This ditch was enfiladed by heavy howitzers, which kept up a constant fire of grape and canister, and the sides and angles of the fort and the ditch itself were covered with the dead and wounded. In the angles of the ditch especially we noticed they lay piled one upon another, and there was no chance to get down into the ditch without climbing over these bodies.

LIEUTENANT DANIEL J. WEST
6th Connecticut Infantry

Pinned down with hundreds of other Yankees on the slope outside the seaward salient, Lieutenant West assumed that reinforcements would soon arrive, and he encouraged the men around him to keep up the fight. But no help was forthcoming, and when Rebel soldiers flanked their position, most of the surviving Federals surrendered. West spent the next 20 months as a prisoner of war.

I crawled up to the top of the fort to see in the darkness what was in front of us. It seemed to be some sort of an entrance from the top of the bombproof into the interior of the fort. Well, we held that angle of the fort for two or three hours, but the Confederates, regaining courage, crawled around our left and got partly in our rear, and we came down out of that into the gun pits, and that was ——!

The dead and wounded covered it so that it was impossible to get around. All of our commanding officers were either killed or disabled and had gone to the rear, but we did not know that at the time. We had kept up the firing wherever we could see the flash of a rebel gun.

We found after a time that Maj. John A. Filler, of a Pennsylvania regiment, was the commanding officer left with us.

As far as I was concerned I had no idea that the assault had been abandoned. I knew that none of the enemy were opposing us in any great numbers.

We had driven them into the bombproof, and we were told after the fight by such men as Col. Bedell, of a New Hampshire regiment, who was taken prisoner early in the assault and taken into the fort, that the rebel officers could not drive the men out to resume the fight. The fort was ours, and if one fresh regiment had been thrown in we should have held it.

We held the gun pits for a long time, but the enemy gradually worked around on our flank and got a howitzer in position that raked the pits, and that was the last of one of the most desperate small battles in that part of the field, if not in any held during the wars.

Some of the boys called on the Pennsylvania Major to surrender, but he had already surrendered. At last some one called out, "We surrender!" and the firing ceased. I took the cylinder out of my revolver and threw it away and that was the commencement of my 20 months' captivity as a prisoner of war.

"We had kept up the firing wherever we could see the flash of a rebel gun."

Shot in the left leg and right hand while urging his troops across Wagner's moat, Colonel John L. Chatfield (above) of the 6th Connecticut was dragged to safety by one of his men. Chatfield was sent north for medical treatment but died at his home in Waterbury on August 10, his wife and three children at his bedside.

A sergeant of the 6th Connecticut holds the regimental colors that were planted on the parapet of Battery Wagner. Despite his grievous wounds, Colonel Chatfield's greatest fear was that the flag had been captured. When told that the colors were safe he wept for joy. "Thank God for that," Chatfield said, "keep them as long as there is a thread left."

"I could hear the sickening thud of case and canister shot slashing through the bodies of the men. How it was possible for a man to reach that fort alive is beyond my comprehension."

BRIGADIER GENERAL WILLIAM B. TALIAFERRO
COMMANDER, MORRIS ISLAND

A Harvard-educated lawyer and veteran of the Mexican War and Stonewall Jackson's campaigns, General Taliaferro (pronounced "Tolliver") was a gritty disciplinarian whose heroic defense of Battery Wagner thrilled the beleaguered citizens of Charleston. In his official report of the action, Taliaferro praised Lieutenant Colonel Peter Gaillard's Charleston Battalion for holding their ground when the 31st North Carolina gave way.

COLONEL ALVIN C. VORIS
67TH OHIO INFANTRY

Most of Strong's brigade was recoiling in defeat by the time Colonel Putnam's brigade—including the 67th Ohio—approached the scene of action. Their ranks torn by shells and musketry, Putnam's men forced their way through the chaos, and numbers of them crossed the flooded ditch and joined the crowd of Federals battling atop the southeast bastion and bombproof. Voris was struck down before he reached the fort, and command of the 67th passed to Major Lewis Butler.

In the meantime, on the left of the work, the Thirty First North Carolina could not be induced to occupy their position, and ingloriously deserted the ramparts, when, no resistance being offered at this point, the advance of the enemy, pushing forward, entered the ditch and ascended the work at the extreme left salient of the land face, and occupied it. I at once directed lieutenant colonel Gaillard to keep up a severe enfilading fire to his left, and directed the field pieces on the left of the fort to keep outside of the sally-port to direct their fire to the right, so as to sweep the ditch and exterior slope of that part of the work thus occupied, and thus, at the same time, prevented the enemy from being supported at that point, and cut off all hope of his escape.

Before my regiment reached the fort, broken and disheartened bodies of our troops were seen making for the rear, but on the Sixty-seventh went, quickening her step, and closing up the ranks upon the colors, and with heroic cheers flung her flag to the midnight breezes on the ramparts of Wagner; but only to bring it away riddled to tatters by shell. Seven out of eight of the color-guard were shot down, and Color-sergeant McDonald, with a broken leg, brought it away. Lieutenant Cochran, commanding company, appreciating the situation, left the fort, went alone to head quarters, 2,500 yards to the rear, for re-inforcements, assuring General Gillmore that we could hold the fort, and then went back to Wagner, and brought off eighteen out of forty men, with which he started in the column in that fatal charge. Poor fellow! He afterward lost a leg, and died of his wounds. Two other lieutenants, with a dozen men, held one of the enemy's large guns for nearly two hours, over which they had hand-to-hand contests with soldiers in charge of the piece. They stayed at the gun till their comrades had withdrawn, and then retired in good order, considering the urgent inducements to get away. I shudder as I think of that awful charge. I could hear the sickening thud of case and canister shot slashing through the bodies of the men. How it was possible for a man to reach that fort alive is beyond my comprehension. I was shot with an Enfield cartridge within 150 yards of the fort, and so disabled that I could not go forward.

ADJUTANT HENRY G. WEBBER
7TH NEW HAMPSHIRE INFANTRY

As the leading unit of Putnam's brigade, the 7th New Hampshire suffered severe-ly; 77 men were killed or fatally wounded. The dead included 11 officers—the greatest such loss of any Federal regiment in the entire war. Lieutenant Webber managed to enter the fort and passed through the fight unscathed. But his career ended in disgrace four months later when he was dismissed for drunkenness.

I found myself, on reaching the crest of the parapet, in a corner where the bomb-proof, rising some six feet higher than the parapet, afforded a protection in front from the enemy's fire, and crowded upon the parapet, the slope of the bomb-proof, and in the corner were one or two hundred men from all the regiments in both brigades, among whom the few that I

In a sketch titled Defense of the Parapet, British artist Frank Vizetelly—who arrived on Morris Island as the battle was raging—depicted the point-blank, hand-to-hand fight atop Battery Wagner's bombproof and seaward bastion.

could make out as belonging to the Seventh New Hampshire were scat-tered. It was in vain that I tried in the tumultuous crowd, to get them to-gether. All was wild uproar, with the groans and cries of the wounded; men calling for their officers, officers calling for their men, and many in wild excitement yelling with no apparent object but to add to the confusion. . . .

Colonel Putnam, delayed by his horse being shot from under him, now appeared upon the fort, and ordered an attempt to charge and silence one of the guns that flanked the sea face, and still swept the top and sides of the bomb-proof with grape.

MAJOR LEWIS BUTLER
67TH OHIO INFANTRY

As Confederate howitzers enfiladed the crowded ditch and outer slope of the fort, Taliaferro ordered Captain William Ryan's company of the Charleston Battalion to counterattack the Yankees trapped in the seaward salient. Ryan was killed and the Rebels recoiled, but lacking reinforcements, the Federals knew they could not hold out much longer. When Colonel Putnam was killed, Butler found himself the ranking officer, and he ordered his soldiers to save themselves if they could.

I well remember the charge of Captain Ryon and the fate that befell him, for in the rebound I was carried into the main body of the enemy in the fort, and my identity being disclosed, three members of the 51st North Carolina raised their muskets to shoot me. Fortunately, every gun missed fire, and I slipped into the second entrance to the bomb-proof, and along the second traverse to the sea front, and thence along the parapet to the southeast bastion, where I met Colonel Putnam, my brigade commander, just coming into the fort. I briefly explained to him the situation as we both stood on the parapet. He turned to me and said: "Major, we had better get out of this." These were the last words he ever spoke. He was shot dead on the parapet. Calling Lieutenant Cate, of his staff, I told him to get the colonel off if possible, but as the latter stooped down to examine him, he was also shot dead and fell across his body. A brief inquiry revealed the fact that I was the only field-officer in the fort, and I at once took what command it was possible to take under the circumstances. I first ordered all colors sent out of the fort, and directed Captain Taylor, of the 62d O.V.I., to take charge of whatever troops he could at the entrance of the bastion, to prevent a repetition of Ryon's charge. I then sent Lieutenant Cochrane, of the 67th O.V.I., with a message to General Gilmore, requesting him to send another brigade to our support, and the message was faithfully delivered, but General Gilmore did not approve, and I next called for volunteers to creep along the glacis and silence the guns that were enfilading the ditch surrounding the southeast bastion. This movement was partially successful. . . .

I directed Captain Cowan, of the 48th New York, to go into the bastion and secure all wounded and all who would go to the rear, while I remained on the traverse with the men that were firing. He came back in about twenty minutes, and said he had got all out that would or could go. We then relieved the men, and left the fort together, and all who remained there did so after they were notified that we were prepared to evacuate.

A graduate of the West Point class of 1857, Haldimand Sumner Putnam had served with distinction on the western frontier and as a staff officer at First Manassas before accepting the colonelcy of the 7th New Hampshire.

BRIGADIER GENERAL WILLIAM B. TALIAFERRO
COMMANDER, MORRIS ISLAND

Referring to himself in the third person in a postwar account of the battle, Taliaferro described the desperate moments when the fate of Battery Wagner hung in the balance. With neither side willing to yield, and repeated Confederate counterattacks failing, Taliaferro drew upon 500 fresh troops of the 32d Georgia that had landed on Morris Island under the command of General Hagood. The Rebel soldiers were soon in a position to surround the Yankee contingent within the fort.

The southeast bastion was weakly defended, and into it a considerable body of the enemy made their way, but they were caught in a trap, for they could not leave it. The fight continued, but it was impossible to stem the torrent of deadly missiles which poured from the fort, the reflex of that terrible tide which had poured in all day, and the Federals retreated, leaving nearly a thousand dead around the fort.

There was no cessation of the Confederate fire. Forts Sumter and Gregg threw their shells along with those of Wagner upon the retiring foe. Nor was the conflict over in the fort itself. The party which had gained access by the salient next the sea could not escape. It was certain death to attempt to pass the line of concentrated fire which swept the faces of the work, and they did not attempt it, but they would not surrender, and in desperation kept up a constant fire upon the main body of the fort. The Confederates called for volunteers to dislodge them, a summons which was promptly responded to by Major McDonald, of the Fifty-first North Carolina, and by Captain Rion, of the Charleston battalion, with the requisite number of men. Rion's company was selected, and the gallant Irishman at the head of his company dashed at the reckless and insane men who seemed to insist upon immolation. The tables were now singularly turned. The assailants had become the assailed, and they held a fort within a fort and were protected by the traverses and gun chambers behind which they fought. Rion rushed at them, but he fell, shot outright, with several of his men, and the rest recoiled. At this time General Hagood reported to General Taliaferro with Colonel Harrison's splendid regiment, the Thirty-second Georgia, sent over by Beauregard to his assistance as soon as a landing could be effected at Cummings' Point. These troops were ordered to move along on the traverses and bomb-proofs and to plunge their concentrated fire over the stronghold. Still for a time the enemy held out, but at last they cried out and surrendered. The carnage was frightful.

Following the Confederate evacuation of Battery Wagner—two months after the second assault—soldiers of the 54th Massachusetts were photographed beside the sandbagged entrance to the main bombproof. It was in this portion of the seaward salient that the heaviest fighting occurred on July 18.

FRANK VIZETELLY

CORRESPONDENT, ILLUSTRATED LONDON NEWS

Vizetelly and his brother Henry were among Britain's most talented newspaper artists. Like many of his countrymen, Frank Vizetelly was sympathetic to the Confederate cause and spent nearly two years with Rebel armies. The zest for action that took Vizetelly to the battlefield of Morris Island ultimately ended in tragedy: In 1883 he perished in the Sudan while on campaign with an Anglo-Egyptian army that was massacred by the Sudanese. His body was never found.

As darkness gathered over the bay, a circle of flame could be seen around the beleaguered fort, while the roar of artillery crashed louder than ever through the still atmosphere. Then there was a silence, when nothing could be heard but the tramp of the troops as they embarked on their way to relieve the garrison. But this silence was of short duration; a fringe of fire leaped from the southern embrasures of Wagner, and succession of rapid discharges from the guns commanding the land approaches told us an assault was being made. As we rowed down the harbor, and drew nearer to the scene of action, we could hear the crack of rifles between the louder reports of the thirty-two-pounder howitzers, and even the shouting of the besieged and besiegers came to us in confused sounds. It was necessary that our approach to Morris Island should be as quiet as possible, for we knew the enemy's ironclads were lying off the front beach ready to open on any party landing to reinforce the garrison; thus our progress was slower than it might otherwise have been. The thickly-packed men covering the deck of the steamer nervously clutched their rifles, and from this

black living mass, almost indistinct in the now dark night, no sound arose, save a few whispers. Suddenly the fire, with a few exceptions, ceased, and there was a moment of intense anxiety to all on board. "Can they have surrendered?" was asked, in undertones, one from another; but nobody ventured to say he thought so. Again, to the relief of every one, the parapet of the battery was illuminated by a thousand flakes of fire, and we then knew that the first assault had been repulsed, and the second was being made. In the flashes of flame, dark figures could be seen moving over the glacis and down into the moat, preparatory to ascending the slopes.

At this moment, the flat-bottomed transport grated on the sand, and, quickly and noiselessly, each man, with his rifle and ammunition held aloft, waded to the shore. Now, indeed, could we hear the tumult of the fight, the Southern yell, and Federal hurrah, mingling with the roar of artillery and rattle of musketry. No time was evidently to be lost: the first companies on the strand were pushed forward at the double. But though too late to share the honor of the second repulse with the brave and exhausted few who remained to meet the enemy, yet they entered the battery in time to capture a score or two of Federals who had succeeded in getting into the work, and who now crouched, panic-stricken, at finding themselves hemmed in a place from which their friends had been driven headlong twice in succession.

In Frank Vizetelly's spirited drawing, Confederate reinforcements surge across Wagner's parade ground to join their embattled comrades in the southeast bastion. The arrival of the 32d Georgia turned the tide of battle and ensured victory for Taliaferro's garrison.

PRIVATE ROBERT D. KELLEY
6TH CONNECTICUT INFANTRY

Shaken by the magnitude of the disaster that had befallen his attacking columns, General Gillmore used his remaining soldiers to forcibly rally the demoralized survivors and walking wounded who streamed southward along the beach. Detailed as a stretcher-bearer with the other regimental musicians, Kelley found himself caught up in the chaotic crowd as he strove to evacuate the casualties before they were drowned by the rising tide.

The sun had set and darkness rapidly settling down over the scene, for the twilight is very short in that latitude, and we were picking up our stretcher to follow the troops, when the officer in command of the battery, which was manned by a company of the First United States Artillery, excitedly exclaimed, "My God! they are coming back! stop them! turn them back!" His men pulled the field gun from the embrasure and placed it at the end of the battery, pointed up the beach. Amazed and startled, for the defeat of that column seemed hardly possible to us, and knowing there was plenty for us to do, and that the sooner we began the better, we started out towards the fort on a run. Pushing our way through the crowds of troops who were thronging back in seemingly confused masses, we kept on until we had passed by a long boat which was lying across the beach and partly on the sands farther in, and then began to look for our own wounded. We had passed many wounded men, but as they were nearer our lines and plenty of stragglers to help them in we let them alone. The crash of bursting shells, the flashes of which lighted up for an instant everything around, leaving a deeper darkness; the whistling of bullets, the hum and whirr of grape, canister and other missiles, the roar of the heavy shot as they flew past and burst behind, the rushing of men as they hurried in the rear, the ceaseless beating and dashing of the surf as it broke upon the beach, the anxious fears for comrades, old and dear friends, some of them schoolmates or playfellows before we ever thought of the possibility of such experiences; and, through all, that all this sacrifice of life was useless, make up a remembrance of that night which is as vivid, now as though it was an affair of yesterday. Wounded men hobbling along singly or supported on both sides by comrades bearing them up were hastening by, anxious to reach the shelter which but a little while before they had left in high hopes and

spirits. We had got beyond the rear of the mass of retreating troops and those who were hurrying back were in small groups or couples, often a wounded man able to walk and companion, carrying the muskets of both, beside him.

A patter of hasty footsteps and a demoralized soldier rushes past as if running a foot-race. We stumble over a man crawling on his hands and knees and recognize one of our own boys. "Hello! old fellow, hurt much?" "Hope not; hit in the feet; got any whisky?" A canteen is handed him and a hearty drink taken. "All right; some behind there pretty bad; the Johnnies have given us —— this time; never mind me, I'll get along bully!" and he toils along cheerfully. A groan is heard close beside us. On the sands above the tide line lie a couple of figures. "Hurt much?" "Yes; this little fellow here's pretty badly hit. I've helped him

Private Walcott Wetherell of the 6th Connecticut was one of 400 veterans of the fighting on Morris Island to receive a bronze "Medal of Honor" by order of General Gillmore. Not to be confused with the Congressional decoration, the so-called Gillmore Medal was to be given to no more than 3 percent of any single unit.

along but I'm played out," said the larger one, "and I'm hit here!" placing his hand near his shoulder. "What regiment? I'm Forty-eighth New York. This's a Connecticut feller." We place the Connecticut "feller" on the stretcher carefully. His face is blackened with powder and dirt; he is bareheaded and his clothing saturated; give the New Yorker a good pull at the canteen; give the other a little one; lift up the stretcher upon our shoulder and hasten back. Sparks of light, like myriads of fire-flies, show that something very much like a fight is going on at our lines. Running and walking we soon reach them and learn the cause of the commotion. The regulars are preventing the retreating troops from passing behind the intrenchments, and are using their revolvers freely, but as far as I saw, more to frighten than to hurt, for in the little time we were trying to pass through with our load one frantic "regular" discharged several shots, pointing his weapon downwards. "Make way for wounded," we called, as we tried to push along near the water. "Ye can't pass here," and a regular with a drawn sabre sprang before us, "Get out the way! Don't you see we're ambulance corps?" showing the white and red bands which we still wore. "Don't give a damn! Ye can't pass here!" And he pushed against one of us with his sabre in a way that left no doubt of his meaning. "What'll we do with this wounded man?" "Put him down there!" said he, pointing in front of the battery, and there, farther away from the water, upon the loose sands, the wounded were lying thickly. Beyond them, stretching into the darkness, were masses of troops whose officers were getting them into some serviceable shape. [We left] our poor groaning burden carefully down beside the others.

COLONEL ALVIN C. VORIS

67TH OHIO INFANTRY

Federal medical personnel were ill prepared to deal with the unanticipated losses from the failed assault on Battery Wagner. Abandoned on the beach and caught in the cross fire, many wounded perished where they lay. Voris was fortunate to find help and was given prompt attention, although the surgeons could not locate the bullet that had struck him. Ten years later it was removed from his bladder.

When struck, I fancied a fragment of shell, many pounds in weight, had torn away a large portion of my left side, in the region of the lower ribs. I plunged forward, whole length, on the ground. In a moment, I raised up partially, and began to feel for the extent of my injury. Ascertaining that I was not lacerated as I had supposed, I thought I would push forward with my men. Getting up, I started to step off with my left leg, soldier like. No sooner had I thrown weight on it, than I fell again, finding myself wholly unable to walk. I was in an awful predicament, perfectly exposed to canister from Wagner, and shell from Gregg and Sumter, in front, and the enfilade from James Island. I tried to dig a trench in the sand with my saber, into which I might crawl, but the dry sand would fall back in place about as fast as I could scrape it out with my narrow implement. Failing in this, on all fours, I crawled toward the lea of the beach, which I hoped might shelter me a little, which was but a few yards distant. Reaching it, I found Sumter, Moultrie, and the batteries on Sullivan's Island had a most uncomfortable range on the beach. The whole dark sky was full of destruction, and the very earth was plowed through and through with the share of death. What could I do, helpless, and these horrors about me? I lay down in the billowy sand to rest and soothe my shocked body and perturbed nerves, strained by the awful tumult raging round me, anxiously wondering what would become of my heroic boys, who were contending against this savage havoc of iron, steel, and gunpowder. A charge of canister, striking all round me, aroused my reverie to thoughts of action. I abandoned the idea of taking the fort, and ordered a retreat —of myself—which I undertook to execute in a most unmartial manner—on my hands and knees, spread out like a turtle. I moved toward the rear at the slowest pace possible and [can't] say that I made any progress. I could hardly move, and then those dreadful guns! . . . My movement not being toward the enemy, whenever I heard a shot following in my line of march, I rolled over on my side, not wishing to be shot in that part of the body never suggestive of valor, and where cowardice is said to place its most notable scars without provoking envy. After working this way for a half hour, and making perhaps 200 yards, two boys of the Sixty-second Ohio found me, carried me to our first parallel, where had been arranged an *ex tempore* hospital, consisting of a huge earth bank, and a surgeon, who, with the zeal of a reformer and curiosity of a philosopher, undertook to fathom the depths of my wound.

"A surgeon . . . with the zeal of a reformer and curiosity of a philosopher, undertook to fathom the depths of my wound."

EMMA E. HOLMES
RESIDENT OF CHARLESTON

Often during the long siege of Charleston, the city's civilians found themselves spectators of military events that could decide their fate. Some, like Emma Holmes, professed a certain nonchalance during the dramatic day-long naval bombardment of Battery Wagner; the Yankee ships had been thwarted several times before. But once the flash of gunfire died away in the darkness Charlestonians waited in suspense to learn the outcome of Gillmore's infantry assault.

July 18 Saturday
From daylight this morning the enemy was bombarding Battery Wagner furiously; they have over 70 guns concentrated from their various batteries & Monitors & they fired at the rate of 20 shots a minute. It was intended to demoralize our troops, preparatory to the assault, which commenced at dark. I spent a good part of the day with an excellent spy glass watching the *Ironsides* and four Monitors: I could see almost every discharge &, when the Yankee shells struck, the earth . . . [sent] up a tall column of sand. I did not feel at all alarmed or excited; I had become so accustomed to the cannonading—but watched everything with intense interest. The *Ironsides* lay like a huge leviathan: long, low & black, discharging broadsides, while at her side, but nearer to Morris Island lying between herself & land, was a Monitor whose peculiar black turrets were instantly recognizable, so distinctly defined against the sky are their huge black forms.

A hand mirror, a combination sewing-and-writing kit, and a pair of drumsticks were among countless souvenirs taken by Confederate soldiers from the fallen Yankees who lay in front of Battery Wagner. Most of the Federal dead were stripped of shoes and useful items of clothing before being buried in mass graves.

MAJOR DAVID HARRIS
Staff, General
P. G. T. Beauregard

A prewar civil engineer and Virginia tobacco farmer, the West Point–educated Harris served on Beauregard's staff for most of the war. During the siege of Charleston he was entrusted with the design and improvement of many vital fortifications, and he was present at Wagner during the July 18 battle. Ten days after the Federal assault, he expressed his views on the use of black soldiers in a letter to his wife.

I have been engaged to the full extent of my physical ability both night and day in the performance of my duties. I was at Battery Wagner during that terrific bombardment to which it was subjected on the 18th Inst. and lent my aid in repelling the assault made on it, at dark that night of which you have doubtless seen accounts in the papers. It was a bold and daring one but later was repelled with immense slaughter of the enemy, both white and black. The parapet and ditches of portion of the battery were covered with the dead and wounded and the entreaties of the wounded the next morning, particularly the poor misguided negroes were piteous. For one I felt more inclined to comfort the negro than the white man. Col. Shaw was killed at the parapet at the head of his negro troops and buried in the same grave with them. The negroes asserted they were put in advance and told to move on, that the sword and bayonet were in their rear. They were then made to receive the first shock of battle and to be as it were a shield for the miserable hypocritical abolitionists.

WILSON ——
32d Georgia Infantry

Writing to his "Home Folks" on July 23, a Confederate veteran of the fight at Battery Wagner, whose full name has been lost to history, described the grisly aftermath of the Yankee charge. Although the writer shared the widespread scorn many Southerners felt for black troops and disparaged their contribution to the fight, Shaw's regiment in fact had suffered the heaviest Union loss: 281 men, of whom only 29 were taken prisoner.

You will be pleased to know that I am still in the land of the living. I am not sick but far from being well, it is now 15 days since we left Savannah Ga in that time we have had no change of clothing—or tents, have been exposed to considerable hardship. No sleep for 5 days or nights at a time. The fighting on Morris Island was very severe. We went over on Saturday returned this morning at 4 Oclk had no Sleep all the time, and but little to eat. The truth is no one wanted to eat. The yankie Iron Clads and Ships keep up a firen all the time, So the men in Battery Wagner have no chance to Sleep in the day time, and at night we all have to work to fix up The damage done in The day by the Shot and Shell which fall into The Fort at the rate of about 400 per hour. There are sum proofs in Battery Wagner but not enough to protect the men from The firen of the gunboats. So our Regt had to take The chances out in the Battery. There we had to cling to the Sides of The Fort and lay down on The ground and protect our selves as best we could. It was very dangerous—Some shell bursting a few feet from our company, and covering us up in Sand, I never in my life thought men could be placed in Such danger and so many get through safe. The Shelling Stop at dark except about 1/2 hour through the night they throw one, just enough to keep them in the Battery from Sleeping or working, but the work must be done, So each night we fix what the Yankes unfixed in the day. Our Regt got over in time on Saturday night to reinforce and change over the Battery and take 96 Yankees prisoners including a number of Officers, one Major of the 55th Pa Regt, I have his Canteen—I saw no Philadelphia Boys with that exception I trust I may never be in such a fight all day long the Yankee Gunboats and the Fort on the Island (for the Yankees have 3) kept up a firen on the Battery. The Bombardment was terrific it kept up until nigh on dusk, driving the men from their Guns, and spreading terror among the troop. The Guns of the Yankees played into the Battery from 3 directions. all at once they stoped and the Yankee Army consisting of the 48th NY. 9th Maine 7th Mass. 62 Ohio. 63 Pa Regts—and two

Black Negro Regts—The 54th Pa and 2d So Ca Regt opened on the Battery. They commenced a charge—coming up in close columns. We opened on them from the Battery with canister shot with deadly effect. but the white men charged gallantly—no mistake—all say so—they came right up into almost certain distruction. The officers leading in the advance—in one place I saw a Col—Lt Col—Captain and two Lieuts killed within 5 feet of each other—twice they planted there flag on the Battery—but each time it was cut down—we did not capture any colors. The having of nigers to fight is no fancy—it is true—I have seen them—two Regt was to have charged one end of Wagner if they had charged as did the white men on our left, the fighting must have lasted longer and more of them been killed—but the nigers would run—only a few being killed in the moat or on the parapit of the Battery, but Fort Sumpter opened fire on them and sent lots of the Damn Scoundrals to the other world. I never saw such a sight as presented itself on Sunday morning at day brake—as far as the eye could reach could be seen the dead and dying on all sides could be seen the result of the fight. I volentered to go out to collect the wounded yankees. I had a chance to see what was to be seen—in the ditch to our left there was 115 killed in a space of about 100 feet—So you can see that there was some brave yankees engaged—I never saw such a sight, men with heads off many with legs shot off—feet, hands and in fact any part of the body—Such complete destruction of life—So wholesale—it makes me shudder to think of it. One poor fellow I saw had a ball shot through his head taking off the forhead both eyes and his ear—I would like to forget his appearance he was alive 24 hours after the fight—others so shot as to be unable to tell if man or beast—the killed was about 8 to 1 wounded generaly it is just the revirse. The men killed was as a general thing fine looking, large men—all the prisoners I talked with seemed to regret the war, but thought it would continue Our loss is killed and wounded was about 100. The yankie boys I think about 1000. It took a whole day to bring the dead—a flag of truce came over the morning after the fight—from the fleet in a surf boat carrying a white flag and the old Stars and Stripes—asking to bury three dead and to provide for there wounded—This was refused—After Staying Some little time the yankee party put back. The land forces of the yankees on Morris Island are very close to us, there Head Qrs being about 700 yds from the fort. We have Rifle pits about 50 yds. It is very dangerous to be on pickett, for the yankees have Sharp-Shooters and Sharp Rifles and Shoot well. to day it is raining very hard, but we have got so we do not mind it. We have no tents I have no blankett except an indian rubber one I got from a yankie.

In Frank Vizetelly's sketch, made on the morning of July 19, Confederate soldiers survey the corpse-strewn slope and ditch of Battery Wagner. Yankee casualties totaled 1,527— seven times the Southern loss. Lacking any other practical alternative, the Rebels heaped most of the 246 dead into trenches in front of the fort.

A Long Season of Siege

Following the disastrous Federal assault on Battery Wagner on July 18, 1863, the Union commander, General Gillmore, resolved to adopt a different tactic. If his infantry could not take the Confederate bastion by storm, he would lay siege to the fort and demolish it with a steady rain of explosives.

Federal troops began digging a network of zigzag trenches, creeping ever closer to Battery Wagner's parapets. Behind the work parties Gillmore sent up howitzers that, along with heavy cannon emplaced farther down Morris Island, began shelling Wagner in an around-the-clock cannonade continuing day after day for six agonizing weeks.

By late July the siege had taken on a murderous life of its own. The Union infantry, digging at the island's sand and muck, broiled in 100-degree temperatures while under constant fire from Confederate mortars and sharp-

....

At Battery Stevens on Morris Island, a Federal gunner holds the lanyard of a 100-pounder Parrott rifle aimed at Fort Sumter. During one 24-hour period in August 1863, Federal shore and naval guns hurled 948 shells at the fort—678 of which found their mark.

shooters. Bloated rats and other vermin roamed everywhere; sea winds brought stinging sandstorms. Men collapsed from heat exhaustion or from malaria and other fevers. "I think," wrote a soldier of the 85th Pennsylvania, "this is the meanest place that I was ever in."

Inside Wagner conditions were worse. To escape the barrage, most of the Confederate defenders spent all day in the fort's bombproof, a vile-smelling burrow that echoed with the screams of the wounded also sheltered there. At night, when Federal fire slackened, the exhausted, ill-fed troops shoveled furiously to shore up traverses and gunports knocked in by Union shells. Still, the Confederates kept their courage and even humor. When General Beauregard, Charleston's commander, asked Colonel Lawrence M. Keitt, one of Wagner's top officers, for a report on the fort's condition, Keitt blithely replied that he and the men could hold out if Beauregard would just "send some more limes, rum and sugar."

The siege ended in early September when Gillmore, his forward trenches now within 200 yards of Wagner's crumbling walls, staged an 8,000-shell bombardment to prepare for a final infantry assault. But by then

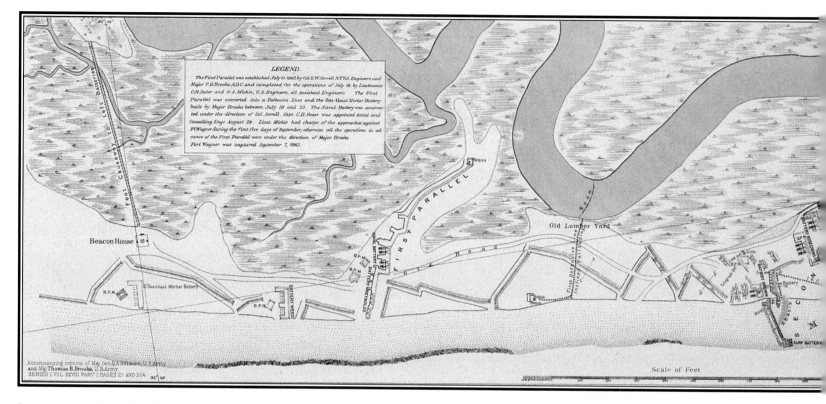

Beauregard had decided Wagner was not worth the sacrifice of more lives and ordered it abandoned along with Battery Gregg to the north. During the night of September 6, the Confederates successfully withdrew 1,000 men by boat. At dawn Union attackers, storming over Wagner's parapets, found only a deserted ruin. It had been, said one bitter Union survivor, the "most fatal and fruitless campaign of the entire war."

Fruitless it largely was. The Federals had Morris Island—at the cost of more than 2,300 men—but Charleston remained in Rebel hands. And so did Fort Sumter, although by now that bastion had been neutralized.

As Gillmore's trenches had approached Battery Wagner, he also came within range of Sumter. On August 17 his 16 long-range Parrott rifles, emplaced on sand dunes south of Wagner, began lobbing shells that easily hit Sumter, about 4,200 yards away. The bombardment—the first of many—continued unabated for a week. The army's guns, joined by the navy's ironclads, fired more than 6,800 rounds that pulverized large sections of the fort's walls. By August 24 Gillmore could boast to Washington that "Fort Sumter is today a shapeless and harmless mass of ruins."

Beauregard soon realized that Sumter was untenable for artillery and began removing the fort's guns, using them to strengthen other batteries around the harbor. He was determined to hold the fort, however, and he replaced the artillerymen with infantry, the troops—like those at Wagner—weathering the repeated bombardments by living like moles in dank bombproofs by day and working at night to shore up the shattered parapets.

On the night of September 8, the U.S. Navy made a move to capture Sumter. A volunteer force of 500 sailors and marines attempted a landing in small boats—with disastrous results. Alert Rebel shore batteries and the infantrymen within the fort swept the boats with fire, and those Federals who managed to land were swiftly cut down or captured. The navy lost 124 men and tried no further amphibious assaults on Sumter.

Gillmore, in the meantime, was waging a campaign of terror against the people of Charleston. His weapon, a big Parrott gun dubbed the Swamp Angel by its crew, rode on a platform in a Morris Island marsh. The gun began sending 200-pound shells filled with an incendiary mixture called Greek fire at the city during the month of August. The firebombs caused much alarm, but far more destructive were the guns set up on the tip of Morris Island during the winter of 1863-1864, whose shells demolished parts of the old lower city.

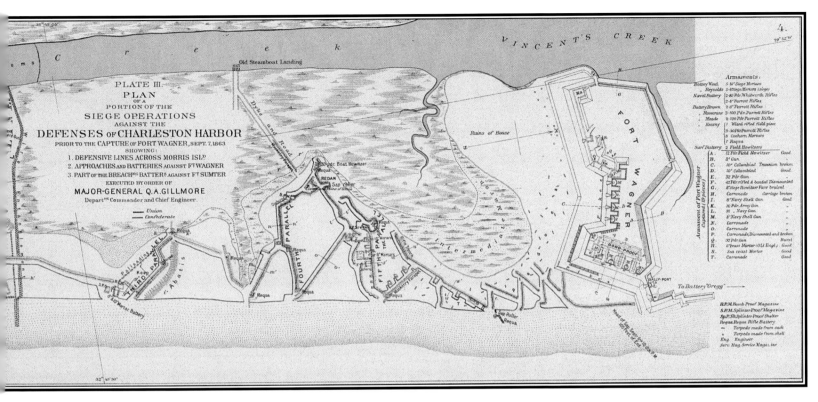

As the Federal guns hammered at Charleston and its defenses, the local Confederate navy did what it could to strike back. On the night of October 5, 1863, an odd little craft called the *David,* carrying a torpedo on a spar, rammed its charge into the hull of the Union warship *New Ironsides,* sending it limping to port for repairs.

Another daring Confederate foray involved a vessel called the *H. L. Hunley,* a bona fide if exceedingly crude submarine, the first ever used in warfare. On the night of February 17, 1864, the *Hunley* sneaked close to the Union sloop *Housatonic* and smashed its torpedo into the warship's hull, blowing off the entire stern section. Most of the Union crew were saved. The *Hunley's* men were not so lucky. The eight-man crew went to the bottom with their bizarre craft.

Such exploits could hardly drive off the Federals. But neither could the Union forces find a way to capture Charleston. So the stalemate continued. Without control of Sumter, Admiral Dahlgren refused to risk his ships by steaming into the reputedly mine-strewn harbor. The Union army for its part made a few halfhearted attempts to creep closer to the city, but they, too, came to nothing.

Charleston finally surrendered in February 1865, when General William Tecumseh Sherman and his 70,000-man army took the state capital of Columbia 100 miles inland. This cut Charleston's major rail and road connections to the rest of the Confederacy, and Beauregard realized that further resistance would be useless. After four years the Union fleet steamed in at last while a brigade of Federal troops paraded through Charleston's streets, a fife-and-drum corps playing the abolitionist hymn "John Brown's Body."

After attempts to seize Battery Wagner by direct assault failed miserably, General Gillmore decided to lay siege to the fort. Gradually moving north along the beach on Morris Island, Federal sappers dug a labyrinth of trenches (blue) that brought Gillmore's guns to within point-blank range of Wagner's parapet. In a classic siege-warfare technique, the trenches were laid out in a zigzag pattern to prevent the Confederate defenders from enfilading—firing directly down—the Federal lines.

CAPTAIN CHARLES P. BOWDITCH

55TH MASSACHUSETTS INFANTRY

In a letter to his mother dated August 5, 1863, Bowditch provided this description of his black troops filling sandbags during their first fatigue duty on Morris Island. Sandbags were indispensable for the Yankees' protection during the 50-day siege of Battery Wagner; the Federals used approximately 46,000 of them in building their trench lines and artillery platforms.

By spring of 1863, the siding, most of the roof, and one of the chimneys of the Beacon House on Morris Island had been stripped away by Federal troops for use in building siege works and bombproofs. Early in operations on Morris Island, the house had provided cover for Federal sharpshooters; later it served as an observation post for spying on the Confederates in Battery Wagner, 1,600 yards away.

We trudged up some two miles on a good sand beach and then struck off and walked through some of the most tiresome sand I ever came across, until we reached a place some three quarters of a mile from Fort Wagner. We were set to work to fill sandbags and a mighty easy work we had of it. It took each man about two hours to do his stent, which was to fill twenty-five bags, and after that each man filled five more for love. In all we filled some 3000 or 4000 bags. One part of Capt. Wales's company was set to work building a bridge in full sight of rebel batteries, but the rebs did not trouble them much, except that they threw three shells about half way between where we were at work and the bridge. It was the first time I had ever heard the whizz of a shell coming toward me. I heard it when it first left the gun and then lost the sound, but caught it again as it came nearer when it sounded just as I should have supposed a solid shot would have sounded if sent through water. The bursting and the whizzing of the shell made some of the men rather timid. One man was so overcome that he fell back into a puddle and came out a most filthy spectacle. The men got through their work in about a quarter of the time allotted to them and loafed and caught crabs the rest of it.

PRIVATE ELIAS A. BRYANT
4TH NEW HAMPSHIRE INFANTRY

As one of the 4th New Hampshire's buglers and later its principal musician, Bryant was not obligated to carry a rifle but chose to do so anyway. One year after the siege of Battery Wagner, Bryant lost his right leg at the hip during the fighting at Petersburg, Virginia. He was discharged in September 1864.

The firing is incessant, both night and day. Our regiment does not lose many men, but still there are two or three or half dozen get hurt every day. The Ninth Maine, who work alternately with our detail, lost many men every few days. The One Hundredth New York was also very unfortunate. We thought it was because they did not take sufficient care. It was necessary to watch the course of the shells from the batteries and the fort and calculate their fall. We got so used to reckoning this from long practice that from the more distant batteries we could tell whether it was a mortar shell or a Columbiad, where it would hit, and how much time we had for getting under shelter. We generally, by order of the officer in command of detail, had a man posted while we worked to give warning when a shell was coming in a particular direction. He would hide behind a heap of sand-bags and as he saw

danger in one direction would call to the men the name of the fort—Simpkins, Sumter, Moultrie—from which the peril threatened. Wagner gave us time only to drop on our faces where we stood, so near was the fort and so direct the course of the shell. The Whitworth gun, too, on Fort Wagner enabled them to fire with great rapidity and accuracy. This gun we could always tell, the report of the explosion following immediately on that of the firing. An alarm from the other forts often gave us time to get under cover of some of the "bomb proofs," which were built with each line of parallels. These were large enough to hold a company.

They were built directly against the line of earthworks. The top slanted down to the fortification of which it was a continuation. They, of course, faced away from the enemy. The framework was a number of upright supported crossbeams and a timber roof. On this the sand was piled. The structure was about high enough to allow a man of average height to enter without stooping.

There was a large one at headquarters, larger, on the ground, than the barn at the farm. One day as I was standing near the mouth of this a shell struck the top and bounded off, bursting as it fell about a rod behind us as we started at the shout of "Wagner" to run under cover. This was an every-day occurrence.

A city of tents—the camp of the 9th Maine—sprouts from the sand on Morris Island. The masts of Union ships in Lighthouse Inlet are visible on the horizon. The 9th Maine lost 182 men killed or mortally wounded and another 239 to disease during the war.

LIEUTENANT WILLIAM E. FURNESS
3D U.S. COLORED TROOPS

A native of Philadelphia, William Furness graduated from Harvard Law School in 1862. Here he describes the difficulties Federal sappers faced while digging their siege lines and zigzag approaches to Battery Wagner. They worked under heavy fire from front and flank and in shifting sands that often turned to mud a few feet below the surface.

"Off in the hazy distance toward Charleston, whose spires shone amid the tropical foliage, a puff of white smoke would curl upward."

Night after night . . . the flying sap was pushed forward, and slowly the works advanced toward the southeastern corner of the Rebel fort. During the daytime lookouts were kept posted under cover, who were to warn the working soldiers of the fort that fired. Off in the hazy distance toward Charleston, whose spires shone amid the tropical foliage, a puff of white smoke would curl upward, and then the warning voice of the watcher would cry, "Cover from Johnston!" and the fatigue party, dropping their shovels, would scatter for the splinter-proofs, whose openings looked seaward, disappearing like rabbits into their holes; and in another second or two the iron messenger would be bursting with hideous roar and scream over the place of work, or ploughing up the sand and debris; then at once the work would be hurried forward again, the party to be scattered next time in the opposite direction by the cry of "Cover Fort Sumter," "Gregg," or "Battery Bee!" Every angle of the approaches, every opening in the parapets, every loophole almost, was covered by the sharp-shooters, and the singing of the minie balls was like the music of immense mosquitoes. Though the missiles were invisible, raw soldiers soon learned the danger of the moment when the singing was heard,—though I have seen a lively negro soldier jump into the air with his hand up to try to catch the fragment of shell, on his first tour of fatigue duty. They soon learned that such Rebel compliments were not to be trifled with; and then the officer in command of the detail had often to hunt those same fellows (who were generally the least courageous, after all) out of the bomb-proofs at the point of his sword.

PAYMASTER HORATIO L. WAIT
U.S.S. Pembina

A member of the Federal blockading fleet, the Pembina, a screw gunboat, was commanded by a South Carolinian, Lieutenant John P. Bankhead, who had sided with the North. According to Wait, when the Pembina appeared off Charleston a former female friend of Bankhead sent him a malevolent gift: "an elegant set of silver coffin handles, and a grandiloquent message to the effect that the coffin to which they belonged was ready and waiting for him in Charleston."

Heavy siege batteries were built to fire over Wagner at Sumter. One, called the naval battery, was served by men from the fleet, mounting the English Whitworth rifles, having hexagonal bores, which had been captured from the Confederates. When these batteries were completed, they, in conjunction with the iron-clads, began the first heavy Union bombardment of Fort Sumter, August 17, 1863, and kept it up day and night for a week. In the bombardment, all of the Union batteries and iron-clads and all of the Confederate batteries participated. At night it made the most wonderful display of pyrotechnics that I ever saw. The air was filled with the luminous curves and flashes of the projectiles. A fifteen-inch gun, when fired with a cored shot, produces such a concussion of the air as to make it unpleasant to the ears of those near it; and when this continues for a week, those firing are as glad of a cessation as those fired at. Hence all rejoiced when Dahlgren and Gillmore concluded that the masonry of the gorge wall of Sumter had been sufficiently pulverized. At this time it had lost all traces of its former face, and had become an irregular mound of brickdust and mortar, in which the fifteen-inch shells would bury themselves, and on exploding throw up a vast red cloud of debris, which would mostly fall back in nearly the same place it came from.

Above, Union sailors man two 70-pounder Whitworth rifles at the naval battery on Morris Island. Purchased by the Confederates from an English manufacturer, the Whitworths were seized by the Federals from a captured blockade runner.

Standing on the sandbag ramparts of Battery Stevens, Federal gunners gaze in the direction of their target—Fort Sumter—more than two miles away. One of eight batteries established on Morris Island, Battery Stevens mounted two 100-pounder Parrott rifles. The tube of a third big gun lies in the foreground.

COLONEL WILLIAM H. DAVIS

104TH PENNSYLVANIA INFANTRY

Davis recounts the tremendous effort and engineering skill required to build the battery dubbed the Swamp Angel. To throw shells into Charleston, five miles away, the battery's 200-pounder Parrott rifle had to be fired at an elevation of 35 degrees and charged with 20 pounds of powder, four more than the normal charge.

It was determined early in the siege to build a battery out in the marsh between Morris and James' islands in the hope that shells from it could be thrown into Charleston. I believe the idea originated with colonel Serrell, commanding the New York Volunteer engineer regiment. The spot selected was about a mile from Morris, and south of a line running from our left batteries to the city, on the edge of a deep creek which made a good wet ditch. It was in the midst of the marsh and a pole could be run down sixteen feet before coming to bottom. It could only be reached by water along the winding creeks which led there, or on a foot bridge across the swamps. Fortunately the enemy had not entirely destroyed the foot bridge that used to lead over to James island, which our engineers repaired, and built up anew out to the spot.

The active part of the work was assigned to a lieutenant of engineers, who, upon being shown the place where the battery was to be erected, said that the thing was impossible. The colonel replied that there was no such word as "impossible" in the matter and that the battery must be built where he had pointed out. To encourage the doubting lieutenant he was told he had permission to call for any thing that might be required for the work. The next day this officer made a requisition on the depot quartermaster for one hundred men eighteen feet high to wade through mud sixteen feet deep. After making the requisition he went to the surgeon of his regiment to inquire whether he could splice the eighteen feet men if they were furnished him.

This piece of pleasantry cost the lieutenant his arrest which, however, did not last long, and the battery was constructed by men of ordinary stature.

It was built entirely of sand bags laid on a heavy foundation of timber sunk several feet into the mud. The bags were filled with sand on the island during the day, and taken round to the place in boats at night. I was told by general Gillmore that the sand bags alone, and by this is meant the material and making, cost the government five thousand dollars. The enemy judged we must be at some mischief so far out in the marsh, but could not divine what it was, for they did not imagine we would be rash enough to attempt to build a battery there. One bright morning they looked across the marshes and saw something that had grown since the last sun went down, which was soon discovered to be the far-famed "Swamp Angel." It was begun on the 4th, and finished on the 19th of August, which was rapid work considering the obstacles to overcome. A 200 pounder Parrott was mounted in it, and great labor and exertion were required to get it into position. It was hauled on a sling cart through the deep sand from the inlet to a creek at the edge of the swamp, where it was embarked on a raft of pine timber, and floated down to the battery at night and mounted.

Colonel Edward W. Serrell of the 1st New York Engineers supervised the construction of the Swamp Angel in seemingly impossible terrain—a marsh between Morris and James Islands, where it was said an iron rod would sink by its own weight.

C. R. BURCKMYER
RESIDENT OF CHARLESTON

A Charleston businessman, Burckmyer returned to his hometown from Europe on a blockade runner shortly before the Federal attack in the spring of 1863. The bombardment he recounts in this letter to his wife occurred late on Sunday night, August 22, the second consecutive night that the Swamp Angel fired on the city. Although shells prompted residents of Charleston's waterfront area to evacuate their homes, little damage resulted.

"The next day this officer made a requisition on the depot quartermaster for one hundred men eighteen feet high to wade through mud sixteen feet deep."

Sunday night I went to bed at 11 and was waked at 12 by a terriffic noise and loud cries in the street. I jumped up and found a crowd before our door who were evidently in a great state of excitement. I rushed into the piazza and found old Jane in her night dress hanging out of her window. She cried to me "O Master, something fell on the shed and has broken in the ceiling." I immediately concluded that it was a shell and hurried up to wake Edwin. He was so soundly asleep however, that not having a light I thought at first that he had been struck by the shell and had become a victim to Yankee malignity and hate. I succeeded in waking him at last and together we went out into the street to investigate matters. We found that a shell had entered the house directly opposite to us, formerly occupied by Mrs. Myers, and commencing at the back garret had descended to the side walk through the house, passing through both floors and penetrating the walls as though they were paste board. Fortunately no one was hurt, although the house was badly damaged. Our door steps were crowded with brick and mortar and some of the bricks from the opposite house broke away a portion of our carriage gate. While we were in the street examining and looking around we heard another shell coming which broke just over the Artesian Well and then another which fell in Chapin's carriage yard. Here a cry was raised in the crowd that the Yankees had the range of that block and that it was no longer safe. No sooner said than the crowd scattered and in two minutes not a soul was left in the lately crowded street.

Federal soldiers guard the remains of the Swamp Angel. The battery consisted of 13,000 sandbags filled with 800 tons of sand laid over a foundation of pine logs hauled from Folly Island seven miles away. The 16,500-pound Parrott rifle exploded while firing its 36th shot. The force of the blast blew the gun tube out of its carriage and onto the parapet.

General Gillmore, commander of the Department of the South, was credited with opening a new era in military engineering and gunnery during the siege of Battery Wagner and the bombardment of Fort Sumter. General in Chief Henry W. Halleck claimed that Gillmore overcame difficulties almost unknown in siege warfare.

LIEUTENANT IRA E. HICKS
7TH CONNECTICUT INFANTRY

Battery Strong, which mounted the 300-pounder Parrott rifle Hicks recalls here and that is shown opposite, was situated on Morris Island southeast of the Swamp Angel. The largest rifled gun ever used in action up to that time, the weapon was fired at intervals of no fewer than 15 minutes; more frequent use would cause the piece to overheat.

August 20, 1863, was a beautiful day. The sun rose in all its grandeur, throwing out heat that was almost overpowering. But the great gun was in position, and all listened for its first call on Fort Sumter. Not far from 9 o'clock the first shot was fired. Those in the battery watched it with anxiety, noting its course, where it struck, and the effect of the explosion of the shell. It fell a little short. At the fifth shot range was obtained, the shell striking the walls of the fort with tremendous effect, throwing up great clouds of dust and brick high in the air. The boys sent up a shout all along the line. The rebs for the time turned their entire attention to the gun and tried hard to cripple it, but without effect. The firing was continued with terrible results all that day. On the morning of Aug. 21 firing was again resumed, but at the sixth shot the shell burst in the muzzle of the gun, blowing off about 18 inches, and upon examination it was found to be fractured about seven inches futher down, breaking the muzzle off in five separate pieces, leaving it in a ragged shape, looking like almost anything but the muzzle of a gun. This was the 27th round that had been fired from it, and it did great damage to the fort. Its loss at this time was a great disappointment to Gen. Gilmore, but he blamed no one—it was the fortune of war. He had put his best man in command of his pet. We had all learned that he could size us up about right; and in this case his judgment did not fail him, for in Capt. Gray he had a gunner as well as a first-class mechanic—one who could as easily repair the monster gun as tell the degrees and minutes of elevation; although many very unjust criti-

'The great engine was once more in order to send its compliments to Fort Sumter in the shape of 300 pounds of iron."

cisms were made by correspondents of several newspapers at that time, one of which was published in a Boston paper and copied into several Connecticut papers. In these communications the officer of this gun was charged with incompetency and neglect. . . .

It was supposed that this gun was entirely disabled, and would be of no further use . . . but the commander of it did not think so. He at once set himself about the task of repairing the gun. Having matured a plan, he asked permission of Gen. Turner . . . to carry his idea into effect, which was at once granted and orders were given to the Colonel commanding Engineer Corps to furnish tools and men to carry out his plans. Immediately the forges were brought into the battery, and with a detail of men, with black-

smith and machinist, the work of repairing the great gun was commenced.

The plan was to cast a new muzzle below the fracture by first chipping off the ends and then enlarging the bore of the gun fully one-eighth of an inch, so the shell or shot would have a free clearance at that point. To accomplish this a stick was placed in the gun and held firmly against the breach. A nail was sharpened and put through the stick at a point below the fracture, at right angles with the bore. In this manner a circle was made around it at the point where the new muzzle was to be formed. The work now begun was pushed forward without any rest, and in 24 hours it was done, and the great engine was once more in order to send its compliments to Fort Sumter in the shape of 300 pounds of iron.

Two federal soldiers enjoy the shade provided by the damaged tube of the 300-pounder Parrott rifle in Battery Strong. The huge gun fired 398 shells during the siege—291 at Fort Sumter, 93 at Battery Wagner, and 14 at Battery Gregg—totaling some 60 tons of iron. Most of the shells were fired after the muzzle had broken off. According to one soldier, "this ragged-nose monster did more solid execution than any half dozen guns during the siege."

PRIVATE ALFRED O. BLOOD
24TH MASSACHUSETTS INFANTRY

By August 26, 1863, the Federals had pounded Fort Sumter into shapeless ruins and completed a succession of four siege works, or "parallels," to within 350 yards of Battery Wagner. The Confederate rifle pits targeted by Blood's regiment lay about 75 yards away, on a ridge of sand about 15 feet high. After capturing the position, the Federals converted it into the fifth siege line, or parallel.

Under command of Wm. H. Redding, Captain of Co. A, we entered the double sap and took position facing the ocean. Capt. Joseph Walker, of the 1st N.Y. Engineers, who was in charge of the engineer work at the front that day, explained to us the situation:

"Men, over there diagonally to your left and parallel with our last parallel is a ridge of sand that the enemy is holding as a line of rifle pits. When you get the order to charge you are to go over those works, cross that field and take that ridge and hold it. You must hold it at all hazards. Capt. Redding and I will go back into the front parallel and order the artillery to open fire on Fort Wagner, and they will keep it up for 20 minutes; then you will get the orders to charge, and remember you must hold that ridge. As soon as you are in possession of it the balance of your regiment will come up with shovels and turn the work to face the other way."

As the two Captains turned to leave us Fitzgerald, one of the wild Irishmen of our company, said: "An', Captain, can we yell?" "Yell?" repeated Capt. Redding, "yes, yell like devils." Almost as soon as the officers disappeared into our parallel all our artillery broke loose on Fort Wagner. The coehorn mortars commenced passing their shells over the field in our front. We could see them and hear the whish, whish, of the burning fuse and the explosions as they dropped along that ridge on which our thoughts were centered.

. . . The 20 minutes came to an end. The firing suddenly ceased. Capt. Redding came into the trench swinging his sword and shouting: "Charge! Charge!" Then the scrambling commenced to get over our earthworks. The sand gave way under our feet; the rear rank had to help the front rank over, and when we were all over we scattered like a flock of sheep. I don't claim to have been the first man on that ridge, for I was in the rear rank, and so was one of the last. I know that we must have been 70 feet from the foremost to the rearmost.

The ridge was a gentle slope on our side, but on their side, where our company struck it, it was almost perpendicular and about 10 feet

down to the men, who stood there in an almost dazed condition. We stood looking at each other, and we yelled: "Surrender!" They shook with fear as they said: "We surrender! We surrender!" We ordered them to drop their guns and come up, which they did with great alacrity. About 20 of their number when they heard the yelling of that Irishman, dropped their guns and struck a double-quick for their fort. As soon as we found the remaining men had surrendered we opened fire on those retreating, and a few of them were killed and wounded. About a dozen of them reached the fort apparently unharmed.

The balance of the regiment soon came up with shovels, and one-third of us held the muskets while the other two-thirds used the shovels. I heard Lieut. Bell sing out: "Here, give these rebels some shovels. They can work as well as any of us." A lot of them grabbed shovels, and I never saw men work livelier than they did. They knew as well as we that Fort Wagner would soon open on us, and they were in as much danger as we were.

PRIVATE JAMES S. SILVA
CLAGHORN'S COMPANY, CHATHAM ARTILLERY (GEORGIA)

Private Silva's Rebel unit was part of the Battery Wagner garrison. In a letter written on September 4, he commented on the speed and energy with which the Federals converted the rifle pits captured by the 24th Massachusetts into a fifth parallel. Two days later, he and his comrades evacuated the fort. By that time, rations had been reduced to four hard biscuits and five ounces of fat bacon per day.

When daylight arrived, to the astonishment of all, it was discovered that the indefatigable yankee had thrown up a breast work across the whole island and they continued to strengthen it during not withstanding a heavy fire was opened on it. You could see the dirt rolling over all along the line but could not get a glimpse of the busy hands thus occupied. Their sharp shooters soon set to work picking off our gunners and so successful were they, that we had to desist from firing. If a man but exposed his head to sight . . . a bullet would almost certainly be put through his head. The General in command, had a ball put through the rim of his hat. At night, a heavy fire was kept up on our side to prevent their working but with little effect, for daylight disclosed another line of entrenchments nearer the fort and running obliquely to the beach the nearest end being about 100 yards from the fort, and so they go on they are still digging and will dig right into the fort in spite of all we can *now* do. We were relieved on the night of the 2nd instead and again arrived at camp without the loss of a man. The duty to which we were assigned was not so dangerous as that to which the heavy artille·y and infantry are exposed. We had charge of two field pieces on the left flank of the fort which were reserved for use in case of assault. At daylight we have to dismount the pieces to prevent the enemy seeing them for could they see them, their big guns would soon knock them to pieces. At dark we remount them and there stay until daylight again no matter how hard the bombardment. We fired them through the night about every ten minutes. During the day we had nothing to do. Seven days service at that place will use up any man. You loose sleep all night and get very little sleep in the day as they are expecting an assault at any time.

The September 26, 1863, edition of Harper's Weekly features fanciful sketches of the August 26 assault by the 24th Massachusetts on the rifle pits in front of Wagner.

Federal gunners of Battery Hays aim their 4.2-inch, 30-pounder Parrott rifles at Battery Wagner, about a mile away. One of the first batteries constructed by Gillmore's forces on Morris Island, Battery Hays was named after Union general William Hays, who was wounded and captured at Chancellorsville.

Photoᵈ by Haas & Peale Morris Island & Hilton Head, S.C.

No. 23.—BATTERY MEADE.
Two 100-pounder Parrot Rifles.   Breaching battery against Sumter.

This picture card of Battery Meade on Morris Island was one of 40 images of the Federal siege of Charleston printed by Haas & Peale, an obscure pair of Union photographers (their full names remain unknown). Unlike more famous Civil War photographers who sold their pictures in formats too large for easy display, or as small carte de visites, Haas & Peale developed their outdoor shots into handy five-by-seven-inch prints. The set represents almost the entirety of their Civil War work.

"Well old fellow our Boat's ready, and I thank God I am getting away from this place. I tell you it is hell, hell."

PRIVATE JOHN HARLESTON
4TH SOUTH CAROLINA CAVALRY

John Harleston was one of a seven-man squad of couriers that was sent to Battery Wagner just before its fall. In four years of war, Harleston was wounded three times and captured twice, but he always insisted that his most trying experience was the six-day assignment to Battery Wagner. Harleston was 32 years old at the time; he lived to be 89, dying in 1919.

On the evening of Aug 31st, about 9 o'clock, the Squad under Sergt. Holland, reported on Southern wharf with Blankets and Revolvers, nothing else, were put in a row Boat with provisions etc. for Morris Island, where we arrived shortly after, and landed on the beach along side of Battery Gregg. As I jumped ashore, the first person I met was Burgess Gordon, of Huger's men. He exclaimed, "Good God Harleston are you here?" I said, "Yes I am here," and told him about taking Moore's place, and he said, "Well old fellow our Boat's ready, and I thank God I am getting away from this place. I tell you it is hell, hell." The next moment he was aboard and off. . . .

After we landed, we went to Couriers' Head Quarters, which was a small low [bombproof] some 100 yards east of Battery Gregg. It faced the City, and was barely large enough to hold our party.

We had scarsely got there, when there was a call for a Courier. One was wanted to carry the dispatches to Wagner, that came from Charleston with us. I don't remember how it happened, but I was detailed to carry them. Now I knew nothing about the rout or way of getting to Wagner, but one of the men garrisoning Gregg, told me to take a Horse from the stable (or pen it was) which was in a corner of the earth works between Courier quarters and Battery Gregg, lead him down to the Beach, Keeping close to the Breast works, until I struck the water, then mount, turn his head up the beach, and let him go. All I had to do was to stick on, and the Horse would do the rest, and advised me to ride a little flea bitten Grey, whose tail had been cut off by a shell, all but six or 8 inches, and was still raw and bloody.

I followed his advice, and when I got to the end of the curtin wall, and near the beach, I jumped on his back, gave him his head, the little Grey was off like the wind. Straight up the Beach we went, until I could see Battery Wagner looming up in the darkness. The Grey made a swerve to the right, and in a minute stopped short under the walls of Wagner to the right of the Sallyport, before an old Gun carriage that he was accustomed to be hitched to. The stop was so short and unexpected, that I shot forward to his ears and came within an ace of going over, but recovered myself and got back into the saddle, which I was very glad of, for the Sallyport was crowded with soldiers, who would have run me to death if I had been thrown. They yelled and cheered and wanted the news, for they knew I was a new arrival, and were looking out for the first comers. This was my first acquaintance with Battery Wagner.

Captain Charles E. Chichester of the Gist Guard Artillery of South Carolina was in charge of the Confederate guns on Morris Island during part of the siege. He was cited for bravery by the Morris Island commander, General Taliaferro.

drew in toward Fort Moultrie a gun was fired and a signal made from the Fort but the Captain seemed to have lost his head and made no response. Instantly, the fire of the Fort was opened upon him and shot and shell tore through the crowds of men on the steamer's deck. The Captain changed her course and essayed to run in between Fort Sumter and James Island but the boat soon became a perfect wreck rolling and tumbling about in the waves. Some of the men were drowned, some were picked up by boats that put out to their relief; others stripped and swam to Fort Sumter and still others came ashore at Fort Johnson—the most utterly demoralized men it has ever been my fortune to meet. . . . That night . . . I heard the sound of troops passing by and went out to find who they were. It proved to be a Regiment that had just been relieved from duty at Fort Sumter and was on the march for the interior of the Island. As the rear came there were the notes of a fiddle played by a soldier in gray, following whom was a singular procession of ghostly figures arrayed in white, dancing and frolicking like a lot of children. These were the men who swam to the fort from the wreck that morning; they had landed naked and had been clad in hospital night-shirts, the only available clothing. All day they had endured the terrific fire that was rained upon Fort Sumter; yet here they were as I saw them. Surely there was never better exemplification of the spirit that animated the Armies of the Confederacy.

COLONEL CHARLES H. OLMSTEAD
1ST GEORGIA INFANTRY

With many of the fortifications guarding Charleston under constant enemy fire, Confederate commanders made regular attempts to supply and relieve the garrisons as often as possible. This dangerous task fell to a flotilla of small vessels that nightly braved detection from Federal picket boats and sentries. Despite a careful system of recognition signals, accidents did occur, as Olmstead relates.

A very tragic event that took place while we were at Fort Johnson was the wreck of the "Sumter." This was a steamer engaged in bringing up troops that had been relieved from duty at Wagner. It was a service that had to be performed at night to avoid the fire of the enemy, and a code of signals was established to pass between the steamer and the forts of the inner harbor, since no chances could be taken of having one of the Yankee vessels slipping in. The Sumter started from Cummings Point crowded with men all looking forward to the relief and rest that had been earned by arduous service at the outpost. As the boat

MAJOR JOHN G. PRESSLEY
25TH SOUTH CAROLINA INFANTRY

On September 1, 1863, Pressley welcomed the news that his regiment had been ordered to Wagner to relieve a part of the garrison. "The 25th South Carolina volunteers were in daily expectation of an order detailing them for the post of honor and danger," he explained, "and were becoming impatient doing camp and picket duty, while the other troops were doing the heavy and dangerous work of the siege."

The regiment, in fine spirits, marched to Fort Johnson in the afternoon. There we found a row-boat large enough to carry one company. This boat was turned over to Company A, under the command of Lieutenant H. B. Olney, which embarked upon it and started late in the afternoon for Cummins Point. The rest of the regiment was embarked on a steamer about dusk. The changes of the garrison were always made at night to prevent the enemy from sinking our boats, nearly the whole of the harbor was under the fire of their batteries. It was the custom to make detail of boats from our naval vessels in the harbor to transfer the troops from the transport steamers to Cummins Point. The steamer, on which the Twenty-fifth was embarked, stopped near Fort Sumter. The usual detail from the navy failed to report, and the steamer was deficient of sailors to man the few boats which she had on board. One boat with a few men pushed off. The captain of the steamer offered me a scow large enough to carry about fifty men if I could find oarsmen. There was no difficulty in this. A number of men, mostly from the Beauregard Light Infantry and Wee Nee Volunteers, expressed their desire to go and ability to row. I soon had the scow full, and with Dr. W. C. Ravenel, our surgeon, Lieutenant F. J. Lesesne, acting Adjutant, and about fifty men and officers, started to Cummins Point. When about half way, the monitors came up and commenced to bombard Fort Sumter. The steamer, with the balance of the regiment on board, being in great danger, returned to Fort Johnson. The harbor was not very rough, the moon shone brightly, and spurred on by the expectation of a shot from the monitors, my oarsmen made rapid progress. We were soon wading out of the water under the guns of Battery Gregg. The boat drew so much water that she could not get near enough to the beach to enable us to land on *terra firma*. Company A had reached Cummins Point, and, with the men brought

with me, I had a command of eighty or ninety. There was no prospect of getting the remainder of the regiment before the next night. This detachment was marched to Fort Wagner, where I reported to General Colquit, who was then in command. As I had not men enough to relieve any of the battalions or regiments in the fort, he ordered me to return to the sand hills, between Wagner and Gregg, and protect my command as well as I could. All that part of the island was under the enemy's fire, and their shell was continually dropping. We retired to what the soldiers call "private bomb-proofs." These were holes in the sand large enough to hold two men. There a man was safe, except from shell bursting immediately overhead or falling vertically. I did not find a "hole in the ground" very comfortable, and so Lieutenant Lesesne and I spread our blanket between two sand hills, and under the shelter of a small bush passed the balance of a very disagreeably cold night. The monitors bombarded Sumter all night. Battery Gregg, on Morris Island, Fort Moultrie and the batteries on Sullivan's Island kept up the fight, and did some excellent shooting. The monitors would belch out columns of flame from their 15-inch guns in their turrets. When the shot from our batteries struck them, they would seem to be covered by sheet-lightning.

Federal soldiers demonstrate for the camera of photographers Haas & Peale how they used a wicker cylinder, known as a rolling sap, to shield themselves from Confederate small arms fire as they laboriously inched along the beach toward Battery Wagner. "The extreme heat of the weather and the excessive fatigue were rapidly wearing down the men," one veteran recalled, "while their constant exposure to death in the trenches was more dreaded than open combat."

MAJOR WILLIAM S. STRYKER

STAFF, MAJOR GENERAL QUINCY A. GILLMORE

Stryker served briefly as a volunteer in the New Jersey militia in 1861. He returned to duty two years later and was assigned to Gillmore's department as a paymaster. An amateur historian who wrote voluminously about the American Revolution, Stryker served as president of the New Jersey Historical Society in his later years.

As the night advanced the discharge of artillery became more frequent. A more beautiful pyrotechnic display was never seen. Balls of fire as if from rockets crossed each other in the heavens above the neutral ground and fell bursting with a shower of brilliant sparks into either works. At time 20 of these meteors would be coursing through the air in a single minute. The rattle of artillery and the explosion of shell was almost constant. I knew from orders which had been given at Gen. Gillmore's Head Quarters that the end was fast approaching. The 5th and 6th parallels were even now just under the sand walls of Fort Wagner. For days and weeks, fatigue parties, white and black, had labored with all the zeal and all the strength they possessed and not a murmur had ever escaped from the worn-out soldiery. Many were very sick! The heat was intense and very enervating, yet the goal was near and every one kept up a good heart and cheered each other as they labored in the batteries and rifle-pits, exposed to shot and shell and the deadly bullet of the sharpshooter.

A detail from the 39th Illinois prepares to load their Requa battery, a new weapon consisting of 25 rifle barrels so arranged on a field carriage that they could fire 175 shots per minute. The cartridges were attached to a brass strip and loaded all at once. The so-called volley guns helped protect exposed areas in the trenches on Morris Island.

CAPTAIN GEORGE W. BARBER

112TH NEW YORK INFANTRY

Barber's vivid depiction of the scene in front of Battery Wagner just before the stronghold fell was written 34 years after the event. His regiment arrived in August 1863 with orders to serve as "grand guard in the trenches." Men from his unit were among the first to discover that the Confederates had evacuated the fort. "Thus," Barber recalled, "after two bloody and unsuccessful assaults and two months' siege, the whole of Morris Island came into General Gillmore's possession."

Passing along the winding passages through the sand, by several mortar batteries and riflepits, where some sharpshooters lay; by the extreme guard and along the line where the colored troops and contraband negroes were busily engaged digging and throwing up and out sand, until you came to the end of the flying sap, looking a little to the left, and one could see within a few yards, apparently, the huge and now shapeless mass of Fort Wagner. There was no sign of life there. A shell would go rushing over head and explode over the fort, lighting up for a moment this ruin. Then again darkness and silence. Passing out again, and looking towards James Island, you could see a sharp flash, hear the smothered sound of a heavy gun, then see a ball with a fiery tail mounting upward very deliberately. Then, having reached its altitude, curving downward. "Now cover!" Every man would seek the bomb-proofs. With a peculiar rushing sound these great shells would explode, scattering iron missiles in every direction.

For several days the parallels approached completion. Our pickets were so near as to converse with the rebel pickets, but woe to the man who showed his head above the embankment. There were on the average five or six casualties daily during the progress of the siege work. The men constantly came upon torpedoes the rebels had buried. Most of these were removed without exploding.

A shell explodes on the rubble-strewn parade ground of Fort Sumter in this oil painting by John R. Key. Key based his painting on a rare but poorly focused photograph taken on September 8, 1863, by photographer George S. Cook of Charleston. Cook made his exposure at the exact moment when a round from a Federal ironclad exploded.

PRIVATE THEODORE A. HONOUR
25TH SOUTH CAROLINA INFANTRY

Honour's attack of dysentery, which he related in a letter to his fiancée, was but a small part of the horrors he experienced during the siege of Battery Wagner. "For Thirty six hours three surgeons did nothing but amputate limbs or dress wounds or pass sentence of death upon the poor fellows," he wrote. "And I was compelled to see all this. Friend after friend was brought in either dead or with arm or leg gone."

The lower regions is perhaps but a similar picture, immajine anything that is truly terrible, and you will perhaps approach the idea. Along with our Regiment was two Regts from Georgia, (27th and 28th) who had been in all the battles of Virginia & Maryland and they all say that nothing they ever experienced before could approximate to Fort W. for the whole time that our Regiment was there they were performing some sort of duty so that for six days and night they were kept constantly on the go, many of them not having had six hours sleep in that time.

On Thursday and Friday the yanks kept up a continuous shelling and we lost a number of our men, but from Saturday daylight or 5'oclock, they commenced in earnest and such a shower as was kept up on poor Wagner as was perfectly terrific. The world has never witnessed such a bombardment. Vicksburg sinks into insignificance along side of it, and our poor fellows were knocked over in crowds. God grant that it might never be . . . my fate to see such sights again. All that could be were drawn into the bombproofs, but of course it was necessary that some men should remain outside to act as sentinals to give the alarm should the enemy attempt an assault, which they might have done at any moment. For Thirty six hours three surgeons did nothing but amputate limbs or dress wounds or pass sentence of death upon the poor fellows.

As chief Confederate signal officer on Morris Island, Lieutenant Frank Markoe Jr. intercepted and decoded Union signals, providing the warning that allowed the Confederates to evacuate Batteries Wagner and Gregg before they could be stormed.

PRIVATE JOHN HARLESTON
4TH SOUTH CAROLINA CAVALRY

The night before the incident described here, Harleston made the last of his many dangerous courier rides between Batteries Gregg and Wagner. He carried a dispatch for Wagner's commander, Colonel Keitt (opposite), informing him that a Union force attempting to surprise Battery Gregg by sea had been repulsed—thanks to a warning from the signal corps, which had deciphered Federal communications.

The morning before the evacuation (I think it was), the firing from ships and batteries had been fearful all night, no let up, and daylight brought no relief. I was at Wagner that night for more than half of it, and when daylight came, I walked to the sally port, where many men had gathered. When I got there, I met Tom Chapman, a member of the 25th Reg' S.C., a Charleston man, and a well-known character. As I came up, he said, "Harleston, had any breakfast?" and I asked him where he expected any breakfast to come from, when there was not a mouthful in the fort. He pointed to the eastern end of the lines, where a small wooden structure had been built and was used to keep Bacon, and hard-tack in. The heavy firing during the night had cut away the wall under which it was hidden, and as soon as seen, was knocked to pieces. We could see sides of Bacon and Hard-tack scattered around in the sand. Chapman was a dare devil sort of a fellow, reckless and bold. He said to me, "I have been watching and thinking for some time, and I'll tell you what we can do. If you

'Now if we wait, until the next volley comes, and then make a dash, one grab a piece of bacon, and the other some biscuit, we can get our breakfast."

notice, you will find the Yanks are fireing from a battery well up the island, and they are firing in volleys, five or six guns at a time. Now if we wait, until the next volley comes, and then make a dash, one grab a piece of bacon, and the other some biscuit, we can get our breakfast. Will you try it with me?" I considered a moment and replied, "I am your man." "Done," he said, "as soon as the next volley comes, and it will be soon, we will start."

The point we were going to was one hundred yards or more from us. While we were speaking, three men had started to do the very thing we had intended. They crept down the wall towards the beach as far as they could get, keeping out of sight of the Yankees. Then they made a break for the food. They got there, but before they had time to do anything, two of them were dead, lying among the Bacon. The other was hit, but I heard got back. We saw all this. It was over in a minute. Chapman turned in a quizical sort of way and said, "Harleston, I ain't hungry," and I answered quickly, "Neither am I," cursed a bit. No breakfast that morning!

On the afternoon of the 5th, the Yankee signals were read, and it was discovered that Battery Gregg was to be attacked by Boats that night, and preparations were made to receive them. Troops were sent down from Wagner after dark (the 27th Georgia Reg') and others, and the embrasure of one of the Big Guns at Gregg was cut away, so as to allow the Gun to bear on the creek through which the Boats were expected, I got down to Gregg from Wagner about 11 or 12 o'clock that night, and after talking with Charley Prioleau, we concluded to take a hand in the fight, with the Georgians, and went over to where they were . . . found them in line lying down, outside and below Gregg. We tried to get Rifles from them but they had none to spare, but told us they [were] spare Guns at Gregg. Prioleau and myself went there; and after a little talk, they handed us out two muskets with some cartridges and a handful of caps. We went back to where our Georgia friends were, and laid down between them. Prioleau was two or three men to the right of where I was.

As soon as I got there, I bit off the end of a cartridge, and ram'd it in the gun, but it stopped some distance from the bottom, and while I was trying to force it down, and cursing the gun, Prioleau sang out to me "John, what's the matter?" and I said, "I can't get my cartridge down." He said, "Oh Lord man, the Gun was loaded when you got it." I tried mine with the ramrod, and found it out. The men around had heard us, and were

tickled to death. They said, "Why partner, you ought to be glad. There you have two bullets, and a handful of buckshot in your gun, and we have only one in ours. You ought to be proud. When that load gets among them Yankees, there won't be none left for us!" I told them I did not feel very much elevated by it, and offered to swap guns with any of them, so they could get the honour, and glory. This turned the laugh on them, and an officer nearby came to see what was the matter. They told him and it made him laugh, and he said to me, "Well Courier, what are you going to do about it?" I replied, "Shoot her when the Yanks come, if it is the last gun I shoot in the war." He said, "Good for you, you can fill them old Muskets chock full, you can't hurt them. If I was you, I would put another in." But I declined. The Guns they had given Prioleau and myself were old U.S. flint and steel muskets, altered to percussion, big heavy things, made for work. I was more afraid [of] the kicking than the bursting.

A former South Carolina congressman, Colonel Lawrence M. Keitt of the 20th South Carolina won praise for his gritty defense and successful evacuation of Battery Wagner. Keitt was mortally wounded at Cold Harbor, Virginia, in June 1864.

"The water was *putrid*, the corpses buried in the sand hills around were torn up by the shell & exposed to the sun, the sick & wounded were unable to be cared for in a place where a sound man could scarcely care for himself."

LIEUTENANT WILLIAM E. FURNESS
3D U.S. COLORED TROOPS

Despite the massive final bombardment of Battery Wagner that Furness recalls here, the Union troops found the fort hardly damaged when they took possession of it on September 7. "Our military engineers learned much from their experience against Fort Wagner," Furness observed. "And first, as I think, they became impressed with the superiority of earthworks over brick and stone structures for military defenses, and of sand over earth."

By the 5th of September all was ready, and final operations were actively begun. For forty-two hours seventeen mortars dropped their exploding shells into the Rebel works, over the heads of our sappers and guards, and thirteen heavy Parrott rifles bombarded the southwest angle of the bomb-proof, while the "New Ironsides" kept a constant succession of shots skipping over the water and exploding in or over the fort. Wagner was silenced even to her sharp-shooters, the whole garrison being forced for shelter to the bomb-proof; and our sappers now pushed forward, troubled only by the flank fire from James Island, till they reached a point so near the Rebel works that these too had to cease their fire. On the 6th of September our sappers, silently pushed past the south face and crowned the crest of the counterscarp, masking all the guns of the fort.

The spectacle during this two days' mortar bombardment was exciting in the extreme. I remember going forward to the Coehorn battery during this time, and watching the fire on the fort. It seemed like tossing heavy balls into a great sand-hill, which the explosions after the dropping of each ball converted into a hell's mouth. The air was thick and murky with smoke, the gunners were grimed and dripping with sweat from excitement and work, and the shells as they left the mortars described the most beautiful curves. Beyond the flag on the Rebel stronghold, no sign of life appeared in Wagner. In the last hours of the sapping the men needlessly exposed themselves, and even crawled forward amid the torpedoes to examine the front of the fort.

PRIVATE JAMES MARTIN
39TH ILLINOIS INFANTRY

On the evening of September 6, five companies from Private Martin's regiment were among the troops ordered to serve as guards for the men digging the advanced trenches. Martin claimed that his commanding officer was so excited by the news of the evacuation of Battery Wagner—brought by the Confederate deserter—that he reported it directly to General Gillmore, bypassing the division command.

About midnight a young man, an Irishman of small stature, whose clothing were dripping with sea brine, was brought to the commanding officer by a Corporal as a deserter from Fort Wagner. He stated that the fort was being evacuated by the rebels, and on being questioned said that he deserted because he had no love for the rebels or their cause. He said he had been taken some months ago, from a vessel that had run the blockade from the Bermudas, and had been placed in Fort Wagner as a soldier. He said he wanted to go home, that a majority of the garrison of the fort had already gone, leaving a squad of men to set fire to the fuse connecting with the powder magazine, with the intent of blowing up as many as possible. He escaped and made his way by swimming around, so he said, to inform the Union soldiers. He was told that the matter would be immediately inquired into, and if the intelligence he brought proved true, he would be rewarded and sent home; but if otherwise, he would certainly be shot. He said he would take his chances, and was given in charge of the guards to be taken to Gen. Gilmore, but not before a rough plan of the fort had been drawn, with a request of him to point out the location of the magazine, which he did.

CORPORAL AUGUSTINE T. SMYTHE

C.S. Signal Corps

Smythe, shown here in a postwar photograph, enlisted in the South Carolina Cadets in January 1861 and joined the signal corps in October 1862. He was serving with the 5th South Carolina Cavalry when the war ended and never officially surrendered. Smythe became a lawyer after the war and served 12 years in the South Carolina Senate.

The yankee flag on Sunday was flying within 40 feet of the ditch of Wagner & the garrison could hear the voices of the men working in the mines. No one dared to show his head over the parapet but at the risk of a bullet from the Yankee sharpshooters. Tho' the round shell fell harmlessly against the ramparts, the heavy Parrotts would penetrate into the middle of them & there burst tearing up the breast works & exposing the wood-work of the bomb-proofs, while the fire, continuous night & day, kept our men in their holes & prevented any attempt even to repair the damages. Communication with them was next to impossible, much less forwarding supplies; the water was *putrid,* the corpses buried in the sand hills around were torn up by the shell & exposed to the sun, the sick & wounded were unable to be cared for in a place where a sound man could scarcely care for himself & at last a virtue was made of necessity & the place was evacuated. It was better to do so while we could remove our men than to wait until all their places of refuge were destroyed & the Yankee miners were in the fort by underground passage, & our men were then forced to retreat in the face of a pursuing enemy. At the time of the evacuation there were 125 sick & wounded in Wagner & on the way from there to Gregg. Some 17 others were killed or wounded. The transporting of the troops was under the charge of Mr. Ward, 1st Lieut. & ex. officer of the Palmetto State & was accomplished in small boats unarmed by the crews of the Chicora & P. S. & by some other boatman from the city. It was in the highest degree successful, every person being brought from the Island,

sick & well. We lost three boats one from the Chicora & two with the city men, in all about 50 men, captured by the Yankees who were coming up in barges to attack Gregg. The magazines, neither at Wagner nor Gregg exploded owing, it is said to the dampness of the trains which had been laid for some time. The soldiers behaved splendidly. No panic, no confusion, no disorder, but quietly as if on parade they marched down the beach, halted in line, & embarked in the boats, exposed all the time to the shell of the enemy which were thick falling around them. Capt. Huguenin & 20 men were left in Wagner as a guard & were to remain until a courier brought them word that all the rest of the troops had left the Island. There was a position for you. With only 20 men, & no reinforcements to call upon, an enemy in force only 40 feet off & the only hope of safety being in their ignorance of the true state of the case. The 20 men were spread along the parapet & kept firing, as on ordinary picket guard, until the orders came, when sending his men before, he set fire to the slow match & made tracks for Gregg. The Yanks never suspected the evacuation until about two hours after, when they cautiously approached. The hated gridiron now floats over both Batteries.

Two 10-inch mortars are angled toward their target in a ditch inside Battery Kirby on Morris Island. Kirby was part of the area known as the Left Batteries, where Gillmore sited his heaviest artillery. The mortars were 4,400 yards from Fort Sumter, 3,000 yards from Battery Gregg, and 1,960 yards from Battery Wagner.

Organized in the fall of 1861 by Captain Charles E. Kanapaux, the South Carolina Lafayette Artillery Battery flew this standard at Battery Wagner until the unit was ordered to evacuate. The Lafayette Artillery remained in the Department of South Carolina, Georgia, and Florida until January 1865, when it was transferred to the Army of Tennessee. After fighting in the Carolinas campaign, the unit was surrendered by General Joseph E. Johnston at Durham Station, North Carolina, on April 26, 1865.

LIEUTENANT FREDERICK T. PEET
CHARLESTON MARINE BATTALION, U.S. MARINE CORPS

The 500 to 600 men of Frederick Peet's battalion were quartered on different ships of the blockading fleet until early August 1863, when they went ashore to assist in the siege. Peet served on the Wabash. The year before, on June 30, he had been wounded and taken prisoner at Frayser's Farm, one of the running fights collectively known as the Seven Days' Battles, which took place outside Richmond at the end of General George McClellan's failed Peninsula campaign. Peet was paroled and exchanged after 18 days.

Our parallels were within a few feet of the ditch and we were ready to attack Wagner. We were ordered to be ready at four A.M. September 7th, and up we went, expecting to storm the fort.

Federal work parties swarm over abandoned Battery Gregg, located at Cumming's Point on the northern tip of Morris Island. The smokestack of a Federal warship is visible behind the dunes. Conrad W. Chapman based this painting on a sketch of the scene that he made while looking through a telescope from the Charleston waterfront.

The marines were up at the front. But the Confederates had gotten wind of the attack and evacuated the fort a short time before our arrival. Some of them were captured by our navy patrol boats when crossing the water between Forts Gregg and Johnson. We soon had possession of all the fortifications on the Island, and then our guns were turned on Sumter.

When I reached the Fort I was surprised to see the havoc our big shells had made. The ramparts were badly torn and some guns dismounted, and the ditches seemed full of fifteen-inch shells which were fired by our monitors. I saw a pile of dead Confederates, all without heads. They must have lost their heads while serving the guns. I then went into the bomb-proofs. Here I saw a dead soldier; he was well dressed in gray, and was a remarkably fine looking man. He had a gold ring on his finger, and he must have been a man out of the common run, for he had a splendid head and his features showed refinement. As I was looking at him a man near me picked up a rebel flag. I saw it had a cord attached to it, and warned him to be careful. I took the line and followed it into the magazine. I presume it was expected some of us would grab the flag and haul at the rope and in doing so blow up the magazine, but I cut the rope on seeing where it led.

"As I arrived on the parapet, I was called upon to surrender my sword, pistol &c, and was then conducted to a casemate in the west face as a prisoner of war."

ENSIGN JAMES WALLACE
NAVAL BATTERY, MORRIS ISLAND

Believing Fort Sumter's garrison to be so weakened that it would now offer only token resistance, Admiral Dahlgren ordered Commander Thomas Stevens to storm the bastion. Wallace was among the 500 sailors and marines who embarked from Federal warships in small boats on the night of September 8. He was in charge of one of the boats and 19 men. The following account is taken from his official report of the failed operation, which cost the navy 124 men.

About 10 p.m. the *Daffodil* took the boats in tow and stood up for Charleston Harbor. About midnight we cast off from the *Daffodil,* and directly after Captain Stevens hailed and ordered me to pull for Fort Sumter. I did so, and while pulling Captain Stevens ordered me to follow the boat on my starboard bow, telling me she was going behind the fort. I followed the boat as directed and passed the side of Fort Sumter which faces Fort Moultrie. Discovering a steamer coming from behind the fort, the leading boat went close in under the walls; we followed her and pulled back toward the sea face, examining the foot of the fort to see if any of our boats had landed. Upon coming to the right bastion of the sea face, I found the marines in boats firing at the fort. I could find no officer to report to regarding the steamer, and no one could tell me whether our men had landed or where they were. Seeing a boat sinking, I pulled toward it, but found that all of its men had been taken out or drowned.

LIEUTENANT COLONEL STEPHEN ELLIOTT
COMMANDER, FORT SUMTER

After Fort Sumter's artillery had been destroyed or removed, General Beauregard ordered Stephen Elliott to replace Colonel Alfred Rhett as commanding officer. As Elliott left for the ruined citadel with about 320 infantrymen, Beauregard told him, "It must be held to the bitter end with infantry alone. There can be no hope of reinforcements."

I saw, before any alarm was given, a long wide broad string of boats approaching the fort from directions somewhat different tho generally from the eastward. My garrison consisted of 300 men. 30 were posted at the south wall the most accessible as its exterior form is that of an inclined plane. 20 at a large breach in the north wall and the balance dispersed as sentries, grenadiers, turpentine-ballers and keg flingers and supports for the several defensible positions, each company and detachment running its assigned post. The wharf was also mined and all these arrangements, which, I may say to you without undue vanity, were all my own, and for which I got materials from Charleston, had been completed only a few minutes when the Navy boys were seen pulling up.

I kept the men quiet until two boats had nearly touched the landing place sending for some of the supports in the meantime. Our fire opened pretty sharply the enemy returning it from his outer boats in a very musical manner which made some of the boys keep time with their heads with more appreciation than pluck. Other detachments now came up and poured in a more rapid fire and the turpentine balls and hand grenades began to work and the *Chicora* and Sullivan's Island and Fort Johnson swept the approaches with grape and shell, some of which took the liberty of bursting in the fort and the jig was up. They had come ashore expecting to find easy access through the broken arches, all of which are filled with sand. Their boats were broken by grenades and masses of masonry and bricks and our muskets would keep popping them over and in pairs and squads they quietly walked round and surrendered to their perfect amazement. In fact they were so perfectly astonished at meeting such a reverse and so delighted at not being shot that they were quite jolly at first but by breakfast time they seemed to realize their position more fully.

LIEUTENANT ROBERT L. MEADE
CHARLESTON MARINE BATTALION, U.S. MARINE CORPS

After the war, Meade was brevetted first lieutenant for his meritorious service during the September 8 navy fiasco at Sumter. He came from a military family: His father was a navy captain; one brother a rear admiral; another brother a navy paymaster. His uncle was General George G. Meade, who led Union troops at Gettysburg.

heavy fire of musketry poured on us from the whole garrison. Moultrie and Johnson also commenced after a few minutes had passed; a rapid and accurate shelling in answer to a rocket from Sumter, the shells falling and exploding all around our boats.

I opened fire and kept it up for a short while when I heard a voice ashore (that of Lt. Commander Williams) to "stop firing and land," which I did as well as possible; my men suffering from the musketry fire and the bricks, hand grenades and fireballs thrown from the parapet. Immediately on striking the beach, I gave orders to land and find cover, which the men lost no time in executing. A short time after, my boat had disappeared. I did not see her any more that night. She was pretty well stove in and had several musket balls through her when we landed.

After I landed, I found that nearly all of our flotilla had left us and that there were only about 90 or 100 men on shore. These were so scattered around the base of the Fort, that they could not well be collected together under the galling fire from the parapet. Poor me! I did not know what to do. I only saw one officer and as I did not know him, I concluded not to report to him, but wait a while or go in search of Captain Stevens or Captain McCawley. As things happened, I became a passive spectator of what was going on around me. It appears that some men on the northeast face had been crying, "We surrender," very loudly, and the garrison ceased their fire for a while to ascertain whether we surrendered or not. They hailed us and the officer I have spoken of (this was Lt. Commander E. P. Williams), after holding a consultation with others who had joined him, answered in the affirmative, no other alternative occurring to us. Escape by our boats was impossible; the boats being stove up, and with the few men and poor facilities we had, it would have been simply absurd, had we pursued the object with which we landed. We were then ordered to ascend the "gorge face" to the parapet, which was accomplished with no little difficulty, the ground up mortar and brick being anything but secure footing—showing to us that even if our whole party landed, we would not have been able to accomplish anything. As I arrived on the parapet, I was called upon to surrender my sword, pistol &c, and was then conducted to a casemate in the west face as a prisoner of war.

LIEUTENANT COLONEL STEPHEN ELLIOTT
COMMANDER, FORT SUMTER

Beginning on September 28, Federal batteries opened a second methodical bombardment of Fort Sumter, and when the firing ended six days later, the fort had been struck by 560 heavy projectiles. Writing to his wife on September 30, Elliott described his living conditions and reassured her that the garrison was well prepared to face any Federal amphibious attack.

I had good sport this morning moving a gun into one of the casemates intended for use. We made a brisk job of it but did not get through before the shelling commenced which made it quite exciting without being dangerous as they came slowly at first and gave us plenty of time to get out of the way after the "lookout" of the sentinels. One of the sentinels . . . gave a good idea of the appearance of one of those heavy guns as it goes off. He gave a false alarm—the shot went at James Island—and when asked why he did so replied "well I seed da smoke a bilin." You have no idea of the vast amount of smoke that comes bursting out from their mouths. The great inertia of the long balls seems to cause both sound and smoke to burst forth with great violence. . . . I have come back to my old room which looks in comparison like a palace, where I am undisturbed except by having to give orders for moving the guns from the parapet. The moon has risen now and probabilities of barges are lessened for the night. I am beginning to take things more quietly, the garrison is in good training and officers and men understand their duty and we will hammer them pretty seriously if they try it. I sleep over here at night—it is so much nicer than the other place which is close and dirty—the necessary attributes of "safety." The mosquitoes are perfectly awful and I have to smoke constantly tonight while writing to keep them from eating me up; my pipe is now out so I must build a smoke. So now the fire is built and I can be comfortable for a little while. I have a nice little mosquito net left here by somebody and get along first rate after I get to bed except in one very important particular which I will leave it to your imagination to suggest.

At left, the Confederate flag flies defiantly from the gorge, or rear wall, of Fort Sumter in this August 23 photograph taken from Morris Island. General Gillmore included the image in his official report to Washington to show the destruction wrought by his heavy guns.

Charleston photographer George S. Cook visited Fort Sumter's beleaguered garrison on September 8, 1863, and recorded this view of two soldiers posing atop the fort's hot-shot furnace, used for baking bread. Cook's photograph shows heavy damage to the eastern barracks and casemates.

LIEUTENANT WILLIAM T. GLASSELL
C.S.S. David

Virginian William Glassell, a lieutenant aboard the U.S.S. Hartford, refused to take the newly required oath of allegiance to the United States when he returned from a cruise to China in December 1861. Imprisoned for eight months and then deported south, Glassell accepted an appointment in the Confederate navy. On October 5, 1863, he commanded the David in a bold attack on the powerful Federal warship New Ironsides.

We passed Fort Sumter and beyond the line of picket-boats without being discovered. Silently steaming along just inside the bar, I had a good opportunity to reconnoitre the whole fleet of the enemy at anchor between me and the camp-fires on Morris Island.

Perhaps I was mistaken, but it did occur to me that if we had then, instead of only one, just ten or twelve torpedoes to make a simultaneous attack on all the iron-clads, and this quickly followed by the egress of our rams, not only might this grand fleet have been destroyed, but the 10,000 troops on Morris Island been left at our mercy. Quietly manoeuvring and observing the enemy, I was half an hour more waiting on time and tide. The music of drum and fife had just ceased, and the nine o'clock gun had been fired from the admiral's ship as a signal for all unnecessary lights to be extinguished and for the men not on watch to retire for sleep. I thought the proper time for attack had arrived.

The admiral's ship, New Ironsides (the most powerful vessel in the world), lay in the midst of the fleet, her starboard side presented to my view. I determined to pay her the highest compliment. I had been informed, through prisoners lately captured from the fleet, that they were expecting an attack from torpedo-boats, and were prepared for it. I could therefore hardly expect to accomplish my object without encountering some danger from riflemen, and perhaps a discharge of grape or canister from the howitzers. My guns were loaded with buckshot. I knew that if the officer of the deck could be disabled to begin with, it would cause them some confusion and increase our chance for escape; so I determined that if the occasion offered I would commence by firing the first shot. Accordingly, having on a full head of steam, I took charge of the helm, it being so arranged that I could sit on deck and work the wheel with my feet. Then, directing the engineer and firemen to keep below and give me all the speed possible, I gave a double-barrel gun to the pilot, with instructions not to fire until I should do so, and steered

directly for the monitor. I intended to strike her just under the gangway, but the tide, still running out, carried us to a point nearer the quarter. Thus we rapidly approached the enemy. When within about 300 yards of her a sentinel hailed us: "Boat ahoy! boat ahoy!" repeating the hail several times very rapidly. We were coming toward them with all speed, and I made no answer, but cocked both barrels of my gun. The officer of the deck next made his appearance, and loudly demanded, "What boat is that?" Being now within forty yards of the ship and plenty of headway to carry us on, I thought it about time the fight should commence, and fired my gun. The officer of the deck fell back mortally wounded (poor fellow!), and I ordered the engine stopped. The next moment the torpedo struck the vessel and exploded. What amount of direct damage the enemy received I will not attempt to say. My little boat plunged violently, and a large body of water which had been thrown up descended upon her deck and down the smokestack and hatchway.

I immediately gave orders to reverse the engine and back off. Mr. Toombs informed me then that the fires were put out and something had become jammed in the machinery so that it would not move. What could be done in this situation? In the mean time, the enemy, recovering from the shock, beat to quarters, and general alarm spread through the fleet. I told my men I thought our only chance to escape was by swimming, and I think I told Mr. Toombs to cut the water-pipes and let the boat sink.

Then taking one of the cork floats, I got into the water and swam off as fast as I could.

The enemy, in no amiable mood, poured down upon the bubbling water a hailstorm of rifle- and pistol-shots from the deck of the Ironsides and from the nearest monitor. Sometimes they struck very close to my head, but, swimming for life, I soon disappeared from their sight, and found myself all alone in the water. I hoped that with the assistance of flood-tide I might be able to reach Fort Sumter, but a north wind was against me, and after I had been in the water more than an hour I became numb with cold and was nearly exhausted. Just then the boat of a transport schooner picked me up, and found, to their surprise, that they had captured a rebel.

The torpedo boat David lies moored to a sea wall near the Charleston docks in this 1863 painting by Conrad Wise Chapman. The 50-foot-long vessel, designed by Julien Ravenel, was steam powered and armed with a 100-pound torpedo fitted to a 14-foot spar at the vessel's bow. The crew of four—captain, engineer, pilot, and a fireman—occupied an open cockpit amidships, behind the boiler.

ACTING ENSIGN ADNA BATES
U.S.S. Canadiagua

Adna Bates volunteered for the U.S. Navy from his hometown of Cohasset, Massachusetts, and spent most of his wartime service on station near the city of Charleston. In an October 1863 letter to his mother, Bates described the precautions taken by the Federal blockaders following the Confederate torpedo attack on the New Ironsides on October 5.

I think I wrote you of the attempt of the rebels to blow up the Ironsides with a torpedo; it was a failure & most of the rebels were taken prisoners, the rest were drowned; the Ironside was not hurt, & only one man killed, but it rather scared them. We send an armed boat now every night in charge of an officer to row guard up by the rebel batteries. I suppose it will be my turn to go pretty soon. They are called to quarters some nights when we see strange vessels, & it is exciting work; a few nights ago we fired into one of our own vessels.

LIEUTENANT COLONEL STEPHEN ELLIOTT
COMMANDER, FORT SUMTER

A devoted husband, Stephen Elliott wrote daily letters to his wife in Charleston. His letter dated October 31, 1863, the final day of the most intense Federal shelling of Sumter, reveals the strain suffered by the entire garrison. In the three-day bombardment the fort was struck by more than 2,900 projectiles, and the garrison suffered 33 casualties.

There I was at the end of the week all right in mind and body though I will own I was a little blue this afternoon. The fact of having lots of stupid people to manage whose stupidity is chiefly attributable to fear

and a parcel of Georgian officers who have no more pride about obeying orders than Benjamin has and having to make out a post return and have all the command returns in and no muster rolls and an adjutant steeped in a mixture of hopeless melancholy and nauseous sycophancy and dead men being toted around the dinner table and men crushed, strangled beheaded and mangled being every now and then lugged in and every body looking at me as if I did it when if I had my way the old fort would be blown tonight in to as many pieces as there are bricks in it and then the constant arrival of some of the nine hundred and two visitors that have come in over the sea and the constant sapping at "m" to which they have at last turned their attention and the mixture of all sorts of people in my private apartment with out my having the power to drive them out and think. I have drawn a picture not by any means agreeable. Last night I placed sixteen men in a position convenient for mounting the parapet in one of the barracks and about 3 o'clock the whole roof knocked down by a shell and fell killing them all except one who was not sleepy and who was standing outside and got out of the way and two others not of the detachment making thirteen in all. I placed the men myself with some encouraging remarks as they would probably be the first engaged and really thought that they occupied the most desirable position of any men on duty. But we cannot always tell about these things. I do not blame myself a bit about it as I am perfectly conscious of having acted for the best. I feel quite hopeful and strong tonight. I expect you will doubt it after the tone of my letter but you know I like to abuse people and I have had a good theme so cut ahead.

Chapman's painting (left) shows Fort Sumter caught in the unearthly glare of a Federal limelight mounted at Battery Gregg. "The appearance of the light would sometimes be striking and beautiful," recalled Confederate engineer John Johnson, "the rays would appear to dart forth and flash upon an expanse of inky blackness; then touching or tipping the crest of the gorge, they would stream across the empty darkness of the interior."

Photographer George Cook returned to Fort Sumter and took this view of the eastern barracks and casemates in a state of total ruin. During the early hours of October 31, a shell struck the already weakened structure and the roof collapsed, killing 13 men who were sleeping inside. The two men posing for Cook stand on a pile of bricks, all that remains of the hot-shot furnace.

MAJOR THOMAS A. HUGUENIN
1st South Carolina Infantry (Regulars)

Under almost daily battering by the Federal heavy artillery, the Fort Sumter garrison suffered a small but constant toll of casualties. Unable to bury the dead in the confines of the fort, the Confederates kept coffins on hand so that bodies could be evacuated by the nightly supply boats from Charleston. Major Huguenin recalled the superstitious effect that a simple careless act had upon one of his officers.

The reserve supply of coffins were stowed in the same casemate in which he and some other officers had their quarters. The piles of coffins was used as a sort of table and he happened to be sitting near it, and as some people will carlessley do, scribbled his name on one of them. He never was satisfied until that particular coffin was used, even going so far as to urge the Quartermaster to use it, without regard to its size for the occupant. When it was used in a day or two he was much relieved, saying he had been afraid it might be used for himself.

"To walk over dead and burning men in your stocking feet is not pleasant but que voulez vous?"

LIEUTENANT COLONEL STEPHEN ELLIOTT
COMMANDER, FORT SUMTER

On the morning of December 11, 1863, during a lull in the Federal shelling, 300 pounds of powder in the magazine located in Fort Sumter's southwestern angle exploded accidentally, killing 11 men and wounding another 41. Slightly wounded in the ankle and head by the blast, Elliott preceded this letter to his wife with a telegram to get the news to her quickly that he was safe.

About nine o'clock yesterday morning while still in bed as I had retired late or rather early a most tremendous explosion took place followed by another. There was a sound of falling matter between the two and I had unbolted and taken down the shutter to our embrasure in a very small space of time. The magazine had blown up and there was not powder enough in to destroy things but enough to kill those who were chowing and doing rations in the next room. The densest smoke filled everything. All who occupied my quarter of the work had to rush for the open air. I soon got round to the inside of the fort and then seeing where the damage lay went through the passage heading back into our room near by the magazine. To walk over dead and burning men in your stocking feet is not pleasant but que voulez vous? I saved everything except my good coat which was in a —— bag hung up and which I have not yet come across. Some of the things were taken out of the room before I got there. I have not yet seen my pistols but I saved all of my papers and books. My pistols were brought round to the battery but such things get lost easily. My sword is all right. I will go up to Charleston in a day or two and have my measure taken for a new suit of clothes. Willis has the cloth ready for me. While running along the slope of the fort a brick was thrown down and rolled on my foot and made me quite lame but an afternoon and night of quiet has relieved me entirely and I have walked over the entire fort this morning without feeling any bad effects. Not long after the fire broke out (which burned everything in that part of the fort) the Yanks commenced to shell; while standing on the entrade near my room a shell

threw down a lot of bricks on our heads. Percy Elliott was knocked cold and I thought he was dead but he fetched after a while. I got three bricks in my head which made the blood spin but after an hour I did not feel them and have not troubled me since. They are only shallow cuts on the lump on the back part of my skull which is thick.

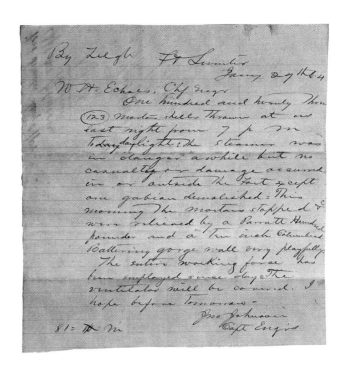

As engineer in charge of Fort Sumter, Captain John Johnson telegraphed daily reports on the condition of the works to his superiors in Charleston. This draft from January 29, 1864, records that 123 mortar shells had fallen on the fort during the night. Johnson's duties included supervising a 100-man crew of conscripted slaves, who nightly repaired damage and reinforced the fortifications.

This portable campaign desk with its multiple cubbyholes and drawers was used by the Confederate officers in charge of Fort Sumter to prepare their official paperwork and personal correspondence. Tradition records that it was also the refuge for the fort's cat during the long siege.

Constructed by the Confederates in 1862, Battery Marshall guarded the eastern end of Sullivan's Island. The battery, shown in this late-war photograph, was built of sand covered with sod and was well provided with deep magazines and bombproofs. It was named for Lieutenant Colonel J. Foster Marshall of the 1st South Carolina Rifles, who was killed at Second Manassas.

PRIVATE W. A. RUSH
7TH BATTALION, SOUTH CAROLINA INFANTRY

Private Rush, from Edgefield County, South Carolina, joined Company H of the 7th Battalion on January 23, 1863. Posted to Charleston Harbor in the autumn of 1863, Rush and his fellow soldiers occupied several posts, including Battery Wagner. Writing from Battery Marshall in late January 1864, Rush described the harsh conditions he and his comrades were forced to endure. On May 16, 1864, he was killed in action at Drewry's Bluff in Virginia.

We are seeing hard time we haven had any meat for five days, dry crackers is all we have to eat, out of sixteen days rashans we only got meat five times. that is enough to make a man swear I hate to write home about our fair. but it gets wors and wors evry day, and I cant help telling you about it, I think they is plenty in the country if we could gets it, All of the Shatterfield Boys are well they are seting about hear as mad as seting hens because we haven drew any meat to day, we have had some as cold weather for the last three weeks as even I felt any whare, rains most all the time, we go on picket evry other night.

COLONEL CHARLES H. OLMSTEAD

1ST GEORGIA INFANTRY

By the winter of 1864-1865, the Confederate naval forces in Charleston Harbor consisted of three iron-clad rams and a host of smaller vessels. Unable to mount big offensive operations against the blockading Federal fleet, Rebel planners turned to unconventional weapons to strike at the foe. Olmstead described the most unusual of them—the submarine H. L. Hunley.

This boat was one day made fast to the wharf at Fort Johnson, preparatory to an expedition against the fleet, and taking advantage of the opportunity, I examined it critically. It was built of boiler iron, about thirty feet in length, with a breadth of beam of four feet by a vertical depth of six feet, the figures being approximate only. Access to the interior was had by two man-holes in the upper part, covered by hinged caps, into which were let bull's eyes of heavy glass, and through these the steersman looked in guiding the motions of the craft. The boat floated with these caps raised only a foot or so above the level of the water. The motive power was a propeller, to be worked by hand of the crew, cranks being provided in the shaft for that purpose. Upon each side of the exterior were horizontal vanes, or wings, that could be adjusted at any angle from the interior. When it was intended that the boat should go on an even keel whether on the surface or under, these vanes were kept level. If it was desired to go below the water, say, for instance, at an angle of ten degrees, the vanes were fixed at that angle,

Conrad Wise Chapman painted the H. L. Hunley at the Charleston docks in October 1863. The submersible was more than 25 feet long and powered by a hand-cranked propeller driven by a crew of six men. By the time of its first operational cruise, the Hunley had suffered a series of accidental sinkings that took the lives of about 32 crewmen.

and the propeller worked. The resistance of the water against the vanes would then carry the boat under. A reversal of this method would bring it to the surface again. A tube of mercury was arranged to mark the depth of descent. It had been the design of the inventor to approach near to an enemy, then to submerge the boat and pass under the ship to be attacked, towing a floating torpedo to be exploded by means of electricity as soon as it touched the keel. Insufficient depth of water in the harbor prevented this manner of using the boat, however, and so she was rigged with a long spar at the bow, to which a torpedo was attached, to be fired by actual concussion with the object to be destroyed.

PRIVATE ARTHUR P. FORD
Buist's Battery, South Carolina Artillery

Despite a string of deadly training accidents, the Hunley still managed to attract volunteers. On the night of February 17, 1864, the vessel attacked and sank the Federal Housatonic with a spar torpedo. Then, returning to harbor, the Hunley sank for unknown reasons, joining her victim in the coastal waters off Sullivan's Island. Private Ford recalled the submarine's strange history.

As I was standing on the bank of the Stono River, I saw the boat passing along the river, where her builder, H. L. Hundley, had brought her for practice. I watched her as she disappeared around a bend of the river, and little thought of the fearful tragedy that was immediately to ensue. She made an experimental dive, stuck her nose in the mud, and drowned her entire crew. Her career was such an eventful one that I record what I recollect of it.

She was built in Mobile by Hundley, and brought on to Charleston in 1863. She was of iron, about 20 feet long, 4 feet wide, and 5 feet deep—in fact, not far from round, as I have seen it stated; and equipped with two fins, by which she could be raised or lowered in the water. . . . She was worked by a hand propeller, and equipped with water tanks, which could be filled or emptied at pleasure, and thus regulate her sinking or rising. The first experiment with her was made in Mobile Bay, and she went down all right with her crew of seven men, but did not come up, and every man died, asphyxiated, as no provision had been made for storing a supply of air.

As soon as she was raised, she was brought to Charleston, and a few days after her acceptance by General Beauregard, Lieutenant Payne, of the Confederate Navy, volunteered with a crew of six men to man her and attack the Federal fleet off Charleston. While he had her at Fort Johnson, on James Island, and was making preparations for the attack, one night as she was lying at the wharf the swell of a passing steamer filled her, and she went to the bottom, carrying with her and drowning the six men. Lieutenant Payne happened to be near an open manhole at the moment, and thus he alone escaped. Notwithstanding the evidently fatal characteristics of this boat, as soon as she was raised another crew of six men volunteered under Payne and took charge of her. But only a week afterwards an exactly similar accident happened while she was alongside the wharf at Fort Sumter, and only Payne and two of his men escaped.

H. L. Hundley, her builder in Mobile, now believed that the crews did not understand how to manage the *"Fish,"* and came on to Charleston to see if he could not show how it should be done. A Lieutenant Dixon, of Alabama, had made several successful experiments with the boat in Mobile Bay, and he also came on, and was put in charge, with a volunteer crew, and made several successful dives in the harbor. But one day, the day on which I saw the boat, Hundley himself took it into Stono River to practice her crew. She went down all right, but did not come up, and when she was searched for, found and raised to the surface, all of her crew were dead, asphyxiated as others had been.

After the boat was brought up to Charleston, several successful experiments were made with her, until she attempted to dive under the Confederate receiving ship *Indian Chief,* when she got entangled with an anchor chain and went to the bottom, and remained there until she was raised with every one of her crew dead, as were their predecessors.

No sooner had she been raised than a number of men begged to be allowed to give her another trial, and Lieutenant Dixon was given permission to use her in an attack on the U.S.S. *Housatonic,* a new gunboat that lay off Beach Inlet on the bar, on the condition that she should not be used as a submarine vessel, but only on the surface with a spar torpedo. On February 17, 1864, Lieutenant Dixon, with a crew of six men, made their way with the boat through the creeks behind Sullivan's Island to the inlet. The night was not very dark, and the *Housatonic* easily could be perceived lying at anchor, unmindful of danger. The *"Fish"* went direct for her victim, and her torpedo striking the side tore a tremendous hole in the *Housatonic,* which sank to the bottom in about four minutes. But as the water was not very deep her masts remained above water, and all of the crew, except four or five saved themselves by climbing and clinging to them. But the *"Fish"* was not seen again.

"I staid at his head and fanned him with a hat until he died, then helped to cut off some curls to send his mother."

No. 27.—BATTERY RENO.
Two 100-pounders, and one 8-inch Parrot Rifle. Breaching battery against Sumter.

Gunners of the 3d Rhode Island Heavy Artillery man Battery Reno, on Morris Island, in this photograph by Hilton Head photographers Haas & Peale.
Completed by August 1863, the battery mounted three heavy Parrott rifles that hurled shells 4,300 yards against Fort Sumter's gorge wall.

SERGEANT MILTON M. LEVERETT
C.S. Ordnance Department

After a period of service in the Beaufort Volunteer Artillery, Milton Maxcy Leverett was appointed an ordnance sergeant in the spring of 1864 and assigned to Fort Sumter. On July 7, after a lull in the bombardment, the Federal batteries resumed their intense fire on the battered fort. In a July 23 letter to his mother, Leverett described the death of his commanding officer, John C. Mitchel.

I have seen a great many wounded and some few killed since being down here. One mortar shell dropped in a crowd of negroes working hitting one outright another died shortly after and wounding ten besides. Poor wretches they see a dreadful time of it, are worked very hard and are very much exposed. I feel very sorry for them, some of them their masters sending down here without any change of clothes for thirty days at a time. It seems to me I would rather pay a fine or stand a prosecution than send a negro of mine down here especially one I cared for. They are treated entirely too harshly. To be sure the answer would be if the negroes don't do the work the soldier will have to and the alternative is die negro or die soldier consequently the negro gets it, but taking that aside they are treated harshly by the overseers.

We have had a very severe loss in poor Capt. Mitchell. He was over with us in our battery chatting saying that he wanted to get out of the noise of the shells around his way but that he found them as bad over here. He was speaking of having a bad toothache said he must get a Yankee shell to cure it. Said he should go next day to Charleston to have it plugged. He was then sent for on some business over at the side of the Fort and five minutes after someone came over saying Capt. Mitchell was wounded. He had gone up on the parapet examining into the condition of things when the sentinel said "Lookout" and told him he had better dodge. He said he wouldn't dodge any of their shells when the shell (a mortar shell) exploded and sent a large fragment right through his thigh and hip mutilating and mangling it horribly taking out the bone clear. He lived about four hours after that. I staid at his head and fanned him with a hat until he died, then helped to cut off some curls to send his mother, assisted in laying him out and dressing him in his full uniform placing him in his coffin putting a large flag we had over him and then sending him off by boat to Charleston. He said he wished to be buried in Magnolia Cemetery without any 'row' quietly as possible. His last message to his mother was quite peculiar. Says

he, "Oh my poor mother when she hears of this," "Percy (speaking to Percy Elliott his adjutant) you must write to my mother, tell her I died like a *gentleman* at *my post* fighting gallantly in the same cause as my poor brother Willie only not as gallantly as he as I have screamed more than he." He spoke of screaming, he didn't scream he only groaned and half cried and fretted and justly so for his thigh was a mutilated mass of pulp so to speak. He said he "had hoped to show the garrison how to die, but couldn't help it he was suffering so much pain." Sometimes he would get stupefied from the effects of the anodyne given him and would speak of everything Ireland and its associations then would speak French fluently but all pretty much disconnected and incongruous. He seemed to be speaking in a cheering manner of France, speaking to at one time "Vive la belle France," &c &c. He was quite disappointed at not being made a Major before. When Capt. Johnson came in he said to him "ah Captain *I am killed* and not made a Major." Capt. Johnson prayed for him with his consent after which he seemed easier. He was a number one man and of great intellectuality. Reminded me in some measure of brother i.e. in his great ambition in his intellect and capabilities and also being a small frail delicate man in his high ideas and estimation of blood—his appreciation of the gentleman. As you know he was a thorough type of the Irish gentleman (don't imagine that he spoke a brogue, his language was pure English, you wouldn't have known that he was an Irishman) and brave as Julius Caesar.

John C. Mitchel, the son of Irish nationalist John Mitchel, shared his father's forced exile to Australia before immigrating to America in 1853. After distinguished service with the 1st South Carolina Artillery on Morris Island, he was appointed to command Fort Sumter in May 1864. Mitchel was mortally wounded by a mortar shell fragment on July 20, 1864.

MAJOR THOMAS A. HUGUENIN

1st South Carolina Infantry (Regulars)

Huguenin graduated from the South Carolina Military Academy in 1859 and was appointed to its faculty that year. With the 1st South Carolina he served in the fortifications on Sullivan's Island and commanded the rear guard during the evacuation of Wagner. In September 1864 he took command of Fort Sumter.

One night a company of the 1st S.C. Regt of Regular Infantry came to take its tour of duty: the company was largely composed of Irishmen. It so happened that the fire the day previous had been very heavy and the garrison had to be called upon to help repair the damages. As this company was fresh I ordered that they should be detailed. During the night the Ladies Relief Association of Charleston sent down some watermelons, and as there was not enough to go around the whole garrison I ordered that they should be distributed to the working parties on duty that night. At daylight these working parties were relieved and received their ration of whiskey and also received the watermelons. One of the officers of the Company the next day overheard the following coloquy. "I say Pat, how dow you like soldiering in Sumter!" The reply came immediately. "By Jabers! Who would'nt soldier in Sumter with melons and whiskey! It is needless to say that these *"luxuries"* were not obtainable at other posts in the harbor.

The shot-torn battle flag of Major Huguenin's 1st South Carolina Infantry, of a pattern issued by the Charleston Depot, was flown from the crumbling ramparts of Fort Sumter during the last seven months of Confederate occupation.

LIEUTENANT WILLIAM T. SAMPSON

U.S.S. Patapsco

Sampson graduated from the U.S. Naval Academy in 1861 and served aboard the U.S.S. Water Witch in the East Gulf Blockading Squadron between Florida and Texas. After a year as instructor at the Naval Academy, he was appointed executive officer of the Patapsco off Charleston in 1863. In a letter to his wife, Sampson described the unsanitary conditions aboard the cramped ironclads.

Well dear we *try* and live here as we do on other vessels; but alas! it is a vain attempt. We have many serious obstacles to contend with. Think Maggie there are only three small openings from the berth to the upper deck. One of those leads to the cabin. Another to the berth deck, down which hatch both men & officers have to pass.

'There is not a prepared dish placed upon the table that does not contain a large proportion of roaches."

When I came on board here, all my ideas of a "man of war" recd a terrible shock. I found everything most disgustingly dirty. This filth extended to every part of the ship. The wardroom seemed to be the dirtiest of all. The table linen was dirty beyond description. I was surprised to find the ship in such a condition, for Mackenzie has the reputation of a fine officer. Experience has taught me that an iron clad cannot be kept clean, there are a thousand reasons why it is impossible. I flatter myself that she has improved considerable—yet oh how dirty! Add to all this the fact that the ship is full of roaches. I have often been shipmates with them before, but not in such numbers as crowd this vessel. While I write I have constantly to brush off 10 or 15 from my paper at a time. They soil everything in my room. Millions of them travel over me every night, crawling into my nose, ears, eyes, & mouth. There is not a prepared dish placed upon the table that does not contain a large proportion of roaches. When I first came on board you can imagine my disgust destroyed my appetite. Now I can sit down & *enjoy* a dish of soup when I can distinctly see more than a dozen roaches in it. I am careful not to eat them of course, at least not the large ones. The butter in a liquid state is full of them. The place I find most difficulty with them, is in baked beans, they look so much like a wild baked bean that it requires a close inspection (which cannot be given by candlelight) to distinguish them. Making a liberal calculation, I suppose I eat, at least, 20 each day. All descriptions of "vermin Exterminators" &c have failed to make a break in their ranks. No school boy could say the multiplication table as fast as they increase. Such is life on board our iron clad. As I expected, another officer has broken down, he has been attached to the ship for over 20 months & has stood it well. There are only 3 watch officers left. I think I will take a watch tho' I had hoped my watches were over. The one thing most detrimental to health on board these I.Cs. is foul air. At night, & indeed at all times when there is a little sea on, all the air holes (called deck lights) have to be closed, there then remains no way for the foul air to escape except thro' one small hatch. The papers may talk of the blowers & ventilation in iron clads; but I know that this want of air is their great draw back. Without the blowers & the system of ventilation which is used, 10 men could not live below 12 hours.

PRIVATE T. F. HAINES
127TH NEW YORK INFANTRY

Impatient at the slow pace of reducing Fort Sumter by artillery fire, Major General John G. Foster, who succeeded General Gillmore in command of the Department of the South in May 1864, conceived a plan to open a breach in Sumter's walls with a gunpowder raft. Several unsuccessful attempts were made in July. Private Haines and his comrades in the 127th New York had been assigned to picket boat duty, and on August 31 they made a third and final attempt.

We made the torpedo of two-inch oak plank in an ordinary pontoon boat. It contained 2,800 pounds of powder.

Now, on the north side of Fort Sumter was a dock about 100 feet long for steamers to come and land supplies. After the torpedo was complete, the next thing was to get a night when the conditions were favorable. We wanted it quite dark and a small sea. Those acquainted with Charleston Harbor know how a sea, a strong wind and the tide may make it impossible to handle a torpedo of that description. This torpedo had a fuse to burn estimated at a certain time of tide while a boat was drifting 40 yards, connected with a sub-marine fuse in a pistol held by Lieut. Abercrombie. Every one of that crew knew the Lieutenant would not fire the fuse till we were as near the fort as 40 yards. We had to pull by the fort in plain sight of the Johnnies to get above, when we could drift down.

We members of the crew were dressed to swim, having on a shirt only. We expected the boat to be sunk, or we might have to fight big

Soldiers huddle around campfires on the rubble-strewn parade ground in Chapman's December 1864 painting of sunrise over Fort Sumter. The artist based his work on a series of sketches by Confederate engineer John Key. As the fort's masonry walls crumbled under the incessant rain of Federal projectiles, the Confederate soldiers nightly reinforced their defenses with sandbags, wicker gabbions, palmetto logs, and wire netting.

odds. We were armed with Sharp's rifles, navy revolvers, and cutlasses.

The first attempt out the sea was too high, and we gave it up; but on the night of Aug. 28, 1864, the weather being favorable, we proceeded.

All the troops on Morris Island expected great results. The forts were ready to pour in their shell the moment we were out of range. It seemed like being in a strange country above the fort, on waters the Johnnies could make boil with grape and canister. The north side of the fort looked like a large hotel, with the ports open and lighted up.

We began drifting down, feeling every minute we might be discovered. We could see the men in the fort and the sentry on the dock. It seemed impossible to sit still in that boat, knowing when the fuse was fired the ball would open, and we would have to pull down by the fort to get home. Forty yards that night was a mighty short distance, and it seemed as if Abercrombie were going to drift into the very fort itself.

Aaron Handy steered the torpedo, and soon the Lieutenant said, "Take Handy aboard," which we did quick. Bang went the pistol. The fuse in the torpedo was ignited. For just one instant the Johnnies seemed paralyzed, then every man in the garrison was on the parapet shooting at us. We could not pull the other way, but had to pull down by the fort about the same distance 40 yards off, for we were in the swash channel. No boat could go through the main channel after the alarm was given.

Not a man in the boat was hit. The blades to the outer oars when out of the water were continually being hit with bullets. There must have been 150 men shooting at one boat's crew, firing at least two shots each before we could get out of range. We were so near them they all fired over our heads. While they were shooting, the torpedo kept drifting. The Johnnies had to run to cover. On the north side was a dock 100 feet long for the landing of supplies. Had it not been for a corner pile to the dock, where the torpedo hesitated and was turned slightly aside by the current, it would have gone to the exact position. There was no way of stopping the fuse from burning. It exploded about 30 feet from where it was designed to go, blowing the dock as high as you could see. The concussion killed a few Johnnies, but did no great damage to the fort.

LIEUTENANT WILLIAM T. SAMPSON
U.S.S. PATAPSCO

On the night of October 23, 1864, the British-owned blockade runner Flamingo ran aground off Sullivan's Island. Sampson's monitor was the first Federal warship to open fire on the stranded vessel. By the next day, the Flamingo had been destroyed by combined shelling from the fleet and the Federal shore batteries. After the war, Sampson rose steadily through the ranks and, as a rear admiral, commanded a fleet at the Battle of Santiago during the Spanish-American War.

About 10:30 P.M. the picket boats discovered a blockade runner coming in. The night was very dark the moon not rising till near midnight. The picket boats fired five times at her with light howitzers striking her three times they say. She kept on at full speed however right up for Charleston, close under the batteries of Sullivan's Island. One of the picket boats followed her & when she got as far up as Moultrie saw that the steamer had grounded. The off. in charge immediately came on board (we were on advance picket) & reported her ashore on a shoal near Moultrie. There is always a great deal of mystery attending blockade runners. It is seldom that two men can agree as to whether one was going out or running in. For that reason I doubted very much whether the picket off. had seen correctly or not. We waited anxiously till the moon got pretty high expecting to see & *know*. It was not till after 5 A.M. that we *thought* we saw something unusual in the direction of Moultrie. The Skipper

Undaunted by fire from Fort Moultrie, a Federal monitor shells the stranded British blockade runner Presto in an engraving that appeared in Harper's Weekly on February 27, 1864. The Presto ran aground on the night of February 2 and was destroyed after three days of bombardment by the monitors Lehigh, Nahant, and Passaic.

gave me orders to open upon it with our 150 pdr. rifle. It was far too dark to see an object well to say nothing of forming an estimate of the distance. I judged the distance to be about a nautical mile or 22 000 yds. & let slip a shell. It fell far short. It now commenced to grow light & we were certain that the reb. had touched bottom. I fired a second shot with increased elevation which also fell short, but very close. The third shot I brought down her foremast. It then had become quite light & the Kaatskill which was on reserve, steamed up & opened with her XI in. gun, but the range was rather too great for her, & as she had no rifle, she fired but a few shots striking her twice. We fired at her with our rifle 43 times & struck her 22 times. The last twelve times I fired I struck her eleven times. She is now half under water & most completely riddled. The Army commenced firing about 6.30 A.M. but made very poor shots. I declare it was the most sport I have had in a long time. I did not get my breakfast till nearly ten; but I would rather lose it than miss a shot with that gun. She puts a shell exactly in the right place every time. I found, after I got the range, that the steamer was a good mile & a half from us. The steamer was a very fine one with two smoke stacks & is supposed to be the celebrated blockade runner "Fox." I intend to ask the captain's permission to try & burn her to night if it is as dark as last night. The rebs. may be able to save a portion of her cargo & will doubtless attempt it tonight. While we were doing the neat thing for the blockade runner, Moultrie opened on us. She made the water boil around us but did not strike us once.

SHELLING A BLOCKADE-RUNNER AGROUND OFF SULLIVAN'S ISLAND.

"She had struck a torpedo and had gone down into the water as silently as a spirit, her smoke-stack alone revealing the fate that she had met in Charleston Harbor."

MAJOR THOMAS A. HUGUENIN
1st South Carolina Infantry (Regulars)

Early in 1865, Admiral Dahlgren issued orders to his monitor captains to search the channels for torpedoes and obstructions. On the evening of January 15, Major Huguenin on Fort Sumter spotted a Union vessel through the shifting fog. He alerted his one remaining battery of three guns, located in the fort's northeast face, to prepare to open fire.

One misty night I was aroused by the officer on duty and informed that a low-lying craft was approaching Fort Sumter from seaward. Hearing this, I immediately ascended the watch-tower, and, after looking steadily through my field-glass, observed what might have been taken for a phantom ship slowly and silently creeping up toward us. This stealthy visitor, I surmised, was nothing less than a monitor, and I presumed that, coming in so unusually close, she must have some evil intention. I thought that either she would open fire at short range to attract our attention while an attack of some kind would be made upon the rear of the fort, or that she was bringing in men to make a sudden dash by barges upon the sea-face, where the debris made by the bombardment shelved down toward the water's edge, inviting assault.

We were prepared to meet either attempt, and got ready to meet whatever might ensue as silently as herself, for I wished to induce her to come as near as possible to the fort, hoping to surprise her by a very warm welcome. Capt. Hal Lesesne's Company, of the First South Carolina Regular Artillery, was doing guard-duty at Fort Sumter just then, and I knew that our only gun-battery, which was mounted on a bomb-proof below, would do effective work in the hands of those experienced artillerymen.

A speaking-tube ran from the ramparts to this embrasure where the guns lay, quietly waiting to be used. I therefore called through this tube to Capt. Lesesne, and said: "Look toward the sea at an approaching object; train your guns upon it, and at the word of command fire, aiming the largest one in the battery yourself."

"Very well, sir," replied Lesesne. "I will open fire on her as soon as you are ready."

Returning to the watch-tower, I waited several minutes, to let the monitor get within range; then, hastening to the tube, gave the order: "Fire!"

Holding my breath, I stood motionless, expecting to hear the quick, responsive roar of the guns; but, to my intense surprise, the silence remained unbroken. Supposing that Capt. Lesesne had not heard my voice, I repeated the command in louder tones, burning with impatience at this delay, fearing that the ironclad might withdraw before we could get a chance to send her to the bottom of the sea, as we had done her companion, the "Keokuk," with the cannon of Fort Sumter. In the silence which still ensued my heart beat so loud that it sounded in my ears like a drum summoning Lesesne to do his part, for I was sure that he could sink her where she then stood. Yet the same unaccountable inaction continued. Calling for the third time, I exclaimed: "Lesesne, in God's name, why don't you fire?"

"I have lost sight of the monitor, sir," answered the artillery captain.

Almost beside myself with excitement and disappointment, I hurried below, raised my field-glass, and gazed seaward; but nothing could I see of this unfriendly visitor, the ghostly war-ship having vanished as completely as if she had been an optical illusion.

To say that we were amazed is to express our feelings very mildly, and we continued to scan the ocean, searching for the missing craft in every direction until dawn began to break over the cold gray sea.

Meanwhile, the tide had gone down during this period of anxious expectancy, and as daylight approached one of us observed what looked in the mist like a post projecting out of the water where nothing had appeared the previous afternoon. Then did we realize the reason of the sudden disappearance of the missing ironclad. She had struck a torpedo and had gone down into the water as silently as a spirit, her smoke-stack alone revealing the fate that she had met in Charleston Harbor on January 15, 1865, carrying with her to a seaman's burial sixty-two men of her crew.

LIEUTENANT COMMANDER STEPHEN P. QUACKENBUSH

U.S.S. PATAPSCO

A veteran of the navy since 1840, Quackenbush had served aboard various blockading vessels off the North and South Carolina coasts and commanded the U.S.S. screw steamer Pequot on the James River in Virginia. He assumed command of the Patapsco in December 1864. Quackenbush retired in 1885 with the rank of rear admiral.

Charleston Roads, S.C., Jan. 16, 1865. . . .

On the evening of the 15th inst. we cast off from our buoy at the lower anchorage and proceeded up to our usual station as advanced monitor. We rounded to, and I immediately called alongside the officers in charge of picket- and scout-boats. I directed them to select as many boats as had grapnels, and to push them up the harbor, using every effort to discover torpedoes or obstructions, the remaining boats to take position on our beams and quarters, keeping within 100 or 200 yards of the vessel.

The command officers of the tugboats were ordered to keep about the same distance ahead and on each bow. The object in assigning these positions was to avoid observation by the enemy and drawing their fire. I then allowed the Patapsco to drift up with the tide until nearly in a line from Sumter to Moultrie, the boats and tugs keeping in their respective positions. From this point, which was the highest obtained, we steamed down to within a few yards of the Lehigh buoy, then stopped and allowed the vessel to drift up, keeping in sight the before-mentioned buoy. On proceeding down the third time, and when within between 200 and 300 yards of the buoy, we struck and exploded a large torpedo or torpedoes, about thirty feet from the bow and a little on the port side.

The instant I discovered that we had been struck I gave the order to start the pumps. In an instant more I discovered that the whole forward part of the vessel was submerged, and, there being no possible chance to save the vessel, I then gave the order to man the boats; but before even an effort could be made to do so the vessel had sunk to the top of the turret.

The boat which hung at the port davits abaft the turret was afloat before Acting Ensign A. P. Bashford and the quartermaster of the watch, who were with me on the port side of the turret, could get into the boat to clear the falls. It was by great exertions that Mr. Bashford and the quartermaster succeeded in clearing the boat from the head of the davits. When I left the turret to get into the boat I could discover nobody on board, and the water was at the time ankle-deep on the turret. My first thought after this providential escape was the safety of such of the survivors as we could pick up. I had the good fortune of saving eleven of the crew. Owing to the disposition of the boats and tugs, which I had previously made to provide against accidents, all those persons who had escaped up from below, and those who were on deck, were rescued, to the number of 43—5 officers and 38 men.

Two officers pose on the deck of the U.S.S. Patapsco in 1863. When the ironclad struck a torpedo 800 yards from Sumter, it sank rapidly with the loss of 64 men.

CORPORAL AUGUSTINE T. SMYTHE
C.S. SIGNAL CORPS

In a February 14, 1865, letter to his mother, written from his observation post in the steeple of Saint Michael's Church, Corporal Augustine Smythe echoes the discouragement that suffused Charleston as General William T. Sherman's army moved north from Savannah.

I am afraid Charleston is doomed. And yet, if as they say it is to save Columbia, I am willing. Much as I love Charleston Columbia is more to me now. Every letter I write I think may be the last from here. We are expecting orders to leave to-morrow or even to-night. Dear old Charleston. My heart is very sad. To leave her now to those wretches after she has so long withstood their assault. Indeed, indeed it is a bitter cup to drink, but if we can assure the safety of Columbia & those in it, we will not complain.

I have arranged for our Gardener, a Scotchman, to live at our house.

This has been a relief to me for it is hard to think of the despoiling of our homes. There is another thing to be done which is hard. I must burn your letters I have here. It is so hard to do that I will leave it for the last. And, if you are obliged to move or you think them in danger of being tampered with, burn those papers of mine that you have. Your letters are with them & if possible I want to save them, but burn if necessary.

The Yankees are shelling away at a great rate. One shell has just burst close by. They might as well save their ammunition. On James Island a heavy bombardment is going on. So we are still alive. But everything is ready to move. Turpentine & rosin have been sent to the gunboats to destroy them. Very few stores are open & provisions cannot be bought. Everybody is excitement personified & the poor quartermaster clerks are flying round in every direction. Oh the loss of ordnance & stores when we leave here! It will be a heavy blow & I cannot but think we could better have spared Richmond. But I trust all will yet be well. Though very blue, my faith in our cause is unmoved & I must believe in our ultimate success. God grant it, & that speedily.

A Confederate sentry lowers Fort Sumter's tattered garrison flag at sunset in Conrad Wise Chapman's painting The Evening Gun. The nightly ritual was accompanied by the firing of a cannon mounted in a bombproof facing the city. During the 567-day siege, the Confederate national flag, flown from a makeshift flagpole on the fort's seaward face, was replaced four times.

This Confederate national flag was the last to fly over the walls of Fort Sumter. Raised for the first time on February 17, 1865, it was taken down that evening when the fort was evacuated.

MAJOR THOMAS A. HUGUENIN
1ST SOUTH CAROLINA INFANTRY (REGULARS)

Just as he had been the last officer to leave Battery Wagner, Huguenin now assumed the duty of overseeing the evacuation of Fort Sumter. At about 10:00 p.m. on February 17, after calling the roll and relieving the sentinels, he ordered the 300-man garrison to board two small steam transports. Major Huguenin himself cast off the mooring lines and was the last Confederate to leave Fort Sumter.

The next morning the 17th a new flag was raised, which was never fired upon, and the garrison were informed that we were ordered to evacuate the fort on that night. At sunset the evening gun was fired—and all the preparations for an assault were made as usual. About nine or ten o'clock two small steamers came to the fort and the troops were marched by detachments aboard. When all had been embarked, except the guard I personally with the Adjt. and Chief Engineer relieved them and ordered them to embark. It was now near 12 o'clock, but singular to say the enemy tho' firing heavily on Sullivans Island did not fire a single shot at us. Under orders received no public property of any description was destroyed except some whiskey which I had emptied into the water for fear the men might get hold of it during the retreat and create a disturbance. My own library of valuable military books I burnt up in the fire-place of my quarters, the official records were sewed up in a pair of my drawers and carried along with us. After visiting every portion of the fort, with a heavy heart I reached the wharf, no one was left behind but many a heart clung to those sacred and battle scarred ramparts, I cannot describe my emotions. I felt as if every tie held dear to me was about to be severed; the pride and glory of Sumter was there, and now in the gloom of darkness we were to abandon her, for whom every one of us would have shed the last drop of his blood.

On the morning of February 18, alerted that Sumter had been evacuated by the Rebels, Major John A. Hennessey of the 52d Pennsylvania acquired a rowboat and set out for the fort. There he raised his regiment's state flag (above).

MRS. LEE C. HARBY
RESIDENT OF CHARLESTON

On February 18, 1865, with the South Carolina state capital of Columbia put to the torch by Sherman's troops, Confederate forces evacuated Charleston. As a young girl, Harby watched preparations for the evacuation of Charleston, and years later she recalled the gloom that settled over the city. "We drew our sable garments of affliction about us," she recalled, "and mourned our dead."

On the 16th, cotton was piled on the public square and burned, that it might not enrich the enemy. The rice—tens of thousands of bushels—at Lucas' Mill was set on fire. On the 17th, the Northeastern Depot, where a large amount of military stores had been collected and abandoned, was thronged with a motley crowd of people, who bore away to their homes provisions of every kind. As the day wore on, explosions were heard on every side; the gunboats "Charleston" and "Chicora" were blown up at the wharves; the "big gun" at the corner of South and East Battery was exploded, and tore out the windows and doors and shattered the roof and piazzas of Mr. Louis DeSaussure's residence, at the opposite corner. The night which followed was a fearful one; no one slept; few went to bed. Fires started everywhere, and there were only negroes to put them out, and they knew the end had come; that the white men had gone or were going, and that the city was helpless and expecting its foe on the morrow. Yet, be it said to their honor, not a case of outrage or violence disgraced their record that night. . . .

Late in the night of the 17th, the "Palmetto State," the gunboat that the ladies built, was blown up at the Gas Company's Wharf, where she lay. Women who had worked and striven and contributed to its building stood at their windows and viewed the flames from the burning boat color the sky, and lo! as the last detonation sounded, the smoke arose and, upon the red glare of the heavens, formed a palmetto tree, perfect and fair, that stood out against the sky, then wavered and broke apart as we watched it through our tears, then crumbled into wreck and ruin and was lost in the darkness and gloom!

It was a terrible, heart-breaking, awful night. The men who were garrisoning Sumter had come over in their small boats, bringing their flags. In the early morning of the 18th, they were gathered in the city on the wharf, and there they cast themselves down on the earth and wept aloud. Some prayed; some cursed; all said they would rather have died in the fort they had so long defended than have her ramparts desecrated by the invader's tread. . . .

All day on the 17th, the evacuation of our troops had proceeded. On the 18th, at ten o'clock, on Meeting street, near Anne, the last body of armed Confederates we were ever to see said good-bye to the weeping women who pressed around them. Yet, even then, some laughed and jested, for, God pity us, we were hopeful still, and they were brave, and we could not think that the end had really come.

The mansion house of Miss Harriet Pinckney, the palace of South Carolina's colonial governors, lies gutted by the fire of December 1861 with its facade cratered by Federal shells. By the time this photograph was taken in March 1865, much of the city's center and waterfront lay abandoned or in ruins.

"Even then, some laughed and jested, for, God pity us, we were hopeful still, and they were brave, and we could not think that the end had really come."

To a chorus of "John Brown's Body," the men of the 55th Massachusetts, a black infantry regiment, march into Charleston on February 21, 1865. The regiment, carrying the Federal colors at right, was greeted with jubilation by the city's newly freed slave population. Colonel Charles B. Fox, the regiment's commanding officer, recalled that "cheers, blessings, and prayers were heard on every side."

GLOSSARY

adjutant—A staff officer assisting the commanding officer, usually with correspondence.

bastion—A projecting portion of a fort's rampart into which artillery is placed. Or, any fortified place.

battery—The basic unit of artillery, consisting of four to six guns. Or, an emplacement where artillery is mounted for attack or defense. A battery is generally open or lightly defended in the rear.

bivouac—A temporary encampment, or to camp out for the night.

bombproof—A shelter from mortar or artillery attack, usually made with walls and a roof of logs and packed earth.

breastwork—A temporary fortification, usually of earth and about chest high, over which a soldier could fire.

brevet—An honorary rank given for exceptional bravery or merit in time of war. It granted none of the authority or pay of the official rank.

buck and ball—A round of ammunition consisting of a bullet and three buckshot.

canister—A tin can containing lead or iron balls that scattered when fired from a cannon. Used primarily in defense of a position as an antipersonnel weapon.

cascabel—A knob or ring projecting from the breech end of a cannon, used with a rope or chain to secure the weapon or shift its position.

chevaux de frise—A movable defensive barrier made of logs with sharpened spikes.

Coehorn—A small mortar, light enough to be carried by four men.

Columbiad—A large cast-metal, smoothbore cannon adopted for all U.S. seacoast defenses in 1860. The largest, a 15-inch Columbiad, threw a 320-pound shell more than a mile.

The tube alone weighed almost 25 tons.

Congreve rocket—A military rocket fitted with an explosive warhead.

contraband—A slave who sought the protection of Union forces.

counterscarp—The exterior wall of a defensive ditch built around a fort.

coup de main—A surprise attack.

Dahlgren gun—A standard U.S. Navy smoothbore developed by John A. Dahlgren. These guns were distinctively bottle-shaped and massive—the barrel alone of a 15-inch Dahlgren weighed more than 10 tons.

double-quick—A trotting pace.

embrasure—An opening in a fort wall through which a cannon was fired.

Enfield rifle—The Enfield rifle musket was adopted by the British in 1853, and the North and South imported nearly a million to augment their own production. Firing a .577-caliber projectile similar to the Minié ball, it was fairly accurate at 1,100 yards.

enfilade—Gunfire that rakes an enemy line lengthwise, or the position allowing such firing.

fatigue duty—A general term for any manual or menial work done by soldiers.

file closer—A soldier marching in the rear of a line of battle to make sure that the formation stayed in order.

flank—The right or left end of a military formation. Therefore, to flank is to attack or go around the enemy's position on one end or the other.

forlorn hope—A desperately difficult or dangerous assignment, or the body of soldiers given such a task.

garrison—A military post, especially a permanent one. Also, the act of manning such a post and the soldiers who serve there.

glacis—The outer rim of the defensive ditch protecting a fort's rampart. It usually sloped down toward the enemy.

grapeshot—Iron balls bound together and fired from a large bore cannon. Resembling a cluster of grapes, the balls broke apart and scattered on impact. At the time of the civil war, grapeshot was reserved for garrison and naval artillery.

hardtack—A durable cracker, or biscuit, made of plain flour and water and normally about three inches square and a half-inch thick.

haversack—A shoulder bag, usually strapped over the right shoulder to rest on the left hip, for carrying personal items and rations.

hawser—A heavy rope or cable used for a variety of purposes on board a ship, including towing.

howitzer—A short-barreled artillery piece that fired its projectile in a relatively high trajectory.

jib-boom—An extension of a ship's bowsprit, usually the foremost part of the vessel.

musket—A smoothbore, muzzleloading shoulder arm.

parallel—A trenchwork for artillery dug parallel to the face of an enemy fortification in order to cover an advancing siege party.

parapet—A defensive elevation raised above a fort's main wall, or rampart.

parole—The pledge of a soldier released after being captured by the enemy that he would not take up arms again until he had been properly exchanged.

Parrott guns—Muzzleloading, rifled artillery pieces of various calibers made of cast iron, with a unique wrought-iron reinforcing band around the breech. Patented in 1861 by Union officer Robert Parker Parrott, these guns were more accurate at longer range than their smoothbore predecessors.

rammer—An artillerist's tool used to force the powder charge and projectile down the barrel of a gun and seat them firmly in the breech. Also, another word for the ramrod of a shoulder arm.

rampart—The main wall of a fort, usually a mound of earth with a flattened top.

ration—A specified allotment of food for one person (or animal) per day. The amounts and nature of rations varied by time and place throughout the war. *Rations* may also refer simply to any food provided by the army.

redoubt—An enclosed, defensive stronghold, usually temporary.

rifle—Any weapon with spiral grooves cut into the bore, which give spin to the projectile, adding range and accuracy. Usually applied to cannon or shoulder-fired weapons.

rifle pits—Holes or shallow trenches dug in the ground from which soldiers could fire weapons and avoid enemy fire. Foxholes.

sally port—A fort's main gate.

sap—A narrow trench dug by a besieging party so that it approaches the enemy's fort or strong point. Or, to dig such a trench.

skirmisher—A soldier sent in advance of the main body of troops to scout out and probe the enemy's position. Also, one who participated in a skirmish, a small fight usually incidental to the main action.

smoothbore—Any firearm or cannon with a smooth, or unrifled, barrel.

solid shot—A solid artillery projectile, oblong for rifled pieces and spherical for smoothbores, used against fortifications and matériel.

taffrail—The railing around the stern of a ship.

terreplein—The horizontal top surface of a fort's rampart, used as a platform for cannons.

torpedo—A floating mine that exploded usually on contact with a ship.

traverse—A trench or other defensive barrier that runs obliquely to the enemy's guns to protect against enfilading fire.

Whitworth gun—British-made steel artillery pieces with reinforcing bands around the breech, designed by Sir Joseph Whitworth.

ACKNOWLEDGMENTS

The editors wish to thank the following for their valuable assistance in the preparation of this volume: Eva-Maria Ahladas, Museum of the Confederacy, Richmond; Beth Bilderback, South Caroliniana Library, Columbia, S.C.; Robert Cornelli, Marietta, Ga.; Robert and Francis Freeman, Hananan, S.C.; John Guy, Washington Light Artillery, Charleston, S.C.; Randy W. Hackenburg, U.S. Army Military History Institute, Carlisle Barracks, Pa.; Corinne P. Hudgins, Museum of the Confederacy, Richmond; Mary Ison and Staff, Reference Library, Prints and Photography Department, Library of Congress, Washington, D.C.; Diane Kessler, Pennsylvania Capitol Preservation Committee, Harrisburg; Teresa Roane, Valentine Museum, Richmond; Bobby Roberts, Central Arkansas Library System, Little Rock; Martha Severens, Greenville County Museum of Art, Greenville, S.C.; Arlene Shy, Clements Library, University of Michigan, Ann Arbor; Anne Sindelar, The Western Reserve Historical Society, Cleveland; June Welles, Confederate Museum, Charleston, S.C.; Sherry Wilding-White, New Hampshire Historical Society, Concord; Michael J. Winey, U.S. Army Military History Institute, Carlisle Barracks, Pa.; Jane Yates, The Citadel, Charleston, S.C.

PICTURE CREDITS

The sources for the illustrations are listed below. Credits from left to right are separated by semicolons, from top to bottom by dashes.

Dust jacket: front, National Archives, Neg. No. 165-C-799; rear, Massachusetts Commandery of the Military Order of the Loyal Legion of the United States and the U.S. Army Military History Institute (MASS-MOLLUS/USAMHI), copied by A. Pierce Bounds.

All calligraphy by Mary Lou O'Brian/Inkwell, Inc.

6, 7: Map by Paul Salmon. 8: Clements Library, University of Michigan. 15: Map by R. R. Donnelley & Sons Co., Cartographic Services. 16: MASS-MOLLUS/USAMHI, copied by A. Pierce Bounds. 17: Library of Congress, Waud #635. 18: MASS-MOLLUS/USAMHI, courtesy Carl Moneyhon. 19: Library of Congress. 20: Frank and Marie-Thérèse Wood Print Collections, Alexandria, Va. 21: MASS-MOLLUS/USAMHI. 23: New Hampshire Historical Society, Concord, Neg. No. F4390. 25: The Western Reserve Historical Society, Cleveland. 26: MASS-MOLLUS/USAMHI, copied by A. Pierce Bounds. 27: Frank and Marie-Thérèse Wood Print Collections, Alexandria, Va. 28: Courtesy Catherine and Evelyn Fishback. 29: Herb Peck Jr. 30: MASS-MOLLUS/USAMHI, copied by A. Pierce Bounds. 31: From *Soldier Life, Secret Service,* Vol. 8 of *The Photographic History of the Civil War,* Francis Trevelyan Miller, Editor-In-Chief, New York, Review of Reviews Co., 1911, copied by Philip Brandt George. 32:

MASS-MOLLUS/USAMHI, copied by A. Pierce Bounds. 33: MASS-MOLLUS/USAMHI, copied by A. Pierce Bounds; *Carolina Light Infantry,* First South Carolina Infantry, Museum of the Confederacy, Richmond, photographed by Katherine Wetzel. 34: MASS-MOLLUS/USAMHI, copied by A. Pierce Bounds. 37: Map by Walter W. Roberts. 38: From *Life in the Confederate Army,* by Arthur P. Ford and Marion Johnstone Ford, Neale Publishing Co., New York, 1905, copied by Philip Brandt George. 39: Library of Congress, Neg. No. B8184-4390— Charles V. Peery, M.D., copied by Henry Mintz. 40: MASS-MOLLUS/USAMHI, copied by A. Pierce Bounds. 41: Frank and Marie-Thérèse Wood Print Collections, Alexandria, Va. 43: Charles V. Peery, M.D., copied by Henry Mintz—Houghton Library, Harvard University, Cambridge, Mass. 44: Charles V. Peery, M.D., copied by Henry Mintz. 45: Old Court House Museum, Vicksburg, Miss., copied by Philip Brandt George. 46: Frank and Marie-Thérèse Wood Print Collections, Alexandria, Va. 47: Houghton Library, Harvard University, Cambridge, Mass. 48: Museum of the Confederacy, Richmond, photographed by Larry Sherer. 49: Confederate Museum, Charleston, S.C., copied by Henry Mintz. 50: Library of Congress, Neg. No. BH824-4742, copied by Philip Brandt George. 51: Courtesy collection of William A. Turner; Frank and Marie-Thérèse Wood Print Collections, Alexandria, Va. 52, 53: Charles V. Peery, M.D., copied by Henry Mintz; Library of Congress; Charles V. Peery, M.D., copied by Henry Mintz. 54: Confederate Museum, Charleston, S.C., copied by Henry Mintz. 55: MASS-MOLLUS/USAMHI, copied by Robert Walch—MASS-MOLLUS/USAMHI. 56, 57: Greenville County Museum of Art, Greenville, S.C. 58: From *The Photographic History of the Civil War,* ed. by Francis Trevelyan Miller, © 1911 Patriot Co., Springfield, Mass. 59: New Hampshire Historical Society, Concord, Neg. No. F2725. 60: Charles V. Peery, M.D. 62: Charles V. Peery, M.D., copied by Henry Mintz. 63: Charles V. Peery, M.D., photographed by Henry Mintz; The Citadel Archives and Museum, Charleston, S.C.—courtesy U.S. Military Academy Library, West Point, N.Y., photographed by Henry Groskinsky. 64: Collection of the New-York Historical Society, New York City. 66, 67: Frank and Marie-Thérèse Wood Print Collections, Alexandria, Va. 70: MASS-MOLLUS/USAMHI, copied by A. Pierce Bounds—Library of Congress, Waud #801. 71: Confederate Museum, Charleston, S.C., photographed by Michael Latil. 72, 73: MASS-MOLLUS/USAMHI, copied by A. Pierce Bounds—Library of Congress, Waud #604. 74, 75: MASS-MOLLUS/USAMHI, copied by

Robert Walch. 76: Frank and Marie-Thérèse Wood Print Collections, Alexandria, Va. 77: New Hampshire Historical Society, Concord, Neg. No. F2724. 78: National Archives, Neg. No. H-620-G-3; courtesy Brian Pohanka. 79: MASS-MOLLUS/USAMHI, copied by A. Pierce Bounds. 80, 81: Charles V. Peery, M.D., copied by Henry Mintz. 83: The Western Reserve Historical Society, Cleveland. 84: Charles V. Peery, M.D., copied by Henry Mintz; Confederate Museum, Charleston, S.C., photographed by Henry Mintz. 85: Charles V. Peery, M.D., copied by Henry Mintz. 86: Library of Congress, Waud #616. 87: Pennsylvania Capitol Preservation Committee, Harrisburg; Division of Archives and Manuscripts, Pennsylvania Historical and Museum Commission, copied by A. Pierce Bounds. 88: Frank and Marie-Thérèse Wood Print Collections, Alexandria, Va. 89: MASS-MOLLUS/USAMHI, copied by A. Pierce Bounds. 90: Charles V. Peery, M.D., copied by Henry Mintz. 91: MASS-MOLLUS/USAMHI, copied by A. Pierce Bounds. 92: MASS-MOLLUS/USAMHI, copied by A. Pierce Bounds; from *History of the Fifty-Fourth Regiment of Massachusetts Volunteer Infantry, 1863-1865,* by Luis F. Emilio, Boston Book Co., 1891, copied by Philip Brandt George. 93: Private collection, photographed by Nicholas Whitman; Bureau of State Office Buildings, Boston, Mass. 94: MASS-MOLLUS/USAMHI, copied by A. Pierce Bounds. 95: Confederate Museum, Charleston, S.C., photographed by Michael Latil. 96: Frank and Marie-Thérèse Wood Print Collections, Alexandria, Va. 97: From *Deeds of Valor: How America's Heroes Won the Medal of Honor,* edited by W. F. Beyer and O. F. Keydel, Perrien-Keydel Co., 1903; Mr. Larry Williams, Apex, N.C., copied by Henry Mintz. 99: MASS-MOLLUS/USAMHI, copied by A. Pierce Bounds. 100: Library of Virginia, Richmond. 101: Houghton Library, Harvard University, Cambridge, Mass. 102: Courtesy Brian Pohanka. 103: MASS-MOLLUS/USAMHI, copied by A. Pierce Bounds. 104: Houghton Library, Harvard University, Cambridge, Mass. 105: Courtesy Stamatelos Brothers Collection, Cambridge, Mass., photographed by Larry Sherer. 107: Confederate Museum, Charleston, S.C., photographed by Henry Mintz; Confederate Museum, Charleston, S.C., photographed by Michael Latil. 108: Courtesy collection of William A. Turner. 109: Houghton Library, Harvard University, Cambridge, Mass. 110: Library of Congress. 112, 113: Frank and Marie-Thérèse Wood Print Collections, Alexandria, Va. 114: MASS-MOLLUS/USAMHI, copied by A. Pierce Bounds; Charles V. Peery, M.D., copied by Henry Mintz. 115: MASS-MOLLUS/USAMHI, copied by A. Pierce Bounds. 116, 117: MASS-MOLLUS/USAMHI,

copied by A. Pierce Bounds; New Hampshire Historical Society, Concord; MASS-MOLLUS/USAMHI, copied by A. Pierce Bounds. 118-121: MASS-MOLLUS/USAMHI, copied by A. Pierce Bounds. 123: Frank and Marie-Thérèse Wood Print Collections, Alexandria, Va.—South Carolina Historical Society, Charleston. 124: New Hampshire Historical Society, Concord. 126: Confederate Museum, Charleston, S.C., copied by Henry Mintz. 127: MASS-MOLLUS/USAMHI, copied by Robert Walch. 128: MASS-MOLLUS/USAMHI, copied by A. Pierce Bounds—Library of Congress. 129: Confederate Museum, Charleston, S.C., photographed by Michael Latil. 130,131: Charles V. Peery, M.D., copied by Henry Mintz. 133: South Caroliniana Library, University of South Carolina—MASS-MOLLUS/USAMHI, copied by A. Pierce Bounds. 134: Confederate Museum, Charleston, S.C., photographed by Michael Latil; from *Personal Experiences in the Civil War,* by Frederick Tomlinson Peet, New York, privately printed, 1905, copied by Philip Brandt George. 135: Museum of the Confederacy, Richmond, photographed by Larry Sherer. 136: MASS-MOLLUS/USAMHI, copied by A. Pierce Bounds. 137: Civil War Library & Museum, Philadelphia, copied by A. Pierce Bounds. 138: MASS-MOLLUS/USAMHI, copied by Robert Walch. 139: Valentine Museum, Richmond. 141, 142: Museum of the Confederacy, Richmond, photographed by Larry Sherer. 143: Library of Congress. 144: Confederate Museum, Charleston, S.C., photographed by Henry Mintz. 145: Confederate Museum, Charleston, S.C., photographed by Michael Latil—MASS-MOLLUS/USAMHI, copied by A. Pierce Bounds. 146: National Park Service, Fort Pulaski National Monument, Savannah, Ga.—Museum of the Confederacy, Richmond, photographed by Larry Sherer. 148: New Hampshire Historical Society, Concord, No. 1992.506.23. 149: Confederate Museum, Charleston, S.C., copied by Henry Mintz. 150: Courtesy collection of William A. Turner; courtesy Washington Light Infantry, Charleston, S.C., photographed by Harold H. Norvell. 152: Museum of the Confederacy, Richmond, photographed by Larry Sherer. 153: Frank and Marie-Thérèse Wood Print Collections, Alexandria, Va. 155: MASS-MOLLUS/USAMHI, copied by A. Pierce Bounds. 156: Charles V. Peery, M.D. 157: Confederate Museum, Charleston, S.C., photographed by Michael Latil; Pennsylvania Capitol Preservation Committee, Harrisburg. 158: Courtesy U.S. Military Academy Library, West Point, N.Y., copied by Henry Groskinsky. 159: Frank and Marie-Thérèse Wood Print Collections, Alexandria, Va.—Bureau of State Office Buildings, Boston, Mass.

BIBLIOGRAPHY

BOOKS

Allardice, Bruce S. *More Generals in Gray*. Baton Rouge: Louisiana State University Press, 1995.

Allen, Albert D., ed. *History of the Forty-Fifth Pennsylvania Veteran Volunteer Infantry, 1861-1865*. Williamsport, Pa.: Grit Publishing, 1912.

Beauregard, Pierre G. T. "Torpedo Service in Charleston Harbor." In *Annals of the War*. Philadelphia: Times Publishing, 1879.

The Blockade: Runners and Raiders (The Civil War series). Alexandria, Va.: Time-Life Books, 1983.

Boatner, Mark Mayo, III. *The Civil War Dictionary*. New York: David McKay, 1959.

Bradshaw, Timothy Eugene, Jr. *Battery Wagner: The Siege, the Men Who Fought and the Casualties*. Columbia, S.C.: Palmetto Historical Works, 1993.

Bryant, Elias A. *The Diary of Elias A. Bryant*. Concord, N.H.: Rumford Press, n.d.

The Burckmyer Letters, March 1863-June 1865. Columbia, S.C.: State Co., 1926.

Burton, E. Milby. *The Siege of Charleston, 1861-1865*. New York: Columbia University Press, 1970.

"Carleton." In *Stories of Our Soldiers*. Boston: Journal Newspaper, 1893.

Carse, Robert. *Department of the South: Hilton Head Island in the Civil War*. Columbia, S.C.: State Printing, 1981.

Chaitin, Peter M., and the Editors of Time-Life Books. *The Coastal War: Chesapeake Bay to Rio Grande* (The Civil War series). Alexandria, Va.: Time-Life Books, 1984.

The Civil War at Charleston. Charleston, S.C.: Evening Post Publishing, 1973.

Clark, Walter, ed. *Histories of the Several Regiments and Battalions from North Carolina in the Great War, 1861-'65*. Vol. 3. Broadfoot's Bookmark, 1982 (reprint of 1901 edition).

Coggins, Jack. *Arms and Equipment of the Civil War*. Wilmington, N.C.: Broadfoot Publishing, 1962.

Confederate General. 5 vols. Ed. by William C. Davis. Harrisburg, Pa.: National Historical Society, 1991.

Copp, Elbridge J. *Reminiscences of the War of the Rebellion, 1861-1865*. Nashua, N.H.: Telegraph Publishing, 1911.

Davis, W. W. H.:
History of the 104th Pennsylvania Regiment: From August 22nd 1861 to September 30th 1864. Philadelphia: Jas. B. Rodgers, Printer, 1866.
"The Siege of Morris Island." In *Annals of the War*. Philadelphia: Times Publishing, 1879.

Deeds of Valor: How America's Heroes Won the Medal of Honor. Vol. 1. Detroit: Perrien-Keydel, 1903.

Denison, Frederic. *Shot and Shell: The Third Rhode Island Heavy Artillery Regiment in the Rebellion, 1861-1865*. Providence: J. A. & R. A. Reid, 1879.

Dyer, Frederick H. *A Compendium of the War of the Rebellion*. Vol. 1. Dayton: Press of Morningside Bookshop, 1979.

Eldredge, D. *The Third New Hampshire and All about It*. Boston: Press of E. B. Stillings, 1893.

Emilio, Luis F. *History of the Fifty-Fourth Regiment of Massachusetts Volunteer Infantry, 1863-1865*. Boston: Boston Book, 1891.

Farenholt, Oscar Walter. *The Monitor "Catskill": A Year's Reminiscences, 1863-1864*. San Francisco, Calif.: Shannon-Conmy Printing, 1912.

Fighting for Time. Vol. 4 of *The Image of War: 1861-1865*. Garden City, N.Y.: Doubleday, 1983.

Ford, Arthur P., and Marion Johnstone Ford. *Life in the Confederate Army . . . Experiences and Sketches of Southern Life*. New York: Neale Publishing, 1905.

Fremantle, Arthur. *Three Months in the Southern States: April-June 1863*. London: William Blackwood & Sons, 1863.

Furness, William Eliot. "The Siege of Fort Wagner." In *Military Essays and Recollections: Papers Read before the Commandery of the State of Illinois, Military Order of the Loyal Legion of the United States*. Vol. 1. Wilmington, N.C.: Broadfoot Publishing, 1992 (reprint of 1891 edition).

Georgia State Division of Confederate Pensions and Records. *Roster of the Confederate Soldiers of Georgia, 1861-1865*. Vol. 1. Comp. by Lillian Henderson. Atlanta: Georgia Division, United Daughters of the Confederacy, 1994.

Holmes, Emma. *The Diary of Miss Emma Holmes, 1861-1866*. Ed. by John F. Marszalek. Baton Rouge: Louisiana State University Press, 1979.

Inglesby, Charles. *Historical Sketch of the First Regiment of South Carolina Artillery*. Charleston, S.C.: Walker, Evans & Cogswell, 1896.

James, Garth W. "The Assault on Fort Wagner." In *War Papers: Being Papers Read before the Commandery of the State of Wisconsin Military Order of the Loyal Legion of the United States*. Vol. 1. Wilmington, N.C.: Broadfoot Publishing, 1993.

Johnson, John. *The Defense of Charleston Harbor: Including Fort Sumter and the Adjacent Islands, 1863-1865*. Freeport, N.Y.: Books for Libraries Press, 1970.

Jones, Iredell. "Letters from Fort Sumter in 1862 and 1863." In *Southern Historical Society Papers: January to December, 1884*. Vol. 12. Wilmington, N.C.: Broadfoot Publishing, 1990.

Little, Henry F. *The Seventh Regiment New Hampshire Volunteers in the War of the Rebellion, 1861-1865*. Concord, N.H.: Ira C. Evans, Printer, 1896.

McCaslin, Richard B. *Portraits of Conflict: A Photographic History of South Carolina in the Civil War*. Fayetteville: University of Arkansas Press, 1994.

Manigault, Edward. *Siege Train*. Ed. by Warren Ripley. Columbia: University of South Carolina Press, 1986.

Mast, Greg. *State Troops and Volunteers: A Photographic Record of North Carolina's Civil War Soldiers*. Vol. 1. Raleigh: North Carolina Division of Archives and History, 1995.

Metcalf, Edwin. "Personal Incidents in the Early Campaigns of the Third Regiment Rhode Island Volunteers and the Tenth Army Corps." In *Personal Narratives of the Battles of the Rebellion: Being Read before the Rhode Island Soldiers and Sailors Historical Society*. Vol. 1. Wilmington, N.C.: Broadfoot Publishing, 1993 (reprint of 1879 edition).

Morgan, James Morris. *Recollections of a Rebel Reefer*. London: Constable, 1918.

National Gallery of Art. *The Civil War: A Centennial Exhibition of Eyewitness Drawings*. Washington, D.C.: Smithsonian Institution, 1961.

North Carolina Troops, 1861-1865: A Roster. Vol. 12. Comp. by Weymouth T. Jordan Jr. Raleigh: North Carolina Division of Archives and History, 1990.

Olmstead, Charles H. "Charleston Harbor: Colonel Charles H. Olmstead's Reminiscences of Service in 1863." In *Southern Historical Society Papers: January to December, 1883*. Vol. 11. Wilmington, N.C.: Broadfoot Publishing, 1990.

Parker, William Harwar. *Recollections of a Naval Officer, 1841-1865*. New York: Charles Scribner's Sons, 1883.

Peet, Frederick Tomlinson. *Personal Experiences in the Civil War*. New York: Private printing, 1905.

Pressley, John G. "Diary of Lieutenant-Colonel John G. Pressley, of Twenty-Fifth South Carolina Volunteers." In *Southern Historical Society Papers: January to December, 1886*. Vol. 14. Wilmington, N.C.: Broadfoot Publishing, 1990.

Price, Isaiah. *History of the Ninety-Seventh Regiment, Pennsylvania Volunteer Infantry: During the War of the Rebellion, 1861-65*. Philadelphia: Isaiah Price, 1875.

Register of Officers of the Confederate States Navy, 1861-1865. Mattituck, N.Y.: J. M. Carroll, 1983.

Reynolds, Clark G. *Famous American Admirals*. New York: Van Nostrand Reinhold, 1978.

Ripley, Warren. *Ammunition of the Civil War*. New York: Promontory Press, 1970.

Rosen, Robert N. *Confederate Charleston: An Illustrated History of the City and the People during the Civil War*.

Columbia: University of South Carolina Press, 1994.

Sauers, Richard A.:

Advance the Colors!: Pennsylvania Civil War Battle Flags. Vol. 1. Harrisburg, Pa.: Capitol Preservation Committee, 1987.

Advance the Colors!: Pennsylvania Civil War Battle Flags. Vol. 2. Harrisburg, Pa.: Capitol Preservation Committee, 1991.

Sifakis, Stewart. *Compendium of the Confederate Armies: South Carolina and Georgia.* New York: Facts on File, 1995.

The South Besieged. Vol. 5 of *The Image of War: 1861–1865.* Garden City, N.Y.: Doubleday, 1983.

Stedman, Charles Ellery. *The Civil War Sketchbook of Charles Ellery Stedman.* San Rafael, Calif.: Presidio Press, 1976.

Todd, William. *Seventy-Ninth Highlanders: New York Volunteers in the War of Rebellion, 1861–1865.* Albany, N.Y.: Press of Brandow, Barton & Co., 1886.

United Daughters of the Confederacy, Carolina Division. *South Carolina Women in the Confederacy.* Vol. 2. Ed. by Mrs. James Conner, et al. Columbia, S.C.: State Co., 1907.

United States Army. *Official Army Register of the Volunteer Force of the United States Army: For the Years 1861, '62, '63, '64, '65.* Vol. 1. Gaithersburg, Md.: Olde Soldier Books, 1987 (reprint of 1865 edition).

United States Navy:

Civil War Naval Chronology: 1861–1865. Comp. by Naval History Division. Washington, D.C.: Government Printing Office, 1971.

Dictionary of American Naval Fighting Ships. Vols. 1-8. Washington, D.C.: Government Printing Office, 1979.

Official Records of the Union and Confederate Navies in the War of the Rebellion. Vol. 12. Washington, D.C.: Government Printing Office, 1901.

Official Records of the Union and Confederate Navies in the War of the Rebellion. Vol. 13. Washington, D.C.: Government Printing Office, 1901.

Official Records of the Union and Confederate Navies in the War of the Rebellion. Vol. 14. Washington, D.C.: Government Printing Office, 1902.

United States War Department:

The War of the Rebellion: A Compilation of the Official Record of the Union and Confederate Armies. Series 1, Vol. 14, Part 1-Reports. Washington, D.C.: Government Printing Office, 1885.

The War of the Rebellion: A Compilation of the Official Records of the Union and Confederate Armies. Series 1, Vol. 28, 2 parts. Washington, D.C.: Government Printing Office, 1890.

Voris, Alvin C. "Charleston in the Rebellion." In *Sketches of War History, 1861–1865.* Vol. 2. Wilmington, N.C.: Broadfoot Publishing, 1991 (reprint of 1888 edition).

Wait, Horatio L. "Reminiscences of Fort Sumter." In *Military Essays and Recollections: Papers Read before the Commandery of the State of Illinois, Military Order of the Loyal Legion of the United States.* Vol. 1. Wilmington, N.C.: Broadfoot Publishing, 1992 (reprint of 1891 edition).

Wallace, James. "Report of Ensign Wallace, U.S. Navy." In *Official Records of the Union and Confederate Navies in the War of the Rebellion.* Vol. 14. Washington, D.C.: Government Printing Office, 1902.

Warner, Ezra J. *Generals in Blue: Lives of the Union Commanders.* Baton Rouge: Louisiana State University Press, 1964.

Wise, Stephen R. *Gate of Hell: Campaign for Charleston Harbor, 1863.* Columbia: University of South Carolina Press, 1994.

PERIODICALS

Barber, George W. "Bombarding Rebel Strongholds." *National Tribune* (Washington, D.C.), July 15, 1897.

Bassham, Ben L. "The Defenses of Charleston, 1863-1864." *Museum of the Confederacy Newsletter* (Quarterly), n.d.

Blood, Alfred C. "In Front of Fort Wagner." *National Tribune* (Washington, D.C.), November 24, 1910.

Bowditch, Charles P. "War Letters of Charles P. Bowditch." *Massachusetts Historical Society,* February-April 1924.

Butler, Lewis. "A Memorable Charge." *National Tribune* (Washington, D.C.), January 10, 1884.

Carney, William H. "Fort Wagner, S.C." *National Tribune* (Washington, D.C.), January 5, 1893.

Eaton, Gilbert. "Fort Wagner Again." *National Tribune* (Washington, D.C.), September 27, 1883.

Haines, T. F. "Men in a Boat." *National Tribune* (Washington, D.C.), June 18, 1896.

Harleston, John. "Battery Wagner on Morris Island, 1863." *South Carolina Historical Magazine,* January 1956.

Harold, James H.:

"Reducing Ft. Sumter." *National Tribune* (Washington, D.C.), April 30, 1891.

"A Stronghold Hard Beset." *National Tribune* (Washington, D.C.), January 14, 1897.

Hayes, John D. "The Battle of Port Royal, S.C.: From the Journal of John Sanford Barnes, October 8 to November 9, 1861." *New York Historical Society Quarterly,* October 1961.

Hicks, Ira E. "Battery Strong." *National Tribune* (Washington, D.C.), December 29, 1885.

Huguenin, T. A. "How the 'Patapsco' Went Down in Charleston Harbor." *Confederate Veteran,* August 1897.

Kelly, Robert D. "The Assault on Fort Wagner." *Philadelphia Weekly Times,* June 5, 1880.

Labay, E. A. "On the Keystone State." *National Tribune* (Washington, D.C.), June 25, 1914.

Leland, Isabella Middleton, ed. "Middleton Correspondence: 1861-1865." *South Carolina Historical Magazine,* 1962, Vol. 63.

Martin, James. "Fort Wagner." *National Tribune* (Washington, D.C.), March 30, 1916.

Michie, Peter. "A Regular at Fort Wagner." *National Tribune* (Washington, D.C.), August 24, 1993.

Morgan, Thomas W. "The Assault on Fort Wagner." *National Tribune* (Washington, D.C.), October 25, 1883.

Olmstead, Charles. "The Memoirs of Charles Olmstead." Part 6. Ed. by Lilla Mills Hawes. *Georgia Historical Quarterly,* 1960, Vol. 44.

Taliaferro, William B. "Fort Wagner." *National Tribune* (Washington, D.C.), September 20, 1883.

Vizetelly, Frank. "When Charleston Was under Fire." *New Age Magazine,* September 1911.

Weigel, John. Letter. *National Tribune* (Washington, D.C.), January 14, 1886.

West, Daniel J. "The Fight at Fort Wagner." *National Tribune* (Washington, D.C.), December 11, 1913.

OTHER SOURCES

Appleton, John W. M. Journal, n.d. Morgantown: University of West Virginia.

Bates family correspondence, 1850-1890. Durham, N.C.: Duke University, Special Collections Library.

Billings, Luther G. Papers, n.d. Washington, D.C.: Library of Congress, Manuscript Division.

Coleman, Philip. Address to the Soldier's Union of the First Congressional Church, Washington, D.C., October 21, 1898. Private collection.

Harris, David B. Letter, July 29, 1863, from the David B. Harris Papers. Durham, N.C.: Duke University, Special Collections Library.

Honour, Theodore. Letter, July 16, 1863, from the Theodore Honour Papers. Columbia: South Caroliniana Library Collection.

Huguenin, Thomas Abram. "A Sketch of the Life of Thomas Abram Huguenin." Unpublished manuscript, n.d. Huger, S.C.: Halidon Hall Plantation.

Leverett, Milton Maxcy. Letter, May 10,11, 1864, from the Leverett Family Papers. Columbia, S.C.: Mrs. Frances Wallace Taylor.

Malloy, John Douglas. Letter, March 24, 1863. Durham,

N.C.: Duke University, Special Collections Library.

Meade, Robert L. "Retrospective." Unpublished journal, n.d., from the Meade Papers. Quantico, Va.: U. S. Marine Corps Research Center.

Rush, W. A. Letters, n.d., from the Flinn Family Papers. Polkville, N.C.: Frank Lattimore.

Sampson, William T. Papers, n.d. Marietta, Ga.: Robert Cornely.

Silva, James S. Letter, September 4, 1863. Paris Island, S.C.: U.S. Marine Corps Museum.

Smythe, Augustine. Papers, n.d. Columbia: South Caroliniana Library Collection.

Stryker, William Scudder. "Three Days in the Civil War." Unpublished manuscript, n.d. Ed. by Stephen R. Wise. Buford, S.C.: Stephen R. Wise.

Swails, Stephen A. Statement to Lt. Henry W. Littlefield, August 12, 1863, from the Cabot J. Russell Papers. New York: New York Public Library, Manuscript Division.

[ ],Wilson. Letter, July 23, 1863. Folder #44. Charleston, S.C.: Fort Sumter National Monument, Manuscript Collection.

INDEX

 Time-Life Books is a
division of Time Life Inc.

TIME LIFE INC.
PRESIDENT and CEO: George Artandi

TIME-LIFE BOOKS
PRESIDENT: John D. Hall
PUBLISHER/MANAGING EDITOR: Neil Kagan

VOICES OF THE CIVIL WAR

DIRECTOR, NEW PRODUCT DEVELOPMENT:
Curtis Kopf
MARKETING DIRECTOR: Pamela R. Farrell

CHARLESTON

EDITOR: Henry Woodhead
Deputy Editors: Harris J. Andrews (principal), Kirk Denkler,
Philip Brandt George
Design Director: Ray Ripper
Associate Editors/Research and Writing: Connie Contreras,
Gemma Slack
Senior Copyeditor: Donna D. Carey
Picture Coordinator: Lisa Groseclose
Editorial Assistant: Christine Higgins

Initial Series Design: Studio A

Special Contributors: John Newton, Brian C. Pohanka, David
S. Thomson (text); Paul Birkhead, Charles F. Cooney,
Ramona Grunden, Steve Hill, Robert Lee Hodge, Henry
Mintz (research); Roy Nanovic (index).

Correspondent: Christina Lieberman (New York).

Vice President, Director of Finance: Christopher Hearing
Vice President, Book Production: Marjann Caldwell
Director of Operations: Eileen Bradley
Director of Photography and Research: John Conrad Weiser
Director of Editorial Administration (Acting): Barbara Levitt
Production Manager: Marlene Zack
Quality Assurance Manager: James King
Library: Louise D. Forstall

Consultants

Brian C. Pohanka, a Civil War historian and author, spent six
years as a researcher and writer for Time-Life Books' Civil
War series and Echoes of Glory. He is the author of *Distant
Thunder: A Photographic Essay on the American Civil War* and
has written and edited numerous works on American military
history. He has acted as historical consultant for projects
including the feature film *Glory* and television's *Civil War
Journal.* Pohanka participates in Civil War reenactments and
living-history demonstrations with the 5th New York Volunteers, and he is active in Civil War battlefield preservation.

Dr. Richard A. Sauers is a historian specializing in the Civil
War. As chief historian for the Pennsylvania Capitol Preservation Committee he directed the research and documentation
of more than 400 Civil War battle flags and wrote *Advance the
Colors!,* the two-volume study of Pennsylvania's Civil War
flags. He is assistant editor of *Gettysburg* magazine. His published works include *A Caspian Sea of Ink: The Meade-Sickles
Controversy* and *"The Bloody 85th": A Supplement to the History
of the 85th Pennsylvania.* He has also compiled a critical bibli-
ography of the Gettysburg campaign.

Stephen R. Wise is a historian and director of the Parris Island
Marine Corps Museum. A resident of Beaufort, South Caroli-
na, Wise received his B.A. from Wittenburg University, his
M.A. from Bowling Green University, and his Ph.D. from the
University of South Carolina. He is a lecturer on Civil War
and Marine Corps history and an adjunct professor at the Uni-
versity of South Carolina, Beaufort. His publications include
*Lifeline of the Confederacy: Blockade Running during the Civil
War* and *Gate of Hell: Campaign for Charleston Harbor, 1863.*

TIME-LIFE is a trademark of Time Warner Inc. U.S.A.

Library of Congress Cataloging-in-Publication Data
Charleston / by the editors of Time-Life Books.
    p. cm.—(Voices of the Civil War)
    Includes bibliographical references and index.
    ISBN 0-7835-4709-9
    1. Charleston (S.C.)—History—Civil War, 1861-1865.
2. Charleston (S.C.)—History—Siege, 1863. I. Time-Life
Books. II. Series.
E470.65.C46 1997   96-47647
973.7'33—dc21   CIP

OTHER PUBLICATIONS

HISTORY
The Civil War
The American Indians
Lost Civilizations
The American Story
Mysteries of the Unknown
Time Frame
Cultural Atlas

SCIENCE/NATURE
Voyage Through the Universe

DO IT YOURSELF
The Time-Life Complete Gardener
Home Repair and Improvement
The Art of Woodworking
Fix It Yourself

TIME-LIFE KIDS
Family Time Bible Stories
Library of First Questions and Answers
A Child's First Library of Learning
I Love Math
Nature Company Discoveries
Understanding Science & Nature

COOKING
Weight Watchers® Smart Choice Recipe Collection
Great Taste~Low Fat
Williams-Sonoma Kitchen Library

For information on and a full description of any of the Time-
Life Books series listed above, please call 1-800-621-7026
or write:

Reader Information
Time-Life Customer Service
P.O. Box C-32068
Richmond, Virginia 23261-2068